Bible promises

DEVOTIONAL

Len Woods
Linda Taylor

ZONDERVAN®

We want to hear from you. Please send your comments about this book to us in care of zreview@zondervan.com. Thank you.

ZONDERVAN

Once-A-Day Bible Promises Devotional
Copyright © 2012 by the Livingstone Corporation

This title is also available as a Zondervan ebook.
Visit www.zondervan.com/ebooks.

Requests for information should be addressed to:

Zondervan, *Grand Rapids, Michigan 49530*

Library of Congress Cataloging-in-Publication Data

Once-a-day Bible promises devotional / written by The Livingstone Corporation.
        p. cm.
    ISBN 978-0-310-41909-9 (softcover)
    1. Promises — Prayers and devotions. 2. God (Christianity) — Promises — Prayers and devotions. 3. Devotional calendars. I. Livingstone Corporation.
    BS680.P68O53   2012
    242'.2 — dc23   2012024684

Devotions taken from *Praying God's Promises for Busy People*
Copyright © 2002, 2012 by Len Woods

Devotions taken from *Praying God's Promises in Tough Times*
Copyright © 2002, 2012 by Len Woods

Devotions taken from *Praying God's Promises for My Child*
Copyright © 2002, 2011 by Linda K. Taylor

Cover design: Jamie DeBruyn
Interior design: Sherri Hoffman and Jamie DeBruyn
Project staff: Len Woods, Linda Taylor, Linda Washington, David Veerman

Printed in the United States of America

12 13 14 15 16 17 /DCI/ 20 19 18 17 16 15 14 13 12 11 10 9 8 7 6 5 4 3 2 1

ABOUT THE LIVINGSTONE CORPORATION

Since our inception in September 1988, Livingstone has helped Christian publishers produce 169 specialty Bibles and more than 500 trade books, devotionals, gift and specialty books, studies and curriculum products. Each year we produce about 70 new titles, including Bibles, reference products, trade books, children's books, studies and curriculum. Our products have won 11 Gold Medallion awards and have been Gold Medallion finalists more than 30 times.

OUR VISION

Our vision is to glorify and enjoy God in and through our lives, relationships and services and support the advancement of the Good News of Jesus Christ.

OUR MISSION

Livingstone's mission is to provide superior ideation, content, design and composition services for religious publishers worldwide.

OUR MOTTO

Ideas to Marketplace. This saying expresses our core brand promise to clients and reflects both the breadth and depth of our capabilities to deliver convenient and effective solutions for marketplace success.

PRECIOUS PROMISES

The LORD is trustworthy in all he promises and faithful in all he does.   PSALM 145:13

You probably are already a person of prayer. As Christians, we know the power of prayer in our lives. There is so much we pray about for ourselves and for others—so many dreams, hopes, plans. So often, however, we get held up by our own doubts. Does God really care about this request?

How valuable, then, to focus on praying back to God the very promises found in his Word. When we speak God's very words back to him, we no longer wonder if this is something God cares about—for he brought it up in the first place. Therefore, this book uses promises from God's Word as the basis for your prayers. The Bible is filled with God's promises, and so we have sought to discuss and pray the reality of those promises into our lives.

It's important to note that some of the promises in Scripture were made to the nation of Israel—God's chosen people. Because we are believers, we can appropriate the truth of many of those promises even though they were not directed specifically to us. However, we need to be careful to look at the context of the specific portion of Scripture and take that into account as we take hold of God's promises. Other verses are promises that declare God's character. We can claim them as promises because the unchanging nature and trustworthiness of God's character naturally flow into the unchanging nature and reliability of his words to us. In addition, some verses come from the book of Proverbs. Here again, we need to consider the context of the book: Proverbs are general truths, not necessarily promises. In these cases, we can pray that these general principles will be true in our lives.

Praying God's promises is not some kind of magic formula. Our prayers always have great power, but we must trust God to work in his way and in his time. We must be patient. If we have to keep praying for years, then we will keep praying for years. In fact, we may not see the answer in our lifetime. But we need to keep praying. Sometimes that is the most powerful thing we can do. And in the end, we can trust that every single one of God's promises will come true.

—Len Woods and Linda Taylor

day1

GOD IS BIGGER THAN YOUR WORLDLY TROUBLES

In this world you will have trouble. But take heart! I have overcome the world.

JOHN 16:33

Have you ever stopped to think how different life would be if we were still living in Eden? No broken relationships. No difficult pregnancies. No squabbles with spouses. No financial woes. No cancer. No feeling far away from God. (And this list doesn't even *begin* to scratch the surface!)

Instead we live in a world marred by the effects of sin. We daily face all kinds of pain, trouble, suffering, weeping, loss and despair.

The temptation is to blame our woes on God, but let's be honest: The human race did this to itself. All God ever did was love us, and—when we rebelled— implement a plan to rescue us.

The promise above—a statement by Jesus to his followers—is a sobering assessment of the way things are. But it is also a hopeful reminder of the once and future Paradise for which we were created.

In light of such truth, author Elisabeth Elliot counsels us: "Refuse self-pity. Refuse it absolutely. It is a deadly thing with power to destroy you. Turn your thoughts to Christ who has already carried your griefs and sorrows." ✤

GOD'S PROMISE TO ME

- Trials and sorrows are part of living in a fallen world.
- I am bigger and more powerful than any worldly troubles you face.

MY PRAYER TO GOD

Heavenly Father, trials and sorrows are a normal part of life. I don't like this truth, but it reminds me of my need for you, God. I can take heart in the fact that you will have the final word. I praise you because you are powerful and sovereign over my life—even the hard times. Always keep me looking to you.

GOD HAS GIVEN YOU ALL YOU NEED IN CHRIST

Being confident of this, that he who began a good work in you will carry it on to completion until the day of Christ Jesus.   PHILIPPIANS 1:6

"Complete" means everything's included or done. Nothing else is needed.

"Incomplete" means something is lacking—and we must either live without that missing something or try to acquire it somehow.

How much of our busyness stems from the reality that our lives our "incomplete" until we are finally united with Christ? Are we playing or vacationing to the point of exhaustion in hopes of acquiring "missing" experiences?

Today's promise says that God will bring his good work in us to completion. Such a bold statement requires us to ask ourselves:

Do we honestly believe Jesus is enough? Are we trusting that he provides ultimate wholeness? Do our lives reflect our belief that our completeness is to be found in him? ❖

GOD'S PROMISE TO ME

- Jesus is fully God.
- You are one with Christ
- I will carry you through to completeness in Christ.

MY PRAYER TO GOD

O Lord, by grace, through faith, I am eternally linked to you. I am part of your body. You are the head. Thank you that my needs are fully met in you. Forgive me for the times I think and act as though you are not enough.

GOD'S PRESENCE GIVES YOU COURAGE

Be strong and courageous. Do not be afraid; do not be discouraged, for the LORD your God will be with you wherever you go.   JOSHUA 1:9

At bedtime the five-year child is afraid. Maybe it's the dark. More likely it's the fear of what might be lurking *in* the dark. The nightlight bulb is replaced, and countless words of assurance are spoken. But still the child trembles. Not until Dad enters the room and sits on the bed for several minutes does the child peacefully drift off to sleep.

There is something about a good and strong father's presence that gives children security and peace.

This was the point of God's promise to Joshua in the key verse for today as the nation of Israel stood poised to move into a strange land filled with strong enemies.

This is the point of God's promise to you. He's with you all the time ... and that is more than enough. ✤

GOD'S PROMISE TO ME

- You do not have to fear.
- You do not need to give in to discouragement.
- I am with you wherever you go.

MY PRAYER TO GOD

O Lord, you tell me to be strong and courageous—to not be afraid or discouraged. With all that I'm facing, such commands seem impossible. Help me believe this pledge, not just in my head, but deep within my heart. Make this truth real to me in my times of trouble.

# day4

YOU CAN TRUST THE POWER OF PRAYER

The prayer of a righteous person is powerful and effective. JAMES 5:16

Can prayer really make a difference? If God knows everything that's going to happen, why pray? Can we really change God's mind?

We might be tempted to live as though our lives are set, and we must sit back and watch them happen. We have no control, so why try to do anything? We picture God with a cosmic cattle prod, having to zap us into action.

That's not how it should be! We were put here on this earth for a purpose, so we need to get moving.

We know that God knows everything, that all our days are in his book and the hairs of our heads are numbered. But *we* don't know everything, and our lives on this earth are a continuous quest to get to know God better. So we need to talk to him, pray for guidance, ask for advice, seek help, plead for healing or protection.

Does prayer change anything? Perhaps the better question is: *Does prayer change us?* The Bible promises that our prayers are powerful and effective. Prayer changes things—but most of all, it changes us. ❧

GOD'S PROMISE TO ME

- Your prayers are powerful.
- Your prayers are effective.
- Your prayers deepen your relationship with me.

MY PRAYER TO GOD

I realize, Lord, that not every prayer is guaranteed a "yes" answer. But I know that my prayers have power and yield results—maybe in ways I will never know. Help me to grasp the awesome power of prayer. Thank you that prayer is the privilege of constant communication with you.

day5

GOD LEADS YOU

You discern my going out and my lying down; you are familiar with all my ways.

PSALM 139:3

How common it is for busy people in a busy world to lose their bearings. We feel disoriented ("I don't know whether I'm coming or going!"). We become discouraged, sometimes even despondent ("I don't understand myself. I don't know how to get off this treadmill."). At our lowest moments, we feel forgotten and alone ("Can't even *one* friend or loved one see what a mess I'm in? Everyone is too wrapped up in their own hectic lives to help me.").

Into our confusion steps the living God with words of assurance. He sees us, our hearts, our situations ... everything! He completely understands not only our complicated personalities, but also our complex problems. And there's more. He pledges to guide us into places of rest. Is there a more comforting promise for people who find themselves caught up in "the rat race"? ✤

GOD'S PROMISE TO ME

- I know where you are.
- I chart your path.
- I will guide you.

MY PRAYER TO GOD

Dear God, you monitor my movements and my thoughts. I want to rest in the truth that I am always on your mind. You promise to guide my steps into places of peace. Thank you, Father, for the comfort of knowing I am known — and cared for.

 **day6**

GOD DOES NOT RESPOND TO THE REBELLIOUS

If I had cherished sin in my heart, the Lord would not have listened; but God has surely listened and has heard my prayer.   PSALM 66:18 – 19

It is bad to be in trouble. It is worse to be in trouble and on the outs with God.

According to the passage above, if we harbor sinful attitudes in our souls or willfully indulge in sinful activities, we should not expect God to respond to our prayers.

This is not because God doesn't love us. He does — more than we realize. It's not because God doesn't want to help us. He longs to deliver. A holy God, however, cannot wink at sin or look the other way. Intimacy with God requires honesty, humility and purity.

For us to attempt to approach God without first addressing the ways in which we have knowingly offended him is an exercise in futility. Sin is the elephant in the room that must be acknowledged and dealt with. Once we do this, we again enjoy sweet fellowship with God. Clean and forgiven, we can be sure he hears our pleas for help. ✤

GOD'S PROMISE TO ME

- I do not hear the prayers of those who have unconfessed sin in their lives.
- I hear the prayers of the righteous.

MY PRAYER TO GOD

Lord, by your Spirit, give me the humility to take a hard look at my life. Show me any wrong attitudes and actions that I need to acknowledge, confess and repent of.

day7

GOD IS TRIUMPHANT OVER DEATH

Jesus said to her, "I am the resurrection and the life. The one who believes in me will live, even though they die; and whoever lives by believing in me will never die."

JOHN 11:25–26

We will not dwell here on the *fear* of death — the terrible uncertainty that so many feel at the thought of caskets and funeral homes and the "hereafter."

We will not try to remedy the *sadness* of death. What sentiments can convey the incalculable sorrow felt at the loss of a loved one?

Instead we will simply ponder the words of Jesus printed above. We will picture Christ standing in a Jewish graveyard, speaking to the weeping friends and family members of a man named Lazarus. There Jesus is — can you see him? — declaring in a clear and calm voice his absolute power over death. Specifically he gives assurance to all who trust him that death is not the end.

Whatever else you think or feel about death today, embrace that truth. ❖

GOD'S PROMISE TO ME

- Those who believe in me do not have to fear death.
- The one who believes in me will live again after death.

MY PRAYER TO GOD

Lord Jesus, keep me from grieving like those who have no eternal hope. I praise you for triumphing over the grave. I do not have to live in fear!

GOD'S WORD ENCOURAGES THE GRIEVING

My soul is weary with sorrow; strengthen me according to your word.   PSALM 119:28

There are so many reasons and occasions for grief. Some reading this page are grieving over the death of a loved one. Others are mourning the end of a marriage or because they have given up hope of ever realizing a deep-seated dream.

In short, grief is about loss. It's the painful anger and emptiness we feel when we have to say good-bye. It's the sharp, soul-shaking sadness that never fully goes away. We don't ever "get over" our grief; we simply learn to not be incapacitated by life's losses.

In deep grief the last thing in the world many Christians feel like doing is reading the Bible. God's words and promises, like strong medicine, can initially sting a wounded heart filled with pain. But applied faithfully, the Word proves to be a soothing balm. It does its healing work by bringing us back again and again to what is really true. ❖

GOD'S PROMISE TO ME

• My Word can encourage you in times of grief.

MY PRAYER TO GOD

Lord, comfort me with your truth.

GOD TAKES CARE OF THE GODLY

Cast your cares on the LORD and he will sustain you; he will never let the righteous be shaken.   PSALM 55:22

What image do you see when you think of the adjective *burdened*? A weary-looking middle-aged couple slumped on a couch in the corner of a hospital lobby? A concerned parent staring through the curtains late at night, wondering about a rebellious 17-year-old? A feeble widow trying—not too successfully—to maintain a big house and yard?

Burdens come in all varieties and sizes (and they come daily), but the promise above is wonderfully reassuring. Whenever we feel weighed down, we can give our problems and worries to the Lord.

And though we sometimes wonder if we can endure long-term burdens, we have the divine pledge that God will never let go of us. ✤

GOD'S PROMISE TO ME

- Give me your burdens, and I will take care of you.
- I will not let you slip and fall.

MY PRAYER TO GOD

Heavenly Father, you see my situation and know my needs. I trust you, Lord. I will cling to you and your promises today.

day10

GOD USES PROBLEMS TO SHAPE YOU

We also glory in our sufferings, because we know that suffering produces perseverance.

ROMANS 5:3

Tell the truth. When you run into problems, what is your first and most common response: complaining? crying? yelling? denial? pouting? rejoicing?

Unless you're highly unusual (or slightly dishonest) you probably didn't answer "rejoicing." Let's face it—it isn't normal to be joyful in the face of trials. But you can develop this trait. According to the promise above, trials are good for you. How so? In the same way that an excruciating exercise regimen is good for you. You sweat and strain through painful and unpleasant workouts. But over time, if you keep at it, you see big changes. You're stronger and healthier.

Viewing your troubles as a kind of "spiritual exercise program" enables you to rejoice (see 1 Peter 1:6–7). It enables you to see your suffering as something good in your life. God is using trials in your life to stretch you and strengthen your faith. Without these pressures, you'd be just another flabby, out-of-shape Christian. ♣

GOD'S PROMISE TO ME

- I allow you to go through trials so that you might grow.

MY PRAYER TO GOD

God, you want me to trust you in the hard times. Rejoicing isn't natural for me, so make it my supernatural response to difficulties and pressures in my life. Teach me to endure, Lord, so that my faith will grow and get stronger.

day11

GOD IS AWARE OF YOUR SORROW

Record my misery; list my tears on your scroll—are they not in your record? PSALM 56:8

Sometimes you're caught off guard by tears. Maybe the sight of your old junior high school does it. Or perhaps you get choked up standing on a beach at sunset or during the playing of the national anthem at a Veteran's Day celebration.

Most times, however, our tears are not surprising. We're exhausted or stressed, frustrated or afraid. We feel helpless and, sometimes, a tad hopeless. And one can only keep such emotions in check for so long.

Psalm 56 is a prayer of David's during one of those bitter times in his life when his enemies were hunting him physically and assaulting him verbally. Weary and worried, he cried out to God. Hot tears and raw emotions—it all came flowing out. But from this dark time in his life David realized the bright promise that God is intimately aware of our sorrows.

We shouldn't be surprised. After all, if God has numbered the hairs of our heads (see Luke 12:7), why not our tears as well? ♣

GOD'S PROMISE TO ME

- I keep track of your sorrows.
- I see all your disappointments and know about all your pain.

MY PRAYER TO GOD

Lord, thank you for loving me—for watching over and caring about all the details of my life. When I suffer for the truth, I can be sure that you see and keep track for the coming day of reward.

day**12**

GOD IS THINKING ABOUT YOU

But as for me, I am poor and needy; may the Lord think of me. You are my help and my deliverer; you are my God, do not delay. PSALM 40:17

Someone has said that companionship doubles our pleasures and divides our troubles.

Haven't you experienced this truth in your own life? You can encounter a tough time, but as long as you're not alone, the situation is somehow tolerable. It's when no one else is around to see or care, when you feel forgotten, that life's struggles become almost unendurable.

On one unknown occasion David lamented: "For troubles without number surround me; my sins have overtaken me, and I cannot see. They are more than the hairs of my head, and my heart fails within me" (Psalm 40:12).

But if you read on in the psalm, you find the truth that gave David peace in the midst of such an uncertain time. It's the promise above—that he was not alone or forgotten. He was comforted by the fact that the Lord was always thinking of him. And that made the difference. ✤

GOD'S PROMISE TO ME

- I am thinking about you right now.
- I am your helper and Savior.

MY PRAYER TO GOD

Thank you, God, for that wonderfully reassuring reminder that I am never forgotten.

GOD DISCIPLINES HIS SINNING CHILDREN

When I kept silent, my bones wasted away through my groaning all day long. For day and night your hand was heavy on me; my strength was sapped as in the heat of summer.
PSALM 32:3–4

All good and wise parents discipline their children. The precise methods vary, but the goal is the same: to train kids to choose right, healthy, God-honoring courses of action. Negative consequences are one disciplinary tool. When certain misbehaviors consistently meet with unpleasant results, a child will eventually amend his or her actions.

God uses this same process with his children. Hebrews 12 explains this "divine discipline" procedure, and Psalm 32 gives us a real-life example. King David had sinned (presumably with Bathsheba). For a while, David refused to acknowledge or turn from his sin. The result was God-induced misery, and a loss of spiritual and likely even physical strength.

It's always wise in the midst of a tough time to ask God if your troubles are a form of divine discipline. Sometimes your messes are self-made. ❖

GOD'S PROMISE TO ME

- I will discipline you, my child, when you stubbornly refuse to confess your sin.

MY PRAYER TO GOD

Your hand of discipline, God, lays heavy on believers who are in sin. You correct your children, Lord, not out of spite or anger, but out of love and concern. You want what is best for each one of us. Thank you for the security of knowing that your love is tough. It will not let me go.

day14 january 14

GOD OFFERS REST

Truly my soul finds rest in God; my salvation comes from him. PSALM 62:1

Between 1861 and 1865, U. S. President Abraham Lincoln is reported to have said, "I am the tiredest man on earth." The photographs from the period bear this out—a care-worn president clearly haunted by the horror of a nation at war.

Ever feel deeply burdened? "Bone-tired" (as they say in the Deep South)? "Chewed up and spit out"?

Such weariness can be spiritual, emotional or physical. But in any case the effect is debilitating. Weary souls feel like they are carrying the world on their shoulders.

Chased by Saul and later carrying the weight of a nation as its king, David knew what weariness was like. He also knew where he could find the ultimate rest: in God.

Feeling weary? You can find "rest in God." ❖

GOD'S PROMISE TO ME

- I see when you are weary and weighed down.
- I want to help you.
- I will give your soul rest if you come to me.

MY PRAYER TO GOD

Lord, I want to trade my heavy burden for the lighter load that you offer. If I am exhausted, maybe it's because I'm not wearing your yoke. Show me how and where I am carrying burdens you did not intend me to bear.

GOD PROMISES GOOD PLANS FOR YOUR LIFE

"For I know the plans I have for you," declares the LORD, *"plans to prosper you and not to harm you, plans to give you hope and a future. Then you will call on me and come and pray to me, and I will listen to you."* JEREMIAH 29:11–12

These powerful words are part of a letter from the prophet Jeremiah to the Jews who had been exiled to Babylon. Their beloved city, Jerusalem, had been destroyed, and the people had been carted away from the land. Things could not have been much worse. Yet this was what God had promised if the people continued their disobedience. Reading 1 and 2 Kings will quickly reveal the depth of the people's faithlessness. So great is God's love, however, that he promised to bring his people home again (see Jeremiah 29:10). Then follows the amazing promise that God has plans for them—good plans—that give them a future and a hope. When they pray, he will listen.

As God's people today, we also can claim this promise. God does have plans for us, plans to prosper and not to harm, plans that will give us a future and a hope.

God's plans are good. Thank the Lord for the promise of good plans full of hope. ♣

GOD'S PROMISE TO ME

- I have plans for your life.
- When you pray, I will listen.

MY PRAYER TO GOD

Thank you for your plans, Lord. You promise that when I pray, you will listen. Help me persevere in seeking you. In seeking you, I know that I will find you.

day16

januaryjanuary 16

GOD FORGIVES THE REPENTANT SOUL

You do not delight in sacrifice, or I would bring it; you do not take pleasure in burnt offerings. My sacrifice, O God, is a broken spirit; a broken and contrite heart you, God, will not despise.   PSALM 51:16–17

Cruising down the highway of life, we are occasionally broadsided by 18-wheelers filled with trouble. In such dark times, about all we can do is cry out for heaven's help.

Sometimes we experience mishaps caused by our own carelessness or foolishness. We are not run off the road by an 18-wheeler, but crash because of our own carelessness or reckless behavior.

The passage above describes a time in King David's life when he ignored God's warning signs and drove straight into trouble. The result was a tremendous wreck that killed two and injured countless others (see 2 Samuel 11–12).

David eventually learned that the only real recovery from such a crash is via humility and repentance. No excuses or pledges will do—just the heartfelt acknowledgement of wrong and the desire to avoid such reckless behavior in the future. ✤

GOD'S PROMISE TO ME

- I will forgive those who are broken by their sin and who want to turn away from it.

MY PRAYER TO GOD

When I sin, Lord, you do not want promises or extravagant attempts at penance. You simply want me to wrestle with the gravity of what I've done. Forgive me, restore me, change me. I want to be a person after your own heart.

GOD HELPS HIS PEOPLE

Then they cried to the LORD in their trouble, and he saved them from their distress ... Let them give thanks to the LORD for his unfailing love and his wonderful deeds for mankind.
PSALM 107:19,21

A few questions for those with a tendency to worry (pause briefly and ponder each one):

- What situations in life are you most worried about right now? Why?
- Of the various situations currently prompting anxiety in your life, which can you personally change? Over what issues do you have absolutely no control?
- What are the inward and outward signs that something has got you really concerned and nervous?
- List all the benefits of worrying. What are some of the drawbacks?
- Is worrying a "sin"? Why or why not?
- How do you think God feels when his children are panicky and anxious?
- Why do some people seem almost immune to worry?
- When is the last time you truly felt at peace?

Instead of worrying, you can cry out to God for help. In times of trouble, trust in God's unfailing love. ✤

GOD'S PROMISE TO ME

- When you cry out to me, I will help you.

MY PRAYER TO GOD

God, I'm crying out to you for help. Help me trust that you will come to my rescue.

day18 january 18

GOD MAKES YOU SECURE

So do not fear, for I am with you; do not be dismayed, for I am your God. I will strengthen you and help you; I will uphold you with my righteous right hand. ISAIAH 41:10

Question: Who among us never struggles with insecurity? Answer: No one.

Insecurity is a universal phenomenon that paralyzes some folks and sends others into a frantic scramble. Insecurity basically means we feel uncertain. We can't relax because we are fearful that something negative might happen to us, and we are unsure as to how to respond.

Today's promise is perfect for all the insecure moments of life. It eases our fear and diminishes our apprehension by reminding us that the living God is always with us. Can we get more secure than that? The One with all power and the ultimate source of help assures his people of the strength and aid they need in every situation. ♣

GOD'S PROMISE TO ME

- I am with you.
- I am your God.
- I will strengthen you.
- I will help you and lift you up.

MY PRAYER TO GOD

I do not have to be afraid, God, because you are with me. Thank you for your strong presence that drives away my insecurity and doubt. Guide me through these uncertain times. Let me be victorious in you.

day**19**

GOD PROMISES YOU ETERNAL TREASURE

The Spirit himself testifies with our spirit that we are God's children. Now if we are children, then we are heirs — heirs of God and co-heirs with Christ, if indeed we share in his sufferings in order that we may also share in his glory. ROMANS 8:16–17

What motivated explorers like Magellan and Columbus to sail across vast, uncharted oceans? What inspires researchers, movie stars, writers or factory workers? The same thing that moves children to dig a hole on a sandy beach. They are all on a search for treasure.

This is what we are — a race of treasure-hunters. We individually pursue whatever we consider supremely valuable — if not the fortune of gold or silver or precious gems, then the "wealth" of freedom, fame, family, friendship or faith.

It's been said that nothing worth having is easy. If this is true, then maybe the greatest treasures of all can be obtained only through the greatest struggles. This might explain the great agonies of the Christian faith. And it also gives us a tantalizing hint of the phenomenal riches that await all who endure to the end. ❖

GOD'S PROMISE TO ME

- You will share all my treasures.

MY PRAYER TO GOD

As your child, Father, I am your heir. All that you have is mine. It is hard to fathom, Lord, such a breathtaking promise. I am wealthy beyond words! Make this life-changing truth more than "head knowledge" to me. Cause it to sink deeply into my soul and to alter the way I live on a daily basis. I want to persevere for you.

day20

GOD TAKES CARE OF THE LONELY

A father to the fatherless, a defender of widows, is God in his holy dwelling. God sets the lonely in families, he leads out the prisoners with singing; but the rebellious live in a sun-scorched land. PSALM 68:5–6

Many people subconsciously believe the notion that God is partial to those in high places—the prominent and powerful; the well-to-do and popular. After all, aren't these the trendsetters and opinion shapers of culture? Aren't these the ones who have the influence to move the masses?

But tucked away in King David's celebration song that is Psalm 68 are two short verses that tell a different story. In this passage we find the startling promise that the God of the universe is concerned not with the rich and famous, but with the poor and obscure.

Downtrodden people have a special place in the Lord's heart. When God sees lonely people, he swings into action, "set[ting] the lonely in families"—that is, providing them with opportunities for rewarding relationships.

If you are lonely today, rejoice in the Lord's care for you, and keep your eyes open for the surprising ways he wants to fill the emptiness you experience. ✤

GOD'S PROMISE TO ME

- I am a father to the fatherless.
- I am a defender of widows.
- I provide for the needs of the lonely.

MY PRAYER TO GOD

Lord God, when I feel lonely, let me look to you to meet my needs. You are a faithful father, deliverer and provider. You are the source of true joy.

day**21**

GOD STANDS UP FOR THE HELPLESS

My whole being will exclaim, "Who is like you, LORD? You rescue the poor from those too strong for them, the poor and needy from those who rob them." PSALM 35:10

In an ideal world, the most vulnerable members of society would be zealously protected by the strong. In our world, the weak and helpless, the poor and needy, are often neglected—or worse, they are mistreated by those with power.

Perhaps you know firsthand about such oppression. Maybe you feel taken advantage of by a tyrannical boss or creditor, harmed by an unfair landlord, or abused by a confusing legal system. Whatever your unique situation, this much is sure: There are few worse feelings than being at the mercy of the mighty.

Take comfort in the words of Psalm 35. There is the story of a mistreated David who found refuge in the promise that God stands up and speaks up for those who are too weak to defend themselves. ✤

GOD'S PROMISE TO ME

• I protect the helpless from those who would take advantage of them.

MY PRAYER TO GOD

Lord, no one cares for the weak and helpless like you. I feel weak and confused. I don't know how to defend myself against those who are after me. Rescue me, God. I look to you and you alone.

GOD RESCUES YOU FROM THE EMOTIONAL DEPTHS

I waited patiently for the Lord*; he turned to me and heard my cry. He lifted me out of the slimy pit, out of the mud and mire; he set my feet on a rock and gave me a firm place to stand.* Psalm 40:1 – 2

Adventure movies often have a "quicksand scene." Someone steps into a "pool" of this mysterious, mucky mess and begins to sink. The more he or she struggles, the worse the situation becomes. In the end, victims survive or not, depending on whether they are good guys or bad. But for the "quicksand scene" to be believable, any survivors will have to be rescued. Everyone knows you don't get out of such a mess on your own.

This is the picture in Psalm 40. David reports the helplessness and hopelessness he felt in the midst of an unspecified trial. Despair is remarkably like being up to one's chest in quicksand. Struggling does no good. In fact, struggling may only make a bad situation worse.

Our only escape from such despair is calling out to God and waiting for him to rescue us. This makes for some dark moments, but if like David, we can bring to mind what we know to be true of the Lord, we will survive to face the next adventure. ❖

GOD'S PROMISE TO ME

- I hear your cry.
- I will deliver you from despair.
- I will give you stability.

MY PRAYER TO GOD

Lord, you see me and hear me when I have lost all hope. Remind me that I need to wait patiently for you and let you deliver me. You are the one who lifts me out of the pit of despair.

day23

GOD HEARS THE CRIES OF THE DESTITUTE

He will respond to the prayer of the destitute; he will not despise their plea.

PSALM 102:17

To hear some tell it, God wants all believers to be financially prosperous.

Such an idea sounds wonderful. Unfortunately it isn't Biblical (not if you take into account *all* of God's Word), nor does it square with the experience of the godly down through the ages. Saints *frequently* do without. Saints *often* suffer. Perhaps even you? Perhaps even today?

Psalm 102 is a moving meditation for believers in crisis. The historical background of this song is unknown. Some sort of enemy seemed to be approaching Jerusalem with evil intent. In this disturbing situation, the frightened and needy psalmist poured out his heart to God. Then, he found comfort in remembering God's care and concern.

One promise—the one above—sticks out. It is not a guarantee of riches, only the assurance that God hears and answers the prayers of his people when they are right on the edge. ✤

GOD'S PROMISE TO ME

- I hear the prayers of the poor.
- I will give you what you need.

MY PRAYER TO GOD

Lord, you hear the prayers of those in financial crisis. I thank you that you know all about my current situation. Show me if I am being disciplined or if this is merely an opportunity to trust you and grow in faith.

day24

january 24

GOD DOESN'T ALWAYS ANSWER "WHY?"

The secret things belong to the LORD our God, but the things revealed belong to us and to our children forever, that we may follow all the words of this law. DEUTERONOMY 29:29

When tragedy strikes, we are quick to look heavenward and ask, "Why?"

Perhaps this reaction reflects a deep-seated belief that God really is in control of all things. Or maybe in our grief and anger we're just looking for someone to blame.

Whatever the reason(s) for our questioning, God apparently does not feel the least bit obligated to explain the cosmic purposes for our pain. C. S. Lewis, in his classic little book *A Grief Observed*, reported that following the death of his wife, he knocked on heaven's door, so to speak, only to hear the sounds of God bolting the lock from the inside. Then? Silence. Nothing.

You may never get satisfactory answers for why you are suffering. And even a detailed explanation might not satisfy. Head knowledge cannot soothe heart pain.

The thing is, God is sovereign. He may choose not to answer "why." But he does hear our cries for help and promises to encourage us (see Psalm 10:17). ✤

GOD'S PROMISE TO ME

- I am in control.
- I may not tell you why you suffer.
- I will comfort you when you do.

MY PRAYER TO GOD

Lord, I may never know the reasons for my trouble. But I must know your comfort. Heavenly Father, I don't need answers, but I do need you!

day25

YOU CAN SAY "NO" TO UNGODLINESS

The grace of God has appeared that offers salvation to all people. It teaches us to say "No" to ungodliness and worldly passions, and to live self-controlled, upright and godly lives in this present age.   TITUS 2:11–12

Jesus' whole life was characterized by his submission to his Father. He said things like, "Very truly I tell you, the Son can do nothing by himself; he can do only what he sees his Father doing, because whatever the Father does the Son also does" (John 5:19).

As believers who have the Holy Spirit in our lives, we too should be living in complete submission to God. Of course, we cannot be perfect as Jesus was, but we are to take Paul's advice and "say 'No' to ungodliness and worldly passions," and "live self-controlled, upright and godly lives in this present age." When we live in this way in our evil world, it *will* make a difference.

Sooner or later, each one of us will be tempted by godless living and sinful pleasures. We can pray that we will keep our focus on our devotion to God in order to maintain self-control and right conduct as we look forward to the return of Jesus. ✛

GOD'S PROMISE TO ME

- When you are devoted to me, you will be able to live in this world with self-control and right conduct.

MY PRAYER TO GOD

Lord, help me know the right thing to do in every situation, and give me the courage to do it. I want to honor you in my choices. Help me to serve you, to build your kingdom and to grow spiritually, so that I will be ready when you return.

day26

january 26

GOD'S WORD IS A STRESS RELIEVER

Trouble and distress have come upon me, but your commands give me delight.

PSALM 119:143

STRESS is what we feel when we **ST**ruggle against all the p**RESS**ures and demands of life.

Typically, stress comes from the realization that our resources are not enough. For instance, we have too many bills and not enough money in the checking account. Or we have ten hours of work to do and eight hours in which to do it. Or we've been given a task we don't have the skills to accomplish.

Psalm 119 offers a little-known, seldom-used stress buster: God's Word. The Scriptures, say verse 143, can bring joy to the child of God who is ready to pull out his or her hair. How? By reminding us of what is true and giving us perspective. God's commands give us delight. When we keep our eyes on our all-powerful, eternal and faithful God, we realize that "our light and momentary troubles are achieving for us an eternal glory that far outweighs them all" (2 Corinthians 4:17). Even though our resources are limited, God's are more than enough for whatever we face. ✤

GOD'S PROMISE TO ME

• In stressful times, my Word can bring you joy.

MY PRAYER TO GOD

Stress seems to bear down on me daily! O Lord, I'm afraid I don't always handle life's pressures well. Keep me from whining and complaining. Show me how to find joy in your commands. What an example I would be if I were to live with joy in the midst of stressful times. Drive me to your word, where I can find life-giving truth and supernatural joy.

day**27**

GOD HELPS THE HELPLESS

*The L*ORD* upholds all who fall and lifts up all who are bowed down.*   PSALM 145:14

The commercial was intended to sell some kind of medical alert device. It featured an elderly actress lying helplessly on the floor, crying out in desperation, "I've fallen and I can't get up!" Within weeks the ad had become a national parody, and the woman's phrase was the punch line to a thousand jokes.

"Really funny stuff!"—only to those who have never taken a tumble, physically or figuratively; only to those who have never experienced the fear of helplessness.

The world snickers at the less fortunate. But God? Never. When he hears one of his children cry, "I've fallen and I can't get up!" or "I'm about to collapse under this crushing weight!" notice what he does.

He "upholds." He "lifts up." He can send such aid in a million different ways. But he will never stand idly by, and he certainly will never scoff at you in your time of need. ✤

GOD'S PROMISE TO ME

- I will uphold you when you fall.
- I will lift you up when you are worn-out.

MY PRAYER TO GOD

Lord, you promise to help the fallen. Sometimes I feel like I spend most of my time on the ground, in trouble. Come to my aid or my situation will never change. You lift up those who are bent beneath their loads. When I am weary and worn-down, prompt me to look to you in faith. And make me sensitive to others who are heavy-laden.

day28 january 28

GOD NEVER ABANDONS HIS SERVANTS

We are hard pressed on every side, but not crushed; perplexed, but not in despair; persecuted, but not abandoned; struck down, but not destroyed. 2 CORINTHIANS 4:8–9

The town skeptic unexpectedly showed up at church one Sunday. He listened attentively to a lively sermon from the book of Acts about the many trials and troubles of the first-century believers. When the invitation was given for sinners to come forward and give their lives to Christ, no one budged. Finally, to everyone's surprise, the skeptic rose from his seat and walked slowly toward the altar. Taking the pastor's hand, the man leaned forward and whispered loudly, "Reverend, maybe more folks would consider joining your church if the Lord wasn't so rough on his most faithful followers!"

Ever feel like that? Shouldn't the children of God be exempt from excessive trouble? That's a nice thought, but it's not reality. The apostle Paul understood as well as anyone that serving God invites opposition and pain and suffering. But notice what enabled him to keep going — the truth that God never abandons his children.

If you are feeling strong spiritual opposition today, let that promise renew your resolve. ❖

GOD'S PROMISE TO ME

- I will not allow you to be crushed.
- I will never abandon you.
- I will give you the strength and courage to keep going.

MY PRAYER TO GOD

Lord, the forces of evil are intent on opposing me. Grant me the faith, courage and perseverance to keep following hard after you. I want to keep going. I want to please you and have an eternal impact on those around me.

day**29**

GOD IS ON THE SIDE OF THE DESPERATE

Blessed are those whose help is the God of Jacob, whose hope is in the LORD their God. He is the Maker of heaven and earth, the sea, and everything in them—he remains faithful forever. He upholds the cause of the oppressed and gives food to the hungry. The LORD sets prisoners free.   PSALM 146:5–7

When life falls apart, if one can cling to the truth that God is good, all powerful, and wise, then it is possible to believe that everything will, somehow and eventually, turn out okay.

Ah, but that's far easier said than done! It takes courage, almost a kind of "spiritual stubbornness" to wait and watch for God to work. Faith is not a breezy, easy act. It does not feel "fun." Trusting God is alternately exciting and terrifying.

So what are we to do in times of trial and crisis? How can we hold on to God? Talking with a mentor can help. So can attending church, journaling and opening up to a small group. God provides a lot of different helps to get us through.

Perhaps the best prescription for difficult times is to practice solitude and try to listen to what God is saying. Take, for example, the promise-filled passage above. Such words can be life to a desperate soul—maybe even yours. ✣

GOD'S PROMISE TO ME

• I will help you in every crisis.

MY PRAYER TO GOD

Lord, you promise so much to those who look to you. Such assurances seem too good to be true. They seem almost mocking, for I am in trouble and I can't find you. I can't see how you are working. Please help me, God. I cannot help myself. You are my only hope.

GOD SETS YOU FREE FROM TERROR

For I hear many whispering, "Terror on every side!" They conspire against me and plot to take my life. But I trust in you, LORD; I say, "You are my God." My times are in your hands; deliver me from the hands of my enemies, from those who pursue me.

PSALM 31:13–15

Lots of days we feel some measure of "minor concern." Occasionally we experience "serious anxiety." Then, there are those times when we are overcome by "outright panic." A 3 a.m. phone call, a heart-stopping lab result, an unexpected pink slip. In those terrifying moments it's as though the earth has given way beneath us and we're free-falling to certain doom.

If you've ever had a full-fledged panic attack, you know how David was tempted to feel in Psalm 31. He was a man in the crosshairs of numerous enemies and rivals. Despite his deep faith, he wrestled with an ominous and imminent sense of dread.

But rather than giving in to wild thoughts and out-of-control emotions, David chose to trust in God's control over all things.

Which is truer of your life right now—terror or trust? Make a commitment today to trust in God in the tough times. ✤

GOD'S PROMISE TO ME

- I am your God.
- Your future is in my hands.

MY PRAYER TO GOD

God, I could make a career out of being terrified by potential trouble. It's a scary world out there. Bad things happen all the time. But I choose to trust you, Lord, and not give in to the temptation to panic.

day31

GOD HAS CANCELED OUT YOUR SIN

Those he predestined, he also called; those he called, he also justified; those he justified, he also glorified. ROMANS 8:30

Someone has said that religion is spelled *d-o*. In other words, it's all the things we think we have to *do* in order to earn God's approval. The problem, of course, is that no matter how religiously we "do' things for God, no matter how active in church affairs, no matter how involved in Christian activities, we can never know for sure if we've done enough.

Christianity is the antithesis of religion. Christianity is spelled *d-o-n-e*. Jesus Christ has already accomplished everything necessary for us to experience God's favor. He purchased salvation for us with his blood. He offers this new life and right relationship with God as a free gift to all who will stop trusting in their own efforts and who will trust him alone. He has *done* it all for us.

It's not wrong to be busy serving the Lord—unless you think that all your "activity" will result in God's favor. Your relationship with God can't be earned. It's a gift. ✣

GOD'S PROMISE TO ME

- I chose you.
- I gave you relationship with me.
- I will give you my glory.

MY PRAYER TO GOD

Lord, you have chosen me and called me to yourself. I do not understand such love, such grace. But I thank you for saving me from sin.

day32 february 1

GOD IS INTIMATE WITH HIS FOLLOWERS

I no longer call you servants, because a servant does not know his master's business. Instead, I have called you friends, for everything that I learned from my Father I have made known to you. JOHN 15:15

In keeping with numerous Biblical descriptions, we think of God in lots of different "roles"—Creator, Sustainer, Provider, Father, Judge, Lord, Savior and King. The Bible also speaks of him as *Friend.*

It's a jarring image, isn't it? Finite creatures in an intimate and affectionate relationship with an infinite Creator? But the concept is thoroughly Biblical. Abraham was called God's "friend" (see 2 Chronicles 20:7 and James 2:23). And Jesus referred to his followers in the promise above as "friends."

We need to be careful not to be flippant with God, or to take our friendship with him for granted. Friends make the effort to spend time together on a regular basis—and it never seems like an effort. The reward is a relationship marked by warmth, love, acceptance and concern. ❖

GOD'S PROMISE TO ME

- You are my friend.

MY PRAYER TO GOD

O God, help me to understand the implications of friendship with you. I want to be loyal, committed and loving. I want to walk with you daily—and make you smile!

day33

GOD WANTS YOU TO EXPERIENCE ETERNAL LIFE

You make known to me the path of life; you will fill me with joy in your presence, with eternal pleasures at your right hand.   PSALM 16:11

Jesus could not have been clearer. He wants us to have the best life imaginable. So why do the vast majority of folks settle for a dreary, superficial existence?

In *The Weight of Glory and Other Addresses*, author C. S. Lewis put it this way: "We are half-hearted creatures, fooling about with drink and sex and ambition when infinite joy is offered us, like an ignorant child who wants to go on making mud pies in a slum because he cannot imagine what is meant by the offer of a holiday at the sea. We are far too easily pleased."

Don't be "too easily pleased"! Realize you were created for so much more than the mindless busyness of mud pie-making. Take Jesus up today on his wild offer of "eternal pleasures" by seeking to be continually in his presence. ✤

GOD'S PROMISE TO ME

- I want to give you a rich, satisfying life.

MY PRAYER TO GOD

You came, Lord Jesus, to give me a full and meaningful life. Forgive me for the times I settle for a drab, ho-hum life. Forgive me, God, for being so busy with the stuff of earth that I fail to seek you.

day34

GOD'S SPIRIT LEADS YOU

What we have received is not the spirit of the world, but the Spirit who is from God, so that we may understand what God has freely given us.   1 CORINTHIANS 2:12

What good is an advantage if you don't capitalize on it? Or a gift you never open?

One of the greatest gifts we've been given as Christians is the indwelling Spirit of God. It is the Holy Spirit who imparts the very life of the Father (God) to us at the time we put our faith in the Son (Jesus Christ). God's Spirit is our "Advocate" (see John 14:26). He gives us the ability to live the way the Father intends for us to live (see Acts 1:8 and Galatians 5:16).

But if we are too busy to acknowledge the Spirit's presence or too distracted to listen to his voice, we squander a valuable resource. He longs to direct us down good paths. He wants to show us the deep things of God.

What needs to change in your life—in your schedule—today so that you can pay closer attention to the Spirit's leadings? Are you willing to slow down and listen? ♣

GOD'S PROMISE TO ME

- I have given you my Spirit.
- My Spirit will show you the depths of my blessings.

MY PRAYER TO GOD

God, you have given me your Holy Spirit. Thank you, Lord! Teach me how to listen to you. Give me ears to hear. I need to better understand grace, forgiveness, eternity—you. Keep me from the distraction of busyness. Draw me closer to you.

day35

GOD HAS CHANGED YOU

Therefore, if anyone is in Christ, the new creation has come: The old has gone, the new is here!   2 CORINTHIANS 5:17

Life stampedes around us and over us. Urgent demands scream at us. How unnatural it feels to deliberately "go against the flow" of our frenetic culture!

Perhaps as you look at your calendar or smartphone or ponder your own personality and habits, you think: *What's the use? I know that excessive busyness is wrong. But I can't change.*

Correction: You already are changed! When God gave you new life—by placing his Spirit within you—a fundamental transformation took place inside you. The old you was replaced with a new nature that has both the desire and the ability to please God. The Christian life is simply the process of working with God to bring that inward change to the surface of your life (see Ephesians 2:10 and 2 Peter 1:4).

Are you willing today to live out the deep changes that God has already begun in you? ✤

GOD'S PROMISE TO ME

- In Christ, you are a brand-new person.
- You are not the person you were. Your old life is gone.
- I have given you new life.

MY PRAYER TO GOD

God, thank you for giving me new life—a rich life that will never end. I am not the person I was—the old me is gone. I praise you, Father, that I do not have to keep living the way I used to live. Because of you, I have the capacity to change and grow into the image of Jesus.

GOD FULFILLS YOUR HOLY PASSIONS

Take delight in the LORD, and he will give you the desires of your heart. PSALM 37:4

In *Confessions* Augustine stated, "You have made us for yourself, O God, and our hearts are restless until they find rest in you." He was referring to the deepest desires of the human heart. Not yearnings for money or sex, power or pleasure — all temporal thrills that leave us hungering for more — but a consuming passion *for* God and the things *of* God.

This is David's point in Psalm 37. God never pledges to satisfy the superficial longings of our worldly nature. Today's promise isn't a divine formula to get that new extended cab pickup or the 3,500-square-foot home on the lakefront.

No, to "take delight in the LORD" means to hunger for his presence, for his will and for his glory. When God is our focus, our desires change. We find ourselves wanting what God wants. And that's when we discover our lives being filled with lasting pleasures. ❖

GOD'S PROMISE TO ME

- When your desires are righteous, you can be sure I will grant them.

MY PRAYER TO GOD

God, I want to delight in you. Forgive me for the times I get overly busy and excited about things that don't matter. I want to enjoy your blessings, Lord, but I want to enjoy you and seek you more than anything else. Stir up the holy passions that you've implanted within me so that the things I want most are the things you want most to give me.

day37

GOD'S CHILDREN ARE CHOSEN OUT OF THE WORLD

If the world hates you, keep in mind that it hated me first. If you belonged to the world, it would love you as its own. As it is, you do not belong to the world, but I have chosen you out of the world. That is why the world hates you.　　　　JOHN 15:18–19

There's an old *Peanuts* cartoon in which Charlie Brown is sharing with Linus his ambition to be rich. But, he adds, while he does want to have lots and lots of money, he also intends to be totally unaffected by his vast wealth. Linus, realizing the impossibility of such a goal, shakes his head and says, "Good luck!"

In a similar way, many Christians want both the world's acceptance and God's approval. "I want to follow Christ," the reasoning goes, "but I don't want my unbelieving friends and neighbors to think I'm weird. I want to live out my faith in such a way that I don't create waves."

"Good luck!" Linus might say.

Truth is, if we really align ourselves with Christ, we will be lightning rods for worldly scorn. A few God-fearing souls will love and respect us. But most people will despise us—or at least what we stand for.

Being hated is a Biblical promise that we don't like to think about. But it's a promise nonetheless. ✤

GOD'S PROMISE TO ME

• The world will hate you if you walk closely with me.

MY PRAYER TO GOD

O God, I don't like the thought of being despised and ridiculed. But I want to stand boldly for you. Make me gentle and winsome like Christ. When I am ostracized and criticized for my faith, help me respond in love.

day38

GOD HAS MADE YOU HIS AMBASSADOR

God was reconciling the world to himself in Christ, not counting people's sins against them. And he has committed to us the message of reconciliation. We are therefore Christ's ambassadors, as though God were making his appeal through us.

2 CORINTHIANS 5:19–20

Good ambassadors lead busy lives. They immerse themselves in the culture of the nation to which they've been sent. They work on refining their language skills. They keep up with current events and government initiatives. They host dinners at their embassy and meet almost nonstop with key advisors and foreign leaders. But in the midst of all this activity, they remember that their real mission is to accurately represent their government.

Isn't this the Christian's job description? We are citizens of heaven, living as "foreigners" in a fallen world. Our task is to represent Christ and his kingdom, to announce his offer of peace and forgiveness.

Only a perspective like this can infuse our daily activities with a sense of urgency. ✤

GOD'S PROMISE TO ME

- I have forgiven your sin and reconciled you to myself.
- I have given you this "Good News" to share with others.
- You are my ambassador.

MY PRAYER TO GOD

God, through Christ, you forgive sins and bring sinners back into relationship with yourself. Thank you, Lord, for drawing me to yourself and saving me. You have given the gospel to me so that I might share it. I'm sorry, Lord, for the times I've been tight-lipped about my faith. Make me bolder and more engaging to those who don't yet know you.

february 8 # day**39**

GOD'S PRESENCE DRIVES AWAY YOUR FEAR

Have I not commanded you? Be strong and courageous. Do not be afraid; do not be discouraged, for the LORD your God will be with you wherever you go. JOSHUA 1:9

Make the decision to follow after God and your life will be anything but dull. He will ask you to attempt "impossible" things. He will lead you in and through some dark and scary situations. Will you, on occasion, feel panicky and uncertain? Count on it. Will you face discouragement? No question about it. Meanwhile, God will call on you repeatedly to keep trusting and keep following.

Take Joshua, for example. When he was tapped by God to fill Moses' sandals and lead the nation of Israel into the promised land, he was uncertain, skittish, fearful—anything but confident. Recognizing this, God told him four times in 18 verses, "Be strong and courageous." And then he gave the reason: "For the LORD your God will be with you wherever you go" (Joshua 1:6,9).

Where is God leading you? What is he calling you to do? Whatever it is, no matter how daunting, the promise is this: You don't have to fear—God is with you to give you success. ✤

GOD'S PROMISE TO ME

- You do not need to be afraid.
- You do not need to give in to discouragement.
- I am with you everywhere you go.

MY PRAYER TO GOD

Heavenly Father, you tell me not to be afraid or discouraged. Given my life situation, these commands seem so impossible. Yet you pledge your presence with me everywhere I go. Thank you, God, for this amazing promise. Help me believe it, not just in my head, but deep within my soul.

# day40

GOD EQUIPS YOU TO HELP OTHERS

Each of you should use whatever gift you have received to serve others, as faithful stewards of God's grace in its various forms. If anyone speaks, they should do so as one who speaks the very words of God. If anyone serves, they should do so with the strength God provides.

1 PETER 4:10–11

In the letter to the believers at Philippi, Paul wrote, "Do nothing out of selfish ambition or vain conceit. Rather, in humility value others above yourselves" (Philippians 2:3). Self-obsessed people are wrapped up in their own lives from sunup to sundown.

Both of these traits — selfish ambition and vain conceit — fly in the face of what we're called to be. As Christians, we've been specially equipped by the Spirit of God with supernatural abilities. God means for us to use these gifts to serve others and to accomplish his plan for the world (see Ephesians 2:10). When we choose to exercise our gifts, God gives us the necessary strength, others find needed help, and most importantly, God gets the glory he deserves.

On the other hand, when we rush around absorbed with own selfish agendas, everyone loses.

Are you so wrapped up in your own hectic life that others are missing out on your unique, God-given abilities? The old saying is true: "If you're too busy for people, you're too busy." ❖

GOD'S PROMISE TO ME

- I have given you unique gifts and special abilities.
- My generosity will flow through you.
- I get glory when you serve in my strength.

MY PRAYER TO GOD

God, thanks for giving me special abilities with which to serve others. I want to be a blessing to others. Most of all, I want to bring you glory. Work in me. Work through me.

day41

GOD HELPS THE WEAK

Those who hope in the LORD will renew their strength. They will soar on wings like eagles; they will run and not grow weary, they will walk and not be faint.   ISAIAH 40:31

Modern life has a way of grinding us down. At the end of a hectic day, we feel tired. By the end of an activity-filled week, we are dragging. After an extended period of nonstop busyness, we feel physically spent and emotionally wasted. What's the answer for those who find themselves weak of body and weary of soul? "Hope in the Lord"—a concept that includes waiting for God to move.

This rare discipline of waiting requires temporarily ceasing your activity (perhaps a half-day retreat or a quiet evening of reflection). It involves analyzing your situation with God's help (talking—and listening). Waiting obviously involves patience (being still, not watching the clock, focusing on being *with* God rather than doing *for* God). Lastly, waiting involves actively trusting God to meet your need for fresh strength—and all your other needs (see Philippians 4:19).

The weak soul who "hope[s] in the Lord" will once again become a strong soul. ✣

GOD'S PROMISE TO ME

- I give strength to those whose hope is in me.
- Those who look to me will fly high and run far; they will never run out of power.

MY PRAYER TO GOD

O Lord, you promise strength to the weak. I am weak, Father. I sometimes feel I can't go on. Without your power, I cannot live as I should. In you there is new power to fly and run and persevere. I want to experience your limitless strength so that I can serve you faithfully and be a light for you in a dark world.

# day42

GOD IS ALWAYS WITH YOU

Surely I am with you always, to the very end of the age.   MATTHEW 28:20

Despite a Herculean effort, Susan isn't able get to the pharmacy, the colleague's surprise birthday dinner, *and* two soccer games between 5:15 and 7:00 p.m. Meanwhile, her husband Jason has so much going on at work and so much on his mind at home, that "even when he's there, he's not there."

What is the lesson in this scenario? Our busyness typically leads to absence. Which is precisely why it is so helpful to remember today's promise. Our busyness does not alter the Lord's *presence* in our lives.

Just before he departed physically from the world, Jesus assured his followers that he would remain with them spiritually in every situation. It's fitting that Matthew would conclude his Gospel with such a statement since he began it by describing Christ as Immanuel, which means "God with us" (Matthew 1:23).

The next time you feel overwhelmed and alone in an endless sea of obligations, remember that Jesus is with you. He won't ever leave you. Will you acknowledge him, lean on him and enjoy his companionship? ❖

GOD'S PROMISE TO ME

- I am with you.
- I'll always be with you.
- You can be sure of this!

MY PRAYER TO GOD

O Lord Jesus, you promised your followers you'd be with them always. Though my busyness and activity often disconnects me from others, it never separates me from you. Your promise is reliable in a world where most promises are not. Thank you, Lord, for the permanent nature of your promise.

day43

GOD GUARDS YOU FROM EVIL

The LORD will keep you from all harm — he will watch over your life.   PSALM 121:7

In a world that has rebelled against its Creator, bad things do happen, and no one is exempt.

With such a sobering truth in mind, many spend their lives nervously, busily and futilely trying to ward off all pain and danger. A better, more Biblical approach is expressed in the promise above.

The verse is from Psalm 121, a hymn of trust sung often by ancient pilgrims on their way to Jerusalem. The verse expresses the calm confidence that God watches over his people. He has us firmly in his heart and hands.

Obviously, this promise is not a guarantee that Christians will never be touched by evil (see the whole book of Acts). Rather it is an assurance that evil will not ultimately triumph over us (see Luke 12:4). We are eternally safe (see John 10:27–29).

The next time you are frightened by a disturbing situation in your life, rather than expending great time and effort trying to protect yourself, busy yourself remembering that in the Lord you are absolutely and eternally safe. ✤

GOD'S PROMISE TO ME

- I will keep you from evil.
- I will preserve your life.

MY PRAYER TO GOD

God, your assurance to your followers is that you will keep them from all evil. Thank you, Lord, that though evil may come, it has no power over me. I believe that you will, as promised, preserve my life. I want to live with the confidence that I am safe in you. Keep me busy trusting, not worrying!

day44

GOD LISTENS TO YOU

The righteous cry out, and the LORD hears them; he delivers them from all their troubles.
PSALM 34:17

One of the great drawbacks of our busy age is that when life gets overwhelming, it's hard to know where to turn. The reason? Just about everyone else is busy too. Even when you manage somehow to get a friend or family member to sit down and chat, do you really have his full attention? Is she truly listening to you—or is she listening to all the pressures swirling around in her own mind? Is he looking *at* you or *through* you?

The Biblical promise above is fantastic news to those with heavy hearts, those without a reliable shoulder to cry on. "The LORD hears" the righteous. Imagine that! The Creator, Almighty God, is *never* too busy to listen to his children. He's a compassionate Father who hears your cries. And he gives you not only his full attention—anytime you need it—but also the help you need in your time of trouble. ✤

GOD'S PROMISE TO ME

- I hear you when you call.
- I rescue you from trouble.

MY PRAYER TO GOD

O Lord, you promised to hear your people when they call for help. What a blessing to know that I have access to you—that you listen intently to the deepest cries of my heart, 24 hours a day, seven days a week. Not only do you listen, but you pledge to rescue your children from all their troubles. I need you, Lord. I look to you to be my deliverer in every confusing and scary situation.

GOD HAS SET HIS AFFECTION ON YOU

See what great love the Father has lavished on us, that we should be called children of God! And that is what we are! The reason the world does not know us is that it did not know him. 1 JOHN 3:1

What does success look like? A close, happy family? An important, well-paying or fulfilling job? Good looks? Material wealth? A set of faithful friends? Athletic or artistic achievement? Something else?

Many Christians busy themselves in the pursuit of one or more of these often elusive success benchmarks, all the while forgetting that they already possess life's most precious treasure.

According to the promise above, Christians are already loved and accepted—fully and completely (see Romans 5:8). When we trust in Jesus to forgive our sins, our status before God changes instantly. We stop being his enemies and become reconciled to him (see Romans 5:10). Better than that, we become God's beloved children (see John 1:12). He actually adopts us into his family (see Romans 8:15) and makes us his heirs (see Galatians 3:29). Think about all that the next time you're tempted to feel insignificant. ✤

GOD'S PROMISE TO ME

- I love you.
- You are my child.

MY PRAYER TO GOD

O Lord, even though you are the Holy One, the Creator of the universe, the God who sits enthroned above the heavens, you actually love me! Thank you for adopting me into your family. I am not just a forgiven sinner, I am your child because of what Christ has done. Help me today to live out my true identity.

day46

february 15

GOD BLESSES YOU WHEN YOU WORSHIP

Few things are needed—or indeed only one. Mary has chosen what is better, and it will not be taken away from her.   LUKE 10:42

How easy it is to fall into the trap of thinking that God is mostly interested in our spiritual activity. Helping this person, serving on that committee, leading a Bible study, assisting with another church project. All of these things may be important, but God wants us to be *with* him more than he wants us to do things *for* him.

When Jesus showed up at her door, Martha rushed into the kitchen and began frantically to whip up a world-class feast. Mary stopped everything she was doing and parked herself in the living room at the feet of Jesus. She lingered in his presence, listening to him, enjoying him, adoring him. When Martha got irritated at her sister, Jesus gently rebuked Martha. He then praised Mary for her priorities.

What about you? Is your tendency to work first or worship first? According to Jesus, your top concern should be to focus on him. When you do, you find a blessing that will never be taken away. ✤

GOD'S PROMISE TO ME

• I will bless those who love me and worship me.

MY PRAYER TO GOD

Christ Jesus, you hold Mary up as a model of following you. O Lord, our task-oriented world tends to view "get it done" people like Martha in highest regard. And sometimes I buy into this kind of thinking—that spiritual busyness is next to godliness. The top priority you want to see in each of your people is a heart that loves you and longs to be with you. Change me, Lord.

GOD HAS MADE YOU HIS HEIR

The Spirit himself testifies with our spirit that we are God's children.   ROMANS 8:16

They were wealthy, middle-aged and childless. So they did what lots of couples do. They adopted a child to love and care for. When they died, everything they had went to their son—a hundred million dollars in assets. What had the boy done to deserve such an inheritance? Nothing. He was their son. The parents chose him. They adopted him.

This true story is analogous to what God has done for us. Reaching out to us. Forgiving our sin. Bringing us into his family. It was *his* decision. We had nothing to do with it, except to respond in faith.

Oh, and what about the infinite, eternal inheritance? That's ours too. *All* of it.

These are important truths to ponder. Can you see how grasping all this might alter the mindset and the habits of an overly striving Christian? ✤

GOD'S PROMISE TO ME

• You are my child.

MY PRAYER TO GOD

Your Spirit, God, reminds me that I am your child. Oh, Father, I will never know why you chose me, why you loved me and adopted me into your family. But I am grateful, and I thank you with all my heart.

day48

GOD'S WORD HELPS SHAPE YOUR ATTITUDES

I delight in your decrees; I will not neglect your word.   PSALM 119:16

Take a day loaded with responsibilities, a day when we're "on the go," trying fever-ishly to get 101 things done. Guess what? That's a day when we are highly vulner-able to sin.

Why? Because we've become task-oriented. We've embraced a clear agenda with definite objectives. Not a problem unless—perhaps *until* is a better word—someone or something blocks our goals. Suddenly we get irritated. We fume at other drivers. Criticize colleagues. Snap at our family. In short, we leave a trail of human devastation all around us.

Today's promise shows a way around this common scenario. We must take God's Word seriously. We must read it, memorize it and think about it throughout the day. We must let it shape the way we think and alter the way we act. It's only as we do this, that we will live a pure life that honors God. ❧

GOD'S PROMISE TO ME

- I have given you my Word.
- Delighting in my Word can keep you from wrong attitudes and actions.

MY PRAYER TO GOD

God, I know I'll never be perfect in this life, but I do want to live in a way that honors you. If I hide your Word in my heart, I can keep from sin. Grant me the wisdom, Lord, to seek you, the discipline to get into your Word—and get your Word into me—and the discernment to apply your truth to everyday situations.

52

GOD CARES FOR YOU THROUGH HARD TIMES

Now if we are children, then we are heirs—heirs of God and co-heirs with Christ, if indeed we share in his sufferings in order that we may also share in his glory.

ROMANS 8:17

We like to focus on the positive. When two people get married, their wedding vows focus on the positive: "To *have* and to *hold* from this day forward, for *better*, for worse, for *richer*, for poorer, in sickness and in *health*, to *love* and to *cherish*, till death do us part." Some negatives are mentioned, but the focus is on the positive aspects of life together. When we actually think about it, most of us realize deep down that in this world we have to take the bad with the good. But we sure don't like to think about hard times, much less live through them.

What's true in marriage is also true in following Christ. Commitment to God involves being faithful *for better, for worse*. Being a child of God sometimes involves sharing in the suffering of Christ (see John 15:20; Colossians 1:24; 1 Peter 4:12).

There are no simple or reassuring explanations for this harsh reality, only the guarantee that trials don't last forever (see Psalm 30:5), and that on the other side of suffering is glory (see 2 Corinthians 4:16–18). Staying focused on these truths during tough times will pay long-term dividends. ❖

GOD'S PROMISE TO ME

- You will one day share my glory.
- You must now share my suffering.

MY PRAYER TO GOD

O Lord, suffering is confusing and painful—something I try desperately to avoid. When hard times come, help me to respond in a godly fashion.

GOD HONORS YOUR FAITH

Without faith it is impossible to please God, because anyone who comes to him must believe that he exists and that he rewards those who earnestly seek him.　　　Hebrews 11:6

Busyness and faith are uneasy neighbors. Busyness says: "Don't just stand there! Do something! Get it done! Get moving! Get busy! Rush! Go! Now! Quick! Work! Press! Push! Hurry! Finish! More! More! More!" In contrast, faith says: "Don't just 'do something.' Stand there. Be quiet. Be still. Wait. Seek. Listen. Trust. Obey. Go against the flow."

Our world prizes busyness. Who gets praised and promoted? Lots of times it's the person with the fullest schedule, the one who logs the most hours at the office.

God, on the other hand, values faith. Without deep trust in the invisible realities of life, the Bible says we'll never encounter the living God or experience the incomparable blessings he wants to give us.

At the end of the day, isn't that what we really want? ♣

GOD'S PROMISE TO ME

- You cannot please me apart from faith.
- I reward those who seek after me.

MY PRAYER TO GOD

Without faith, God, I cannot please you. Forgive me for the times I wrongly imagine that a busy life is the way to fulfillment. Real faith believes that you, the God of the Bible, are the one true God. O Heavenly Father, deepen my trust in you. Reveal yourself to me in new ways.

day51

GOD'S WORD POINTS THE WAY TO SUCCESS

Keep this Book of the Law always on your lips; meditate on it day and night, so that you may be careful to do everything written in it. Then you will be prosperous and successful.
JOSHUA 1:8

It's the same every weekend. Tens of thousands of people pack convention centers and hotel ballrooms across the country to hear self-help gurus and financial experts speak on how to be successful. Most of these events are slick and entertaining, with attendees caught up in the possibility of "realizing their potential" or "seeing their dreams become a reality." And many of the people come away feeling motivated and helped. But how much of the advice they hear really squares with what God has said about how to succeed?

According to today's verse, true success isn't about making money, positive thinking or getting people to do what you want. God defines success as knowing and doing his Word. We achieve lasting glory when our sole goal is to honor the Lord. ✤

GOD'S PROMISE TO ME

- If you study, meditate on and obey my Word, you will have success.

MY PRAYER TO GOD

You have given me your Word, Lord. Thank you for revealing yourself and for showing me the right and best way to live. True success requires me to be immersed in and submitted to your truth. Give me the discipline to study, the desire to meditate on and the courage to obey the Scriptures.

day52

GOD PROVIDES A SOLUTION FOR HARRIED SAINTS

The LORD longs to be gracious to you; therefore he will rise up to show you compassion. For the LORD is a God of justice. Blessed are all who wait for him! Isaiah 30:18

George Santayana once observed, "Those who cannot remember the past are condemned to repeat it." This is precisely the reason the church (i.e. the modern day people of God) is wise to ponder carefully the experience of the Jews in the Old Testament.

By the time Isaiah arrived on the scene in 739 BC, Judah was in big-time trouble. Like the ten tribes of Israel to the north, the two southern tribes had forgotten God and were beginning to experience life apart from his blessing. Isaiah urged them to turn around ... or else.

The details vary, but the principles and promise are still valid today. To experience all that God wants for us, we must turn to him—and wait for him in faith. If we ignore him, we do so at our own peril. ❖

GOD'S PROMISE TO ME

- Return to me, wait for me and I will deliver you.
- You will find strength when you trust me.

MY PRAYER TO GOD

Lord, you are sovereign and holy. Forgive me for acting as though I am in charge of my own life and for doing unholy things. I will turn to you and wait for you.

GOD REJOICES OVER YOU

The LORD your God is with you, the Mighty Warrior who saves. He will take great delight in you; in his love he will no longer rebuke you, but will rejoice over you with singing.   ZEPHANIAH 3:17

How do you show your delight in the ones you love? Perhaps you say it with flowers or candy, a card, a trip to a nice restaurant, or doing a chore for the person you love.

This delight is especially welcome after a rebuke. Consider the look on your child's face when, after a scolding, you hug her and remind her of your love.

God shows his delight in his people in a special way: with a song. Is that an image you can readily grasp? Most of us, if we're honest, would find that notion difficult to believe. This is due to a flawed view of God—as a stern disciplinarian who is would rather rebuke than rejoice. Yet the opposite is true. The Creator of the universe sings his delight in you.

If you've sensed the discipline of the Lord in your life, be assured by this promise from Zephaniah. God sings over you! ♣

GOD'S PROMISE TO ME

- I take delight in you.
- I will rejoice over you with song.

MY PRAYER TO GOD

Heavenly Father, I feel so blessed that you love me so much that you would sing over me. I offer you my heart unreservedly.

day54

GOD HONORS HIS FAITHFUL SERVANTS

Anyone who loves their life will lose it, while anyone who hates their life in this world will keep it for eternal life. Whoever serves me must follow me; and where I am, my servant also will be. My Father will honor the one who serves me. JOHN 12:25–26

Look carefully at each of the verbs in today's promise passage. *Loves. Lose. Hates. Keep. Serves. Follow. Am. Be. Honor.* These are serious words with serious implications.

Basically, if we opt for a petty, self-absorbed life (*loves*), we miss God and the eternal blessings he offers (*lose*). On the other hand, if we exchange our self-centered, temporal agendas (*hates*) for Christ's, the deepest desires of our hearts are fulfilled in ways we cannot anticipate (*keep*).

Are you following Christ (*serves*)? Embracing his attitudes and values (*follow*)? Imitating his lifestyle (*am, be*)? At home? In the neighborhood? In the workplace?

If so, there's just one more word: *honor.* ✤

GOD'S PROMISE TO ME

- I bless those who give their lives away.
- I honor those who follow Christ.

MY PRAYER TO GOD

Thank you, God, for saving me—for showing me that you and your glory are the main thing in life. I am not. You are worthy of all that I am—my attention, my affection, my adoration, my life. How easy it is, Lord, to forget my purpose, to forget that I was made by you and for you.

day55

GOD'S SPIRIT INSTRUCTS YOU

I will pour out my Spirit on all people. Your sons and daughters will prophesy, your old men will dream dreams, your young men will see visions. Even on my servants, both men and women, I will pour out my Spirit in those days.　　　　JOEL 2:28–29

Ever stop to think about how often we seek counsel? Engaged couples—wise ones, anyway—pursue premarital advice. Folks with money woes often make appointments with financial planners. Businesses routinely hire consultants. Let's face it—getting good guidance is a smart way to either get out of trouble or stay out of it.

This is equally true in the spiritual realm. God has given us his Spirit to be our permanent, resident counselor. The Holy Spirit not only shows us which direction to go, he also gives us the power to live as we should.

Today as you engage others and immerse yourself in a full schedule, listen to the quiet voice of the Holy Spirit. He is a perfectly wise counselor who longs to show you the best course of action in each situation. ❖

GOD'S PROMISE TO ME

- I have given you my Spirit.
- As you listen to the counsel of the Spirit, you will live as you should.

MY PRAYER TO GOD

Thank you, God, for coming to live inside me that I might have continual counsel. Keep me from doing what my sinful nature craves. Lord, make me more desirous of following the leading of the Holy Spirit.

day56

february 25

GOD SATISFIES YOUR DEEPEST LONGINGS

Whoever drinks the water I give them will never thirst. Indeed, the water I give them will become in them a spring of water welling up to eternal life. JOHN 4:14

Mark Twain once observed, "You don't know quite what it is you want, but it just fairly makes your heart ache, you want it so." It's a shame the great humorist never took to heart the words of Augustine (see February 5).

The fact of the matter is we are restless, aching people. Look around you. Look at the myriad ways people are trying to fill the gnawing emptiness inside them. This frantic soul-searching helps explain much of our behavior.

Ultimately only one Person can quench our thirst fully and finally: Jesus. If your heart is parched and your soul is thirsty, you need to know that Jesus offers the living water of salvation ... to you and to all who will come to him in simple faith. ✤

GOD'S PROMISE TO ME

- I alone can quench your spiritual thirst.
- I give eternal life.

MY PRAYER TO GOD

Jesus, you are the only one who can satisfy the deep longings of my soul. Remind me that nothing in a temporal world can bring lasting fulfillment to an immortal soul. The life that you give is my internal source of continual refreshment. Teach me the holy habit of looking to you alone for whatever my soul needs.

day57

GOD SETS YOU FREE IN CHRIST

Live as free people, but do not use your freedom as a cover-up for evil; live as God's slaves.
1 PETER 2:16

Christ came to set us free (see John 8:36). Wonderfully free from sin's grave penalty and its terrible power. Gloriously free from guilt and shame. Marvelously free from a life of empty religious drudgery.

But if you look around you—and maybe even within you—you don't always see the glad signs of freedom. You see Christians trapped in unhealthy habits and destructive lifestyles. You see exhausted believers who view the Christian life as an oppressive list of dos and don'ts.

Christ came to set us free. Free to enjoy the rich banquet of endless grace. Free to throw back our heads and laugh at the wonder of forgiven sin. Free to give ourselves fully to the task for which we were created—the only task which can fill our hearts—serving our gracious God.

Are you living like the free person you are? ✤

GOD'S PROMISE TO ME

- I have set you free.
- You will experience true freedom when you serve me in grace.

MY PRAYER TO GOD

I am truly free in Christ. O Lord, this is a phenomenal truth! But I do not always live it out. Instead of joyful delight in your refreshing salvation, I often feel like I am barely making it. I am free, not to live as I want, but as you desire.

GOD WILL CAUSE YOU TO OVERFLOW WITH HOPE

May the God of hope fill you with all joy and peace as you trust in him, so that you may overflow with hope by the power of the Holy Spirit.   Romans 15:13

It's a pretty grim world out there, don't you think? Grouchy, grinchy neighbors. Dour, sour co-workers. Journalistic purveyors of doom and gloom.

A cynical outlook is the opposite of hope. Cynicism says, "I already know the outcome, and it's grim." If ever anyone had a right to be cynical, that person was the apostle Paul. Take a look at his record of hardships (see 2 Corinthians 4:8–9). Yet Paul encouraged believers to "overflow with hope by the power of the Holy Spirit." Having a hopeful outlook despite hardship is proof of the Holy Spirit's presence. The hope he provides is anchored in trust—trust that God sees, that God loves.

Perhaps trials have made you doubt. Maybe hope seems impossible to grasp, and you're feeling like a fountain without water today. God understands. Turn your heart to him. Let him fill you to overflowing with hope. ✤

GOD'S PROMISE TO ME

- If you trust me, I will fill you with hope.

MY PRAYER TO GOD

O God, restore my hope. Help me take my eyes off my problems as I hope in you and wait on you to act.

day59

GOD CONTROLS EVERY SITUATION

Remember the former things, those of long ago; I am God, and there is no other; I am God, and there is none like me. I make known the end from the beginning, from ancient times, what is still to come. I say, "My purpose will stand, and I will do all that I please."
ISAIAH 46:9–10

We love feeling "on top of things." We like to believe that we are "in command" of our life situation. We loathe feeling "out of control."

But control is an illusion. We can't script our days any more than we can plan out next week's weather. The reality of life is that life throws curve balls. People act and react in unexpected ways. Each new day brings events we did not plan. You would think that we'd catch on to the fact that we're mere mortals and that we actually control very little.

The promise above is a good reminder for those times when our plans don't work out. The promise tells us that God is in control. Coupling that truth with the fact that God is good is the first step to finding peace in busy, tense or unexpected situations. ♣

GOD'S PROMISE TO ME

- I am God.
- I am in charge of history.
- My plans cannot be thwarted.

MY PRAYER TO GOD

Your fingerprints, O Lord, are all over human history. Thank you, God, for being in control of not only my life, but the whole world. You alone know the future and can orchestrate the events of life. Keep me from foolishly believing that I can plan out my life. Give me the grace to trust that you know best and that you will work for my good and your glory.

GOD USES PURE PEOPLE

In a large house there are articles not only of gold and silver, but also of wood and clay; some are for special purposes and some for common use. Those who cleanse themselves from the latter will be instruments for special purposes, made holy, useful to the Master and prepared to do any good work.   2 TIMOTHY 2:20–21

It's been said that every person longs for two things—relationship and impact. We were designed to connect with God and others; we also were designed to make a difference. No wonder we want to do something lasting and significant with our lives.

The promise above weaves together these two longings. It tells us that if we are relating rightly to God, then he will use us to do important things in this world.

Reflect on your own life. Is God using you? If not, it might be because of disobedience. Would you knowingly drink out of a dirty glass? Neither will God choose to use a believer who is harboring unconfessed sin in his or her heart.

Admitting our sin and thanking God for his forgiveness (see 1 John 1:9) is the way we find ongoing cleansing. That's the necessary first step for becoming a powerful utensil in the hands of God. ❖

GOD'S PROMISE TO ME

- I want to use you.
- If you are spiritually pure, I will use you for my purposes.

MY PRAYER TO GOD

You want to use me for your purposes God—to do big things. Thank you for allowing me to participate in your eternal plan. Only if I am clean will you choose to work through me. Show me any failures or wrong choices that I need to see, admit and turn from. I want to be clean. I want to be used by you.

day61

THOSE WHO BELIEVE WILL BE SAVED

If you declare with your mouth, "Jesus is Lord," and believe in your heart that God raised him from the dead, you will be saved. For it is with your heart that you believe and are justified, and it is with your mouth that you profess your faith and are saved.

ROMANS 10:9–10

If your child or some other loved one is not a believer, you are surely hurting. Perhaps you only recently became a believer yourself and want your loved ones to know the faith you now profess. Perhaps you think you did everything wrong in your relationship with your child or loved one and now you are punishing yourself. Perhaps you think you did everything right in showing the love of God, and now you can't believe this is happening.

Whether we were "right" or "wrong," we need not punish ourselves or wonder what we could or should have done better. It's better to spend our energy on our knees in fervent prayer for our children and other loved ones. God works in every person in a different way. He promises that every person who believes and confesses Jesus as Lord will be saved. We can pray for others, but we can't make them believe. The Holy Spirit must work in them. ❖

GOD'S PROMISE TO ME

- I will save those who confess and believe.
- By believing in me, you are made right with me.
- By confessing your faith in me, you will be saved.

MY PRAYER TO GOD

Dear God, you promise that those who believe in Jesus and confess him as Lord will be saved. I pray that my loved one will see their need for you. I pray they will call on you. Please guide them toward confession and belief.

# day62

GOD IS YOUR PLACE OF SHELTER

The Lord is a refuge for the oppressed, a stronghold in times of trouble. Psalm 9:9

Every action movie worth its weight in popcorn features some kind of chase. An evil villain or ominous fate threatens the main character; he or she is trying to make it to safety. Therein lies the tension.

Of course, most movies are simplistic and predictable. Life is not. Our enemies don't always come dressed in black, looking suspicious. We don't have stunt doubles to leap from balconies for us — nor, thankfully, are we called upon to do that in an average week.

What we do have for our moments of uncertainty, fear and panic is the sure promise of God as our refuge. He is the one to whom we can run. In him we find safety, peace and rest. ♣

GOD'S PROMISE TO ME

- I am a shelter for the oppressed.
- I am a refuge for those in trouble.

MY PRAYER TO GOD

O Lord, sometimes I do feel oppressed by life — by concerns and worries and complicated situations. Help me to remember that you are a shelter for those who are weary and scared. You are my refuge in times of trouble.

GOD REWARDS THOSE WHO SEEK HIM

Without faith it is impossible to please God, because anyone who comes to him must believe that he exists and that he rewards those who earnestly seek him. HEBREWS 11:6

People may try all kinds of things in an attempt to please God. Many think that going to church will do it. Some try being generous and kind, living a good life, or keeping all kinds of rules. But the Bible makes it clear that it is impossible to please God *without faith*. In other words, all of our "doing" amounts to nothing. We can attend church, give our money, serve others and flawlessly keep all kinds of rules we set for ourselves, but if we do not have faith in God, we cannot please him.

When we have true Biblical faith, we believe in God and his goodness. We come to him, believing that he exists and, even more, believing that he rewards those who search for him. Jesus said, "Ask and it will be given to you; seek and you will find; knock and the door will be opened to you" (Matthew 7:7). God rewards us with himself and his presence forever. It's a simple process—with eternal rewards. ❖

GOD'S PROMISE TO ME

- It is impossible to please me without faith.
- I will reward those who sincerely seek me.

MY PRAYER TO GOD

Lord, you say that anyone who wants to come to you must believe that you exist. Draw me to you and help me to sincerely believe in your existence as an almighty yet loving God.

# day64

GOD GIVES ETERNAL LIFE

Whoever believes in the Son has eternal life, but whoever rejects the Son will not see life, for God's wrath remains on them.   JOHN 3:36

It doesn't get much clearer than this. God promises eternal life to those who believe; he promises his eternal wrath to those who live in unbelief. There are only two choices. We either believe Jesus is who he said he is or we don't. We either choose to follow him or we don't.

The choice is clear; the promise is clear. John repeated this same sentiment in another book: "Whoever has the Son has life; whoever does not have the Son of God does not have life. I write these things to you who believe in the name of the Son of God so that you may know that you have eternal life" (1 John 5:12–13). John wrote these words so that we could know that we have eternal life — not *hope* that we have it, but *know* it.

Do you know that you have it? ✤

GOD'S PROMISE TO ME

- Any person who believes in me will have eternal life.
- You can trust my promise to give you eternal life.

MY PRAYER TO GOD

Lord, thank you for the promise of eternal life — a life that begins now. I look forward to being with you forever.

GOD BLESSES HIS PEOPLE

Who may ascend the mountain of the LORD? Who may stand in his holy place? The one who has clean hands and a pure heart, who does not trust in an idol or swear by a false god. They will receive blessing from the LORD and vindication from God their Savior.

PSALM 24:3–5

When the Israelites sang this psalm, possibly every Sabbath in the worship services at the temple, they were acknowledging God's holiness and their need to be pure before him.

In our own strength, none of us can be totally clean, perfect and acceptable to God. If that were true, Christ would not have had to die. We must pray that those we love will accept the sacrifice of Christ and so receive the gift of the Holy Spirit. As the Holy Spirit works in them, they will be able to turn from idolatry, stay pure and have truthful speech. The glorious promise is that they will "receive blessing from the LORD and vindication from God their Savior." They are welcomed into God's presence. What more could we ask for? ✤

GOD'S PROMISE TO ME

- I will bless and give right standing to those who accept my sacrifice and seek to follow my Spirit's leading.
- The one who trusts in me will be welcome in my presence.

MY PRAYER TO GOD

Oh Lord, I desire to be in your presence. May the Holy Spirit work in my heart so that my actions will always be pure before you. I pray that my desires will always be pure and that I will continue to pray for those I love that they will receive your Spirit.

day66

march 7

GOD WILL MAKE YOU SECURE

It is God who arms me with strength and keeps my way secure. He makes my feet like the feet of a deer; he causes me to stand on the heights.　　　2 SAMUEL 22:33–34

Have you ever seen a deer spring over a fallen log? Their cloven hooves and dew-claws give them the traction they need to easily traverse a forest landscape. They can leap over surfaces that seem slippery or dangerous without the fear of falling.

Some of the challenges we face in life make us feel insecure and doubtful. Our fears tell us that if we take a wrong step, we'll fall into danger, temptation or even further into doubt. But there's good news. David used the feet of a deer as a reminder of the assurance and strength God provides. His assurance and direction powers us to do whatever we're called to do. He exchanges our slippery feet—our doubts—for the deerlike feet of the overcomer. And the best part of all is that we don't have to do anything in our own pitiful strength.

Need assurance? Call on the Lord. Then get ready to take on any terrain! ✤

GOD'S PROMISE TO ME

- I offer you my strength.
- I help you stand secure.
- I enable you to do what you thought was impossible.

MY PRAYER TO GOD

Oh Lord, I crave your assurance. Please put a spring in my step as I follow where you lead.

70

day67

YOU CAN TRUST GOD

Those who know your name trust in you, for you, LORD, have never forsaken those who seek you.   PSALM 9:10

What does it mean to trust someone? According to the dictionary, to trust means to rely on a person's integrity, strength, ability or surety. When we trust someone, we have confidence in that person; we know that we can rely on them.

Today's verse tells us that those who know God trust him. We can rely on his integrity, strength and ability; we have confidence in him. He has shown us his trustworthiness through his Word, in the lives of other people and in our own lives. The promise is that God never abandons anyone who searches for him.

Are you struggling with trusting God? Perhaps you're in a questioning, doubtful frame of mind because of circumstances beyond your control. If so, keep seeking. God will not abandon those who are seeking him. May your search lead you back to God. ❖

GOD'S PROMISE TO ME

- I always know when and why you're searching.
- I will not abandon you in your search for me.

MY PRAYER TO GOD

You promise, Lord, that you have never abandoned anyone who searches for you. Lead me to your truth.

YOU CAN LIVE A GODLY LIFE

His divine power has given us everything we need for a godly life through our knowledge of him who called us by his own glory and goodness. Through these he has given us his very great and precious promises.   2 PETER 1:3–4

Living a godly life sounds difficult and intimidating, doesn't it? After all, we're so imperfect. We can be glad God promises that we don't have to do it alone; Jesus' divine power will give us everything we need to live godly lives. We don't need to keep an exhausting number of rules or lock ourselves away from the world. That is not God's plan. Instead, we are to draw on the divine power Jesus gives us.

Peter goes on to say that Jesus' divine power also gives us all the promises of God's Word. If God's power gives God's promises, then those promises are sure and steadfast. As we apply the benefits of those promises to our lives, we can live "a godly life."

Where does it all begin? "Through our knowledge of him who called us by his own glory and goodness." We can pray for spiritual growth—to know Jesus better. Many rich and wonderful promises are ours as we grow. As we learn to apply these promises, our faith will produce moral and spiritual excellence. ✣

GOD'S PROMISE TO ME

- I will give you everything you need to live a godly life.
- Your faith will produce a godly life.

MY PRAYER TO GOD

You promise, Lord, that as we get to know Jesus better, his divine power will give us everything we need for living a godly life. Help me grow spiritually. May I live for you.

YOU CAN FIND TRUE LIFE

Jesus said to his disciples, "Whoever wants to be my disciple must deny themselves and take up their cross and follow me. For whoever wants to save their life will lose it, but whoever loses their life for me will find it."   Matthew 16:24–25

The crux of the gospel seems at first glance to be a contradiction: To follow our Lord and Savior, we must shoulder his cross. To find true life, we must be willing to lose our lives. God specializes in taking what makes sense to us and turning it upside down.

Confessing our belief in Christ as our Savior is only the first step. *After* we have done that, God calls us to follow him. That means that we must do as he did and go where he went. It requires that we set aside every selfish goal and seek first what God wants for and from us. This attitude transforms self-centeredness into God-centeredness. To shoulder our cross means that we obey no matter what, even to the point of death.

Do you understand the cost of following Christ? Are you willing to pay it? As you give up your life in order to be used by God, you will find true life. That's a promise. ✤

GOD'S PROMISE TO ME

- When you give up everything to follow me, you will not be disappointed.
- As you live for me, you will find true life.

MY PRAYER TO GOD

Lord, you say that your followers need to set aside their selfish ambition and shoulder their crosses. Help me to always seek your will, to set aside selfish ambitions and desires, and to trust that you have something far better in mind.

day70

GOD TRANSFORMS YOU

Do not conform to the pattern of this world, but be transformed by the renewing of your mind. Then you will be able to test and approve what God's will is — his good, pleasing and perfect will.   ROMANS 12:2

Have you ever been asked, "How will I know what God wants me to do?" Maybe you've asked that question yourself.

Most people who have walked with Jesus for many years can see that a steady walk with God, seeking to follow him with small steps of faith, has transformed their lives. It's the small steps that lead to the big goals. The quivering steps of faith keep us on solid foundations.

So how can you know the will of God? Take the daily little steps. God never shows us the entire path ahead. We probably couldn't handle that anyway. Instead, he promises that his Word will be a lamp to light our feet, lighting up just a small portion of the path ahead (see Psalm 119:105). God want his children to be different from the world by our faith and to ask him to transform us as we learn more about him. Then we will be guaranteed to stay on the right path, doing God's "good, pleasing and perfect will." ✤

GOD'S PROMISE TO ME

- I will transform you into a new person as you seek to follow me.
- I will let you know my perfect will as you walk with me.

MY PRAYER TO GOD

Lord, help me grow closer to you, to understand the difference between what you desire and what the world offers. Teach me not to copy the behaviors and customs of this world but to be transformed into a new person.

day71

YOU ARE GOD'S FRIEND

You are my friends if you do what I command. I no longer call you servants, because a servant does not know his master's business. Instead, I have called you friends, for everything that I learned from my Father I have made known to you. JOHN 15:14–15

Jesus is our friend. That's a mind-blowing thought! Jesus, the glorious God of the universe, took on a frail human body, walked on the earth, faced ridicule and rejection, and was murdered by the people he had created. He faced pain and suffering because he loved us. He laid down his life. Why? So we could be his friends.

Friendship takes good communication and time spent together if the relationship is to grow. We can pray that our relationship with Jesus will be a "best friend" relationship, that we will love him, spend time with him and talk to him daily. When we are best friends with Jesus, we will have all the tools we need to love others as much as Jesus loves us. To love sacrificially, to love when that love is not returned, to love even the unlovable—that is Jesus' kind of love. ❖

GOD'S PROMISE TO ME

- I loved you so much that I died for you.
- You can be my friend.

MY PRAYER TO GOD

Lord, you command us as believers to love one another as you have loved us. You exemplified that love when you died for us. I pray that you will help me follow your command to love others with your kind of love.

GOD BLESSES YOU WHEN YOU OBEY YOUR PARENTS

Children, obey your parents in the Lord, for this is right. "Honor your father and mother"—which is the first commandment with a promise—"so that it may go well with you and that you may enjoy long life on the earth."   EPHESIANS 6:1–3

If you're a parent, have you ever tried to throw the weight of this verse around with your children: "See, the Bible says obey your parents! And see, one of the Ten Commandments says to honor your parents!"? The approach doesn't work, but the reality is that God has told us something important about our relationship with our parents in these verses. Paul noted that the command to honor one's parents ends with a promise directly from God—that those who do obey and honor their parents "may enjoy long life on the earth."

This verse is manifest as children respond with obedience. When they do, they are learning an attitude of respect that will carry over into their relationship with God. As they obey their parents, they will also be kept safe from harm—thus paving the way for a long, full life.

Children learn to honor their parents based on the way that parents model that respect. They observe our interactions with our parents and note the respect—or lack thereof—we offer. As parents—or spiritual parents—we can be good examples by demonstrating a respectable and honorable manner in our interaction with our children and with others. ✤

GOD'S PROMISE TO ME

- I will bless you when honor your parents.
- I can help you to be a wise and discerning parent.

MY PRAYER TO GOD

Lord, help me to be respectful of others and to teach respect in my own children. Help me to be wise in the obedience I require and in the discipline I give for disobedience.

day73

A SPOUSE CAN BE A TREASURE

He who finds a wife finds what is good and receives favor from the LORD.

PROVERBS 18:22

If you're married, think back to the time before you married. Did you pray for your future spouse, even if you didn't know who that person was? Perhaps your parents or some other loved one prayed for you to find the right person.

Today's proverb says that "he who finds a wife finds what is good and receives favor from the LORD." Of course, proverbs are just that—general truths. Although we can't technically call them promises, we can pray that the general truth will be true for those we're praying for: our spouses, our children, other loved ones, even ourselves. We can pray that if it is God's will that they (or you) marry, he will give them (or you) wisdom, discernment and a willingness to listen carefully to his guidance. We can pray that our sons will find wives who will be "treasures" to them and that they will be godly husbands. We can pray that our daughters will find godly husbands to whom they will be priceless treasures.

If you're praying for a mate for yourself, pray for God's choice, and for God to make you ready for this next step in your life. ✤

GOD'S PROMISE TO ME

- Marriage has my stamp of approval. I can help your marriage be a great success.
- I can help you be a treasure to your spouse—and help your spouse to see it.

MY PRAYER TO GOD

Lord, you know how tough marriage can be. In fact, the world doesn't often give us the picture of spouses truly treasuring one another and receiving your favor. I pray for my marriage, and thank you for the priceless treasure of my spouse.

# day74

YOU ARE GOD'S TEMPLE

Do not be yoked together with unbelievers. For what do righteousness and wickedness have in common? Or what fellowship can light have with darkness?... What agreement is there between the temple of God and idols? For we are the temple of the living God. As God has said: "I will live with them and walk among them, and I will be their God, and they will be my people." 2 CORINTHIANS 6:14,16

If you've ever seen two yoked animals, you know that a matched pair of animals is necessary. Otherwise, they won't move as a team. That's why you would never yoke a horse with an ox.

These verses from Corinthians offer excellent advice for all kinds of relationships. To be yoked with someone means you are working with them as a team.

Sometimes believers read these verses and they are tempted to think they need to build a high wall around themselves, close the drawbridge and never come out lest they be infected by the evil world. That's not what the rest of the Bible tells us, however, nor was that Jesus' example to us.

We need to pray that we can be around unbelievers—at school, at work, in the neighborhood—and yet not be influenced by them. We need to discern how to have friendships with unbelievers and yet know where to draw the line. We need to interact with them, but not be yoked to them. We need to pray that we will shine for Christ and influence unbelievers—not the other way around. ♣

GOD'S PROMISE TO ME

- You are my temple.
- I am your God and I walk beside you.

MY PRAYER TO GOD

Heavenly Father, because we are your temples, you command that we not make lasting commitments with unbelievers. Thank you for the promise that you will walk among us and be our God.

day75

GOD BLESSES THOSE WHO CHOOSE WISE COMPANY

Blessed is the one who does not walk in step with the wicked or stand in the way that sinners take or sit in the company of mockers, but whose delight is in the law of the LORD, and who meditates on his law day and night. PSALM 1:1–2

Who is your oldest, long-term friend? Is this someone who has been in your life since childhood? While your neighborhood determined many of your friends in your younger years, this changes as you grow up and move on in life. Some newer acquaintances probably have developed into life-long friendships.

Many of us can probably attest to at least one or two unwise friendships we've had in our lives. We can recognize the quality of a friendship by the "fruit" it bears in our lives.

Prayer is a good resource to use when choosing positive friendships. We can pray to avoid close friendships with the "wicked," the "sinners," and the "mockers" as the psalmist suggests, while also praying that we will be positive witnesses to the non-Christians in our sphere of influence.

"Meditat[ing] on [God's] law day and night" is another good resource for developing good friendships. It helps us avoid the temptation to follow the wrong crowd. ✤

GOD'S PROMISE TO ME

- I bless those who do my will.
- I can help you choose close relationships wisely.

MY PRAYER TO GOD

I know, Lord, that you want me to delight in doing your will, and that's what I want more than anything. Help me choose positive relationships and build good Christian friendships that will support me in my faith.

day76

GOD BLESSES HONORABLE BEHAVIOR

Live such good lives among the pagans that, though they accuse you of doing wrong, they may see your good deeds and glorify God on the day he visits us ... For it is God's will that by doing good you should silence the ignorant talk of foolish people. 1 PETER 2:12,15

When we ask, "What is God's will?" we tend to think in terms of some grand cosmic plan God has for us. While God does have a plan for humankind, we should do what we can to discover God's specific path for us. We need to take note that Peter makes "God's will" a simple daily act. It is God's will that our good lives should honor him before our unbelieving neighbors. It sounds simple, but it's a high calling and a challenge. It makes us consider what the unbelievers around us think of us. Do they consider us honorable? Are our lives "good"? Are our lives a positive witness to them, no matter how much they may disagree with us or even dislike us?

God promises that when we live honorably before unbelievers, we are doing his will. We can pray daily to be able to live good and honorable lives among the unbelievers around us. We also can pray that God will protect us in times of spiritual warfare and that any false accusations against us would be silenced. We can pray that our God-honoring behavior will help bring others to faith while it brings glory to God. ❧

GOD'S PROMISE TO ME

- I will bless your honorable behavior.
- Your good behavior among unbelievers brings honor to me.

MY PRAYER TO GOD

Lord, I pray that my life will be such a shining example of you that others—even accusers and troublemakers—will be drawn to you.

day77

GOD BLESSES YOUR LOVE FOR OTHER BELIEVERS

Finally, all of you, be like-minded, be sympathetic, love one another, be compassionate and humble. Do not repay evil with evil or insult with insult. On the contrary, repay evil with blessing, because to this you were called so that you may inherit a blessing.

1 PETER 3:8–9

We may live in a world of unbelievers, but we also have many relationships with believers. Peter has some good advice for us because sometimes relationships with fellow believers can be difficult. We have all been saved by grace, but we are all still works in progress. So when frustration and conflict arises between believers, we must all be patient.

At times we may have honest disagreements with other believers. We may not agree about child-rearing or schooling or how to worship or what to wear or how to spend our money. That's when we need to be willing to let God work in another's life and in ours as well. God gave us room for lots of disagreement, and we need to learn how to handle it. "Like-minded" does not mean zero disagreements; it means majoring on the truly important things and not nit-picking about the rest.

We need to pray that God will make us positive examples in our relationships with other believers. God promises to bless his people when they treat one another in a Christlike manner. ✤

GOD'S PROMISE TO ME

- I will bless your kindness toward other believers.
- My Spirit will help you act as I desire.

MY PRAYER TO GOD

Lord, you promise blessing for your Christians who treat other believers well. Please give me sympathy, love, humility and a tender heart toward others.

day78

GOD PROTECTS YOU IN TEMPTATION

No temptation has overtaken you except what is common to mankind. And God is faithful; he will not let you be tempted beyond what you can bear. But when you are tempted, he will also provide a way out so that you can endure it.   1 CORINTHIANS 10:13

It doesn't get much better than this! Not only does God care about our needs and concerns, but here's a promise that says our faithful God cares about our individual temptations.

Satan is a powerful adversary. He knows our weaknesses, and he deftly fashions temptations that are just what we desire. Think of it: custom temptations. But God promises that *no* temptation will ever be too strong for us to resist; he will always show us a way out.

We will face temptations every day. We can pray to God and hold on to his promise that he will help us resist every temptation and escape from it. ❖

GOD'S PROMISE TO ME

- I will be faithful to keep the temptation you face from becoming too strong for you to resist.
- When you are tempted, I will always show you a way out.

MY PRAYER TO GOD

It's a tough world out there, Lord, with temptations lurking around every corner. You don't promise to protect me from temptation, but you do promise your help in resisting temptation when I face it. Thank you for your promise that no temptation will ever be so strong that I can't stand up against it.

YOU CAN COME BOLDLY TO GOD'S THRONE

We do not have a high priest who is unable to empathize with our weaknesses, but we have one who has been tempted in every way, just as we are—yet he did not sin. Let us then approach God's throne of grace with confidence, so that we may receive mercy and find grace to help us in our time of need.   HEBREWS 4:15–16

When you've messed up, what's your first response? Many of us, if we're honest, might follow the example of our first parents, Adam and Eve—we hide. We also tend to take this approach when we wrestle with temptation.

Hebrews 4:16 gives us some advice to take us out of hiding: "Let us then approach God's throne of grace with confidence." When we're tempted to doubt, worry, throw in the towel, become afraid or "lose it" emotionally, we have the assurance that Jesus was tempted with the same things we are, and he understands our weaknesses. Therefore, he can help us when we come to his throne.

The Savior understands your temptations. He knows your weakness, and he can help you. You can go boldly to God's throne to receive his mercy, grace and help. You can go boldly—confidently—because you are his beloved child. ✤

GOD'S PROMISE TO ME

- I have gone through suffering and temptation and understand what you are facing.
- You can come boldly to my throne anytime and receive mercy and grace in time of need.

MY PRAYER TO GOD

Lord, I am so thankful for your promise that I can come boldly to your throne. Thank you for that access to you day or night.

day80

march 21

GOD WILL GIVE YOU DISCERNMENT

Dear friends, do not believe every spirit, but test the spirits to see whether they are from God, because many false prophets have gone out into the world.   I JOHN 4:1

"I'm sure this is the truth." "I had a feeling that was wrong." "God told me to tell you …"

Ever fall victim to a "word" someone claimed to have from God? Many lives have been damaged because they acted on a "truth" they received, a "truth" that turned out to be false. We sometimes base our actions on our opinions, feelings or even hearsay. We're so sure we're right that we don't even bother consulting God. But the apostle John challenges us to seek the Lord's discernment.

In John's day, false teachers blatantly professed untruths about God and caused problems for the first-century believers. John urged his readers to test the "prophecies" the prophets claimed were God's. How could they do that? Through God's Word and the Holy Spirit.

God will give us the discernment we need to know what's true. In that way, we don't have to rely on our own, sometimes faulty, logic. ✤

GOD'S PROMISE TO ME

- I can help you discern truth.
- You can ask me to help you.

MY PRAYER TO GOD

Lord, I need your help to discern what's true. Help me to find the answers I need through your Word and the wise counsel of those you send to me. Help me never to pass on false doctrine.

day81

YOU CAN BE PURE

How can a young person stay on the path of purity? By living according to your word.

PSALM 119:9

Is there anyone who would want to relive their middle school or high school days? Consider the bids for power, the blows to self-esteem, the angst. Consider also the numerous temptations to compromise your principles, to follow the crowd.

It is difficult to be young, but young people can learn to value purity and thereby to live honorable lives. Though many will say that purity is an "old-fashioned" concept, remaining pure is possible.

God promises that we can stay pure by obeying his Word. As we read the Bible, God will speak to us. As we memorize Scripture, it will be available to us for whatever situation arises. When we are tempted—and we can expect to face temptation daily—we will have God's words at our disposal, and the choice to obey will be much easier. ✤

GOD'S PROMISE TO ME

- You can stay pure by obeying me.
- Memorizing Scripture will help you remain pure.

MY PRAYER TO GOD

Lord, the world doesn't value purity. The expectation is that no one can remain pure. I pray that you will help me continue to see the value of purity and desire it in all areas of life.

SHELTER FROM THE STORM

Then the LORD will create over all of Mount Zion and over those who assemble there a cloud of smoke by day and a glow of flaming fire by night; over everything the glory will be a canopy. It will be a shelter and shade from the heat of the day, and a refuge and hiding place from the storm and rain. ISAIAH 4:5–6

Famous British preacher Charles Spurgeon once wrote, "Our Savior is the harbor of weather-beaten sails." We get beat up sometimes, don't we? We face times of trial, difficulty, pain and suffering that tear our sails and seem to leave us stranded in the middle of the ocean. But then God gently breathes his peace and guides our battered ship into the safe harbor of his love.

Difficulties, pain and suffering will not cease until we get to heaven. In the meantime, we must face into the wind, never doubting God's promises to us during these times of trial.

We will not be spared suffering—it comes to all of us. When suffering strikes, we need to sail our ships through the trials, relinquish control by lowering our sails, and let God take the wheel.

Hunker down with God. The waves will wash over you, but calmer seas are ahead. God himself will be a refuge and hiding place from the storm and rain. ♣

GOD'S PROMISE TO ME

- Life is full of stormy seas, but I am always with you.
- Stop trying to control your ship. Lower your sails and let me guide you through the storm.

MY PRAYER TO GOD

God, the storm is pounding. I'm soaked and terrified. I give you control of my ship. Guide me to safe harbor.

day83

GOD VALUES YOU

Flee from sexual immorality. All other sins a person commits are outside the body, but whoever sins sexually, sins against their own body. Do you not know that your bodies are temples of the Holy Spirit, who is in you, whom you have received from God? You are not your own. 1 CORINTHIANS 6:18–19

Sex is everywhere, isn't it? Walk by a newsstand, turn on the TV, go to most movies, or go online. But notice that the Bible doesn't say, "Run from sex!" God created sex and gave it as a wonderful gift to the man and woman he created for their pleasure and for procreation. But Satan twisted what God created and made it into a destructive force. Therefore we need a healthy view of sex and sexuality while being aware of and avoiding sexual sin.

There are ways to develop a God-centered view of sex. Find Christian books on this topic. Set guidelines that work for you and your family—from what you watch to what you wear. If you have children, teach them modesty and purity. Teach them that sex is good within God's boundary—marriage. Discuss as a family what constitutes sexual sin and how to run from it. ❖

GOD'S PROMISE TO ME

- You were bought at a high price and are indwelt by the Holy Spirit.
- You can honor me with your body.
- I can help you run away from sexual sin.

MY PRAYER TO GOD

Oh Lord, I see unwanted pregnancies, sexual disease, families torn apart, pain—all from the misuse of your good gift. You tell us to flee from sexual sin. Help me to appreciate your gift of sex and to use it as you intended.

day84

YOU CAN HELP OTHERS

Brothers and sisters, if someone is caught in a sin, you who live by the Spirit should restore that person gently. But watch yourselves, or you also may be tempted. Carry each other's burdens, and in this way you will fulfill the law of Christ.   GALATIANS 6:1–2

With maturity comes responsibility. God desires our spiritual maturity so that we can help others. Praying for others is one way that believers older in the faith can help other believers, particularly those who may have fallen into sin. It is through prayer that we can be equipped to restore others and give wise counsel.

Yet we must also pray for a wall of protection around us. Satan hates it when believers step in and thwart his plans. We need to pray that God will protect us from pride—thinking that we got the person we prayed for back on track—and from being tripped up by the same temptations faced by those we are trying to help. We are especially vulnerable if these are areas in which we are already weak.

God says that we are obeying the law of Christ when we reach out to help other believers and share their burdens. We are all on this path together. We need to help and encourage one another. ❖

GOD'S PROMISE TO ME

- I desire that you mature so that you can help others.
- You obey my law when you share other people's troubles and problems.

MY PRAYER TO GOD

Lord, equip me to serve you. Help me be compassionate and share others' burdens. I also pray for a wall of protection around me as I help others. Guide me as I walk along your path so that I can willingly pick up those who have fallen and help them along the way. Protect me from pride and from falling into sin.

day85

GOD DOES NOT PLAY FAVORITES

Peter began to speak: "I now realize how true it is that God does not show favoritism but accepts from every nation the one who fears him and does what is right." ACTS 10:34–35

When you were a child, did you ever play favorites when choosing teams or inviting people to a birthday party? Did you ever have to watch from the sidelines as someone else played favorites? It hurts to be the one not chosen. Many lives have been severely damaged through favoritism.

God shaped the people of Israel into his special nation. The Messiah—Jesus—came from this nation. But after Jesus returned to heaven and the Holy Spirit came to earth, God extended his family membership to the Gentiles. Peter initially balked at the idea of even entering the home of a Gentile, having never done so before. But God assured Peter of the promise above: God does not show favoritism. He accepts anyone who comes to him—Jew or Gentile.

Sometimes we play favorites, fearing people who are different from us. God reminds us that favoritism has no place in his kingdom. God's love has no color or national identity. All are welcome to join his family. ❖

GOD'S PROMISE TO ME

- I do not play favorites.
- I accept everyone willing to do what is right.

MY PRAYER TO GOD

Lord, sometimes I fear that I'll say or do the wrong thing around people I don't know or don't understand because they are different than I am. Grant me boldness to love all people and to never play favorites.

GOD WATCHES OVER YOU

I will instruct you and teach you in the way you should go; I will counsel you with my loving eye on you. PSALM 32:8

What an incredible promise! Have you ever wondered how people who aren't Christians handle decision making? Whenever a big decision comes into their lives, they have nothing but their own wits to depend on as they consider their options.

Even as believers, we might sometimes forget to ask God for his guidance in our decisions, especially if we think he will disagree with our agenda. So, we go our own way, at times falling into one of life's potholes. When trouble comes as a result, we blame God, wondering why he didn't "save" us from hard circumstances.

God never forces his counsel on anyone. When we choose to trust him, we choose to place ourselves under his authority. He promises to guide us along "the way [we] should go." It's all a matter of trusting that his desires for us are best. ❖

GOD'S PROMISE TO ME

- I will guide you along the very best pathway for your life.
- I will advise and watch over you every step of the way.

MY PRAYER TO GOD

You promise that you will guide your people along the best pathways for their lives. Guide me today, Lord. Give me the strength to step out with courage and faith as I sense your leading.

day87

GOD KEEPS YOU FROM FALLING

The LORD makes firm the steps of the one who delights in him; though he may stumble, he will not fall, for the LORD upholds him with his hand. PSALM 37:23–24

When is the last time you walked across an icy parking lot? Maybe you avoided doing so out of fear that you would fall. One false move and you'd slip and break your arm or leg.

We sometimes have this tentative approach to life, fearing that we'll slip in some way. The Lord understands our frailty. He promises to direct our steps. And even though we will stumble, God promises that we won't fall, for he will hold us up.

When we ask for God's direction for our lives, we can also pray for the humility to follow God's guidance ... step-by-step. Rarely does he give us the big picture; rarely does he show us the destination. Instead, he expects us to follow him with baby steps, to follow in the daily details of our lives.

There will be difficulty, failure and frustration, and days when we might stumble. But God promises that we will not fall, for he holds us up. ❖

GOD'S PROMISE TO ME

- I direct your steps
- I delight in the details of your life.
- I will not let you fall.

MY PRAYER TO GOD

Lord, I'm grateful that you promise to direct my steps. I trust that you will hold me tightly with your hand. Please give me encouragement, comfort and an arm on which to lean.

day88

GOD DIRECTS YOU AS YOU SEEK HIM

Trust in the LORD with all your heart and lean not on your own understanding; in all your ways submit to him, and he will make your paths straight. PROVERBS 3:5–6

If you've hiked through a wooded area, you know the value of staying on carefully marked paths. The paths are there to help you navigate through the area. When you veer off the path, you might find yourself in trouble.

Like Pilgrim in John Bunyan's *The Pilgrim's Progress*, we need to stay on the clearly-marked path in order to avoid all kinds of trouble. God promises that when we trust him and seek his will instead of depending on our own understanding, he will direct our paths. That doesn't mean that we never think through a problem or ask others for advice, but it does mean that we take what we know and the advice we get and still seek God's guidance.

With God's guidance we'll stay on the path, step around the rocks and boulders, and not get pulled in other directions. As we walk the path, we can seek God's will and walk in step-by-step obedience. ❖

GOD'S PROMISE TO ME

- When you trust in me and seek my will, I will direct your path.

MY PRAYER TO GOD

Lord, I truly need your direction. Help me to trust you wholeheartedly and to seek your will in all I do. Give me wisdom and the peace that comes from knowing that you are directing my path.

day89

GOD USES TROUBLE TO BUILD CHARACTER

Consider it pure joy, my brothers and sisters, whenever you face trials of many kinds, because you know that the testing of your faith produces perseverance. Let perseverance finish its work so that you may be mature and complete, not lacking anything.

JAMES 1:2–4

Some Christians in the midst of trouble feel an obligation to pretend things are better than they are. Just watch their forced smiles or listen to their overly rehearsed declarations of faith and praise. Clearly these folks are trying hard, but they appear to be playing—badly—the role of a "mature Christian"—rather than responding authentically.

There are believers who react to those in crisis by bombarding them with Bible verses and Christian clichés. Their intent is to help, but in times of pain even true words can ring hollow and sometimes even have a stinging effect. *"God is with me"—okay, I guess that's true. But I sure can't sense his presence. Why do I feel so alone?*

The James passage above suggests that trouble is a fact of life. It also declares God's goal that we develop depth of soul, not a superficial "Christian persona." In other words, it's okay to wrestle honestly. In fact, that's the only path to a strong character. ♣

GOD'S PROMISE TO ME

- I allow you to go through trials so that you might develop a strong character.

MY PRAYER TO GOD

O Lord, forgive me for the times I buy into the silly idea that you or others are impressed by superficial saints who mindlessly parrot Bible verses. Help me to remember that you want me to endure and grow strong in character. Make me attractive to others not because I wear a plastered-on smile but because I show that I'm working out my faith in an authentic way.

GOD GIVES THE DESIRE AND POWER TO OBEY

Therefore, my dear friends, as you have always obeyed—not only in my presence, but now much more in my absence—continue to work out your salvation with fear and trembling, for it is God who works in you to will and to act in order to fulfill his good purpose.

PHILIPPIANS 2:12–13

Think back to your college days. Perhaps they weren't so long ago. Your parents sent you off, trusting that you would remember all that they had taught you over the years. They hoped you would be a credit to them while you were absent from them.

Paul had similar advice for the believers in Philippi—his "spiritual children." Now that he was a prisoner, he reminded them of his teachings and how they were to continue in obedience in his absence. He greatly desired that they would pass the true test of lessons received—living out those truths on a daily basis without being nagged to do so.

Today, we can pray, with Paul, that we will be careful to remember and follow all that we've been taught. We can obey God with "fear and trembling." And what does God promise? That he is working in us. That he will give us the desire to obey and the power to do what pleases him. ✤

GOD'S PROMISE TO ME

- I can give you the desire to obey me and the power to do what pleases me.
- I will help you put your faith into action and obey me with reverence and fear.

MY PRAYER TO GOD

Lord, help me remember all that I have learned and to put my faith into action in every part of my life. Help me to obey you with reverence. You promise that you will work in me, helping me to obey. Help me to hold on to that promise.

day91

BECOMING LIKE CHRIST IN HUMILITY

Therefore, whoever takes the lowly position of this child is the greatest in the kingdom of heaven.
MATTHEW 18:4

The disciples had asked Jesus a question: "Who, then, is the greatest in the kingdom of heaven?" (18:1). In response, Jesus brought a child into their midst and explained that they needed to become as humble as little children. What did he mean?

Jesus said of himself, "Take my yoke upon you and learn from me, for I am gentle and humble in heart, and you will find rest for your souls" (Matthew 11:29). Paul wrote, "Have the same mindset as Christ Jesus ... He made himself nothing by taking the very nature of a servant, being made in human likeness" (Philippians 2:5,7).

To be humble like a child is to have a sincere and trusting heart. That kind of faith pleases Jesus. As children trust and depend on their parents, so we can completely trust and depend on God. Children aren't concerned about climbing the ladder of success or where they are in the social strata, and we shouldn't be either. As children, we can be more concerned about living for God and humbly serving others than about our own "position." ❧

GOD'S PROMISE TO ME

• As you humble yourself before me, you become great in my kingdom.

MY PRAYER TO GOD

You promise, Father, that those who are humble will be the greatest in your kingdom. I pray that my humble faith and service to you will accomplish great things for your kingdom.

day92 april 2

BECOMING LIKE CHRIST IN SERVICE

You, my brothers and sisters, were called to be free. But do not use your freedom to indulge the flesh; rather, serve one another humbly in love.   GALATIANS 5:13

Along with humility comes an attitude of service. Jesus came to serve: "Just as the Son of Man did not come to be served, but to serve, and to give his life as a ransom for many" (Matthew 20:28).

Paul told the Galatian believers that they had been called to live in freedom from sin because of what Jesus had done for them. However, that freedom did not mean that they could do anything they pleased and not be held accountable. Instead, this freedom allowed their normally selfish, sinful nature to be overruled by a desire to serve others in love.

No matter what kind of employment we have, how much money we make or how busy we are, we can still be characterized by our willingness to serve others. We can pray that we will never be "above" doing certain acts or "too busy" to be involved in activities that help others.

Pray that you will find areas of service where you can make a difference. ❖

GOD'S PROMISE TO ME

- I have given you freedom to serve others in love.

MY PRAYER TO GOD

Lord, you have given me freedom to serve others. Thank you for freeing me from my sinful nature and giving me a desire to selflessly reach out and serve others. Show me where I can use my gifts to really make a difference for your kingdom. May an attitude of humble service infuse every part of my life.

day93

GOD DELIVERS THE FAITHFUL FROM SHAME

Those who look to him are radiant; their faces are never covered with shame.

PSALM 34:5

Has this ever happened to you? You're in a tough spot, a real mess. But instead of looking to God and responding to your situation in faith, you panic. You end up making decisions that you later regret.

First Samuel 21 records how David, while fleeing from the murderous King Saul, pretended to be insane when he encountered a Philistine king. This is Israel's greatest war hero and most faithful follower of God, in enemy territory, depending on a manmade trick rather than God to save his skin!

Later, in reflecting upon this incident in Psalm 34, David declares that God is faithful to deliver his people from shame. Could it be that David regretted his failure to demonstrate faith before the king of Gath? Could it be that David was saying when we come back to God after making choices we are ashamed of, we find the forgiveness and cleansing that puts our shame to flight? ♣

GOD'S PROMISE TO ME

- Look to me and I will give you joy.
- I will not allow shame to touch you.

MY PRAYER TO GOD

Lord, there is joy—not shame—for the troubled soul who looks to you in faith. When I am in trouble, keep me from the temptation to take matters into my own hands. Rather than devising some kind of human scheme to avoid trouble, give me the courage to trust in you. And when I fail, keep me from wallowing in shame. Prompt me to turn back to you so that I might know your forgiveness and peace.

day94

BECOMING LIKE CHRIST IN INTEGRITY

Whoever walks in integrity walks securely, but whoever takes crooked paths will be found out. PROVERBS 10:9

People with integrity are trustworthy. They speak the truth and live the truth. Perhaps that is why Proverbs describes them as "walk[ing] securely." They don't worry about which person they told what story to in order to keep their lies straight. Instead, they always tell the truth.

Jesus called for people to trust him: "Whoever believes in me does not believe in me only, but in the one who sent me. The one who looks at me is seeing the one who sent me. I have come into the world as a light, so that no one who believes in me should stay in darkness" (John 12:44–46). Why do we know we can trust Jesus? Because every word he said came true.

We can be people of integrity. We can pray to be known for integrity and to always walk securely in God's truth. ✤

GOD'S PROMISE TO ME

- I will help you to have integrity.
- With integrity, you will walk securely all the days of your life.

MY PRAYER TO GOD

Lord, I want to be a person of integrity, a person known for honesty and truthfulness. Sometimes it seems that integrity is in short supply in our world. I want to maintain integrity in my friendships, marriage, family, occupation — wherever you place me.

BECOMING LIKE CHRIST IN SELF-DENIAL

Whoever wants to save their life will lose it, but whoever loses their life for me and for the gospel will save it ... If anyone is ashamed of me and my words in this adulterous and sinful generation, the Son of Man will be ashamed of them when he comes in his Father's glory.   MARK 8:35,38

It can be tough to take a stand, to stand out, to stand up. We don't want to call attention to ourselves. So we try to blend in and lay low. We aren't ashamed of Jesus and his words, we just don't want to put them "out there" for people to criticize.

Can't our faith just be a private matter?

Jesus says no. If we are ashamed to acknowledge him before the people in our lives, he will be ashamed to acknowledge us before his Father.

Doesn't that make your blood run cold?

Far better to be ready to lose whatever you have for the sake of your Lord.

We need to pray that we will be willing to give up everything else for the sake of Jesus and the Good News. Jesus came to deny himself, to lay down his life (see John 10:15). We need to pray that we will never be ashamed of the gospel. When we pray this way, we will find true life. ❖

GOD'S PROMISE TO ME

- You will find true life when you are completely committed to me.
- When you acknowledge me, I will acknowledge you.

MY PRAYER TO GOD

You promise, Lord, that we find true life by denying ourselves. Grant me the humility and courage to do so. May I never be ashamed of your gospel.

day96

april 6

BECOMING LIKE CHRIST IN FORGIVENESS

If you forgive other people when they sin against you, your heavenly Father will also for-give you. But if you do not forgive others their sins, your Father will not forgive your sins.
MATTHEW 6:14–15

When Jesus hung in agony on the cross, he said these words: "Father, forgive them, for they do not know what they are doing" (Luke 23:34).

The bottom line of our relationship with God is forgiveness. If God were not willing to forgive our sins, we would be completely without hope. But he continues to forgive us every day. While it's true that we are already forgiven, we still need to come to him in repentance, seeking forgiveness for the sins that plague us. And in order to have a Christlike spirit, we must learn to forgive others in the same way that Jesus forgives us.

People who forgive are set free from grudges and the cycles of hurt and revenge. When we refuse to forgive another, we harbor the hurt that person has caused us and allow it to continue to fester. We carry it around with us. As a result, we give that person way too much power over us. Even more importantly, when we refuse to forgive others, we show that we don't understand the great gift of mercy that God has given us. Being able to forgive shows that we understand that we are forgiven people even though we don't deserve to be forgiven. ✤

GOD'S PROMISE TO ME

- You will understand more about my forgiveness as you learn to forgive others.

MY PRAYER TO GOD

Father, help me be forgiving. I willingly relinquish any grudges or hurts that are a detri-ment in my life. Make me more sensitive to those who need my forgiveness.

100

day97

BECOMING LIKE CHRIST IN PATIENCE AND COMPASSION

We urge you, brothers and sisters, warn those who are idle and disruptive, encourage the disheartened, help the weak, be patient with everyone.   I THESSALONIANS 5:14

Jesus acted with great compassion toward many people. With the masses of people, Jesus showed great love and concern. Even at those times when he went away for a rest and the crowds followed, Jesus was not angry or impatient. Instead, at one point, "when Jesus landed and saw a large crowd, he had compassion on them, because they were like sheep without a shepherd. So he began teaching them many things" (Mark 6:34). Jesus knew people's needs, and he responded accordingly. At times he spoke warning to the disciples, for they would soon carry great responsibility. And he spoke the harsh truth to the Pharisees about their self-righteousness.

Paul wrote that God's people need to care about one another. Many times compassion is the key—we need to encourage the timid and take care of the weak. We need to pray for wisdom to respond correctly with the right words at the right time. ❧

GOD'S PROMISE TO ME

- You can learn to love others and have compassion just as I have compassion for those in need.

MY PRAYER TO GOD

Father, give me the kind of compassion that is like yours. When I reach out to help others, may they see you.

day98

GOD GIVES WISDOM

If any of you lacks wisdom, you should ask God, who gives generously to all without finding fault, and it will be given to you. JAMES 1:5

We fight aging. We buy creams and gels to fix our sagging skin and our graying hair. But there's a good thing that comes with aging—at least for most people—a little bit of wisdom gained in the trenches of life experiences. Where we used to look up to older people for advice, now we *are* those older people. It behooves us to ask God for wisdom to make sense of our lives so far and to be able to share that wisdom with others.

While it's true that much of our wisdom comes from the experience of serving God over the years, it's also true, as God's promise says, that if we need wisdom, all we have to do is ask him for it. He promises to give wisdom for every situation and to help the one asking to continue to grow in that wisdom.

Pray that you will gain the wisdom of experience that comes from walking with God and that you will continue to ask for the wisdom you need for every day, every situation, every conversation. God promises to give it. ✤

GOD'S PROMISE TO ME

• When you ask me for wisdom, I will gladly give it.

MY PRAYER TO GOD

Lord, I need wisdom for the decisions I make every day. May your wisdom guide the choices and decisions I make, so that I will gain valuable wisdom to pass on to others.

day99

THE GODLY CAN GIVE GOOD ADVICE

The mouths of the righteous utter wisdom, and their tongues speak what is just. The law of their God is in their hearts; their feet do not slip. PSALM 37:30–31

Having wise people to go to for advice and guidance is a precious gift. God says, "Plans fail for lack of counsel, but with many advisers they succeed" (Proverbs 15:22). While God is our ultimate source of wisdom, he understands that we need people to talk to, to bounce thoughts and ideas off of, and to help us work through a situation or make a decision. We should seek out wise believers who can offer good counsel. We need to ask God to help us be wise believers ourselves, those who fill our hearts with God's law so that we will never slip from his path. Then we can offer godly counsel to others.

As we navigate through life, we need to seek out wise, godly people for advice. We need to pray for our friends and family that they too will find others to guide them. And as we mature and grow older, we can ask God to help us to be godly advisors who can offer wise counsel to others. ✤

GOD'S PROMISE TO ME

- I can guide you to people who will give godly advice.
- I can help you give godly counsel to others.

MY PRAYER TO GOD

Lord, give me discernment to know what advice is godly advice. Then help me make a good decision. I want to be known as a godly person who knows right from wrong and can give others solid guidance.

day100

THE WISE GAIN KNOWLEDGE OF GOD

My son, if you accept my words and store up my commands within you, turning your ear to wisdom and applying your heart to understanding ... then you will understand the fear of the LORD and find the knowledge of God. For the LORD gives wisdom; from his mouth come knowledge and understanding. PROVERBS 2:1,5–6

More than anything in this world we should desire wisdom. King Solomon knew that. When God offered him anything he wanted, he chose wisdom in order to rule God's people well (see 1 Kings 3:9–10). His advice to us is to seek wisdom with everything we've got (see the book of Ecclesiastes).

We can discern wisdom when we hear it so that we will know what is wise and what is not. Sometimes wisdom comes through experience, and we will need to figure out what we've learned.

God's Word invites us to search for wisdom as we would for lost money or hidden treasure. God promises that when we do, we will understand what it means to fear the Lord, and we will actually gain "knowledge and understanding." Now that's a promise worth pursuing!

God is the source of true wisdom. If our search for wisdom doesn't lead to him, we will find only a poor imitation of wisdom. ❖

GOD'S PROMISE TO ME

- As you gain wisdom, you will gain a deeper knowledge of me.

MY PRAYER TO GOD

Father, open my ears to your wisdom. Help me to recognize wisdom when I hear it. I pray that in all of my seeking, I will find it, for you are the giver of wisdom.

day**101**

WISDOM BRINGS GREAT REWARD

Get wisdom, get understanding; do not forget my words or turn away from them. Do not forsake wisdom, and she will protect you; love her, and she will watch over you. The beginning of wisdom is this: Get wisdom. Though it cost all you have, get understanding.

PROVERBS 4:5 – 7

When we pray for wisdom, we may echo these words of King Solomon in today's promise. Living wisely is important, for wisdom is a protection. Wise people are saved from lots of stupid mistakes and consequences. They have an honorable reputation.

This doesn't mean that wise people never make mistakes or are not attacked. In fact, sometimes the wisest people are the focus of the harshest criticism. Even then, however, they will sustain the blows because their reputation goes before them.

Pray that you will hold on to wisdom and gain a good reputation because of it. Then when attacks come, you will be able to stand firm. Wisdom will exalt and honor you. ❖

GOD'S PROMISE TO ME

- You can learn to be wise and develop good judgment.
- Wisdom will exalt and honor you.

MY PRAYER TO GOD

Lord, work in my life to develop wisdom. May I never turn my back on wisdom but always love and embrace it. You have said that when I prize wisdom, it exalts me; when I embrace wisdom, it honors me.

day102

THOSE WHO OBEY ARE WISE

Not everyone who says to me, "Lord, Lord," will enter the kingdom of heaven, but only the one who does the will of my Father who is in heaven ... Therefore everyone who hears these words of mine and puts them into practice is like a wise man who built his house on the rock. MATTHEW 7:21,24

In order for us to be able to obey, communication with God and relationship with him are necessary. We can't obey when we don't know the rules. People who are believers are constantly seeking to know God better so they can obey him.

Even in obedience, all believers don't look alike. God gives us all enough room for a range of choices in some areas. Unfortunately, many today are mixed up about those areas. Some try to make sin an option or a lifestyle choice. Other issues—such as how we school our children, worship or spend our money—offer us many options, and each of us can be in God's will even though we may do those things a bit differently.

We are responsible to know God's Word in order to discern what's sinful and to be sure of God's guidance. The responsibility to obey is ours. If we continue to seek God's guidance sincerely and obey what he says, our lives will be built on solid rock. ✤

GOD'S PROMISE TO ME

• You will have great wisdom when you listen to my teaching and obey me.

MY PRAYER TO GOD

Lord, give me discernment so that I won't condemn others in areas where you have allowed for freedom. Help me build my life on the solid rock of your Word. May I not only hear your teaching but also listen and obey.

day103

OBEDIENCE PROVES YOUR FAITH

What good is it, my brothers and sisters, if someone claims to have faith but has no deeds? Can such faith save them?... Faith by itself, if it is not accompanied by action, is dead. But someone will say, "You have faith; I have deeds." Show me your faith without deeds, and I will show you my faith by my deeds.   JAMES 2:14,17–18

As believers, we are to show our faith by the good deeds we do. We don't do these good things in order to earn God's favor or to somehow hold on to our salvation. Instead, we do them because the Holy Spirit is working in us, changing our lives and our focus.

So what kind of good deeds does God want? He wants obedience, whether that means trusting him, setting straight a lie, dealing with a gossip, taking time to study the Bible and pray, or doing an act of kindness for someone. A lifestyle of obedience requires a moment-by-moment decision to obey God in the little and big things that occur each day. Will we fail? Of course. Does messing up mean we aren't believers? No. God works on us and in us little by little, like Michelangelo sculpting his famous *David*. God doesn't make us perfect the moment we believe. Instead, we grow, mess up, learn from our mistakes and move on.

And we pray that our faith will show itself in good deeds as God continues carving his masterpiece little by little. ✤

GOD'S PROMISE TO ME

• Your faith will show itself through your obedience.

MY PRAYER TO GOD

Lord, may my faith reveal itself in obedience as you continue to work in my life.

GOD WILL REDEEM THE TIME

I will repay you for the years the locusts have eaten — the great locust and the young locust, the other locusts and the locust swarm — my great army that I sent among you.

JOEL 2:25

It was that last slice of pizza, cake or lasagna that did it. Your stomach tried to tell you it was full while you reached for another serving, and now it's getting back at you. That last slice was one too many.

There are countless times when we struggle to listen to our conscience. Ignoring that still, small voice, we make mistakes. At the time, the decision seemed like the right one, but we are left hurting. Regretting those times can feel like a necessary penance, but regret without redemption can become agonizing punishment.

The prophet Joel had the sad task of bring messages of judgment to God's people. Yet he was also able to temper those messages with news of God's mercy. Yes, judgment would come, but God would give back the years the locusts had eaten.

In other words, God forgives. His mercy is great. He wants us to learn from our mistakes and allow him to bring good from them. Time is too precious a gift to spend wallowing in regret. After we've repented, God forgives us and moves on. We should too. ✤

GOD'S PROMISE TO ME

- When you ask for forgiveness, I will give it.
- I will redeem your past by guiding your future.

MY PRAYER TO GOD

Lord, thank you for understanding and forgiving my mistakes. Help me to learn from them that I may grow closer to you.

day105

GOD SWEEPS YOUR SIN AWAY

I have swept away your offenses like a cloud, your sins like the morning mist. Return to me, for I have redeemed you. ISAIAH 44:22

Meteorologists are the professional fortune-tellers of our time. Even with Doppler radar, most of a weathercaster's job involves him or her being wrong more often than right. Large storms can often be predetermined, but small things, like rain or clouds, can't be accurately predicted.

Fortunately, God is much more reliable than the weather report. It's never guess-and-check with God. He knows what is in store for all of us. He's told us that there will be hard times and cloudy days, but he has also promised that just as the sun is somewhere behind those clouds, he too will always be there for us.

Sin can overshadow our lives and demoralize us if we let it. Trusting in God to forgive us and lead us when we repent is our only assurance of eternal happiness. He is always ready to sweep our sins away. God's forecast? Partly cloudy with a 100 percent chance of redemption. ✤

GOD'S PROMISE TO ME

- If you repent, I will forgive.
- I know the plans I have for you.
- I will always be with you.

MY PRAYER TO GOD

Father, I am gratefully astonished by your willingness to forgive. Thank you for your faithful presence in all I do, and help me to seek out the sun when there are cloudy days in my life.

day106

GOD KNOWS YOU

Before I formed you in the womb I knew you, before you were born I set you apart.

JEREMIAH 1:5

If you had good parents, then plenty of wonderful things happened while you were in the womb. The moment your parents became aware of your existence, they began making plans. They got baby books. They put together a place for you in their house or apartment. They got clothing, books, diapers, toys and all sorts of accessories. They went to doctor's appointments. They decided on what they would name you.

Your parents had dreams for you. They wanted to be great parents. They wanted to raise you well and give you every opportunity.

Another person had some plans in place as well—God himself. In fact, he knew you'd be showing up in the womb before your parents did. He knew every decision they'd make and every mistake. In short, he knew everything about you.

Jeremiah was set apart for a special task, but we know that God makes each of us special with special tasks to do on this planet. If you're still wondering, go to the Source for an answer. He had you in mind from the beginning. ✤

GOD'S PROMISE TO ME

- I have chosen you.
- I know you completely.
- I want to guide you.

MY PRAYER TO GOD

Lord, thank you for knowing me from before I was even born. Show me the tasks you have for me.

day**107**

GOD GIVES YOU A NEW HEART

I will give you a new heart and put a new spirit in you; I will remove from you your heart of stone and give you a heart of flesh. And I will put my Spirit in you and move you to follow my decrees and be careful to keep my laws. Ezekiel 36:26–27

When we're born, our parents take care of us, clothe us and teach us. In many ways, we become versions of them. Brought into the world as blank slates, our parents help shape who we are.

As a believer in Christ, we're part of another family. Committing ourselves to God, we offer up all that we were so that we can be remade. Once his, God does just that—he remakes us so that we may become a version of him. Though sin makes us an imperfect version, we can still aspire to be like our Father.

Being born again gives us a new start. God takes our slate and erases all the evil and sin, leaving only the good. He take our hearts, hardened by the hurt and sin and evil in the world, and gives us hearts of flesh, able to accept his love and share it. He gives us the Holy Spirit, clothes us in his righteousness and teaches us through his Word. We have a chance now, no longer shaped into who we are but rather into what we should be. ✤

GOD'S PROMISE TO ME

- Through me, you can be a new creation.
- The Holy Spirit is a gift I will never withhold.
- I can soften your hardened heart.

MY PRAYER TO GOD

Lord, thank you for giving me new life in you. I rededicate myself to you as your servant. Help me to continue to follow your ways and learn from your Word.

day108

GOD WILL FIGHT FOR YOU

The LORD your God, who is going before you, will fight for you.   DEUTERONOMY 1:30

In this world of instant news, there are many things that frighten us. We fear natural disasters, terrorists, accidents and wars. We know that God is in control, but watching the news can bring us to a state of anxiety.

When the Israelites heard about the people in Canaan, they were fearful too. They felt the same fear we do today—an irrational fear. After all, isn't all fear irrational when God is on our side? The punishment for their irrational fear was a lifetime wandering the desert. God was ready to give them the promised land; their fear gave them the desert.

When we watch the next news story about a tragedy or disaster, we can remember that God promises his presence no matter what we encounter. Trusting God means taking on our fears head-on and moving to a place of peace. ❖

GOD'S PROMISE TO ME

- You can overcome your fear, for I am with you.
- I will always be your protector and fortress.

MY PRAYER TO GOD

God, thank you for always being there for me as comforter and protector. Help me to remember in times of trouble that you are with me.

day109

GOD REWARDS YOUR QUIET TIME WITH HIM

But when you pray, go into your room, close the door and pray to your Father, who is unseen. Then your Father, who sees what is done in secret, will reward you.

MATTHEW 6:6

There is a thriving breed of people in America known as the Coffee Shop Writers. They cannot work anywhere else except in the bustling coffee shop of their neighborhood. They settle in, get their coffee and work tirelessly on their novel, article or screenplay. They seem to believe that their work needs an audience—both before and after publication.

Even though this is a specialized group, in reality you can find people with a similar perspective in all walks of life: lifting weights, taking pictures, cooking, running, working or even eating. People are beginning to find it difficult to do anything without an audience.

The last thing God wants our spiritual life to become is a show we put on for others. Prayer should be a time of personal reflection and divine conversation. It needs to be between us and God. That's it. Even when you're not on your cell phone, your webcam is off and you're not engaging in social media, you still have an audience of One—and he knows your heart. ❖

GOD'S PROMISE TO ME

- I will always be personal, and I will always be with you.
- Others look on the outside, I will always look at the heart.

MY PRAYER TO GOD

Lord, thank you for always listening to me. Help me to remember that even though I follow you in deed and in word, our relationship is a personal one.

YOU BELONG TO GOD

Know that the LORD *is God. It is he who made us, and we are his; we are his people, the sheep of his pasture.* PSALM 100:3

If someone asked the question, "What do you own?" we'd probably look around and start listing our furniture, clothing, books, cars or houses. But what if the question was, "What do you take pride in owning?" We would probably turn to things we've made or, at the very least, fixed ourselves. We value things where we can say, "I did that."

If we were to ask God the same question, he probably wouldn't say anything. He would simply smile gently and hold a mirror up in front of us. It might be hard to believe sometimes, but we are God's cherished creation. Even when we make mistakes, doubt him or even reject him, he still takes pride in us. We can never escape his love.

Feel special yet? You should. Because when you reciprocate God's love through the way you live, he looks down on you and says, "I did that." ♣

GOD'S PROMISE TO ME

- You will always be my creation, my child, my loved one.
- I will always be proud of you.

MY PRAYER TO GOD

God, thank you for making me. Help me to do your will.

LOVE NEVER FAILS

Love does not delight in evil but rejoices with the truth. It always protects, always trusts, always hopes, always perseveres. Love never fails.   1 CORINTHIANS 13:6–8

It's the theme in every Disney princess story. We preface the word with descriptors like "puppy" and "true." Sometimes it happens at the top of the Empire State Building. Whatever it is, however it happens, we are obsessed with *love*.

The irony is that love is hard work. While the movies have given us love stories and romantic comedies that bring us a warm and fuzzy view of finding love, actually *keeping* love is an entirely different story. Divorce statistics bear this out. To always trust, hope and persevere is hard work.

But love can do it.

Love doesn't exist in a purely scientific world. Without the soul, all we have are the primal instincts of attraction, protection and reproduction. Love has always been God's greatest gift, and the strongest proof of his existence. So the next time someone asks you to prove God's existence, refer them to their favorite love story, and remind them that only God's kind of love can make it last. ❖

GOD'S PROMISE TO ME

- Love will always persevere.
- My love for you is never-ending.
- I will help you to love.

MY PRAYER TO GOD

Lord, thank you for creating love and loving me. Help me to love others, especially when it feels difficult or even impossible.

day112

YOU WILL RECEIVE A CROWN THAT LASTS FOREVER

Do you not know that in a race all the runners run, but only one gets the prize? Run in such a way as to get the prize. Everyone who competes in the games goes into strict training. They do it to get a crown that will not last, but we do it to get a crown that will last forever. 1 CORINTHIANS 9:24–25

Every year an elementary school holds races for every grade. Two boys in the fourth grade have been waiting for this day since the school year began. Each wants more than anything to win and, when the whistle is blown, each runs as hard as he can toward the finish line. Who won? One judge says it was the first boy while another judge says it was the second. The boys look at each other in astonishment. Did we really tie?

It's generally known in sports that anything is better than a tie. Even though statistically a tie is better than a loss, when you're a player or a coach, it makes you wonder how much more work would have gotten you the win. It leaves you dissatisfied.

Heaven is a tie we can be satisfied with. Everyone racing for the prize of heaven will be happy to discover that it is a prize to be shared. In heaven there's no question about who won because—thanks to Christ—we all did. ✤

GOD'S PROMISE TO ME

- There is a place waiting for you in heaven.
- As long as heaven is your goal, you will always win.

MY PRAYER TO GOD

Father, thank you for giving me eternal life in your kingdom. Help me run to win so that I may reach the goal of eternity in heaven.

FILLED WITH THE FRUIT OF RIGHTEOUSNESS

That you may be able to discern what is best and may be pure and blameless for the day of Christ, filled with the fruit of righteousness that comes through Jesus Christ—to the glory and praise of God. PHILIPPIANS 1:10–11

Paul's loving words to his dear friends in Philippi are echoed by Christians everywhere. We want those whom we serve to understand what really matters in life—not how they look, not how they dress, not how popular they are. What really matters is their relationship with Jesus Christ and their continued growth in him.

We want them to live pure and blameless lives until Christ returns. Purity seems to be a rare commodity these days, judging from what we see on TV, in movies, and in magazines. Yet when we live in purity, we exhibit a character trait that is valuable.

Praying for this fruit is a prayer that requires perseverance. Let's pray that we will always be filled with that fruit and the good things that Jesus produces in our lives through the presence of his Holy Spirit. Then our lives will bring much glory and praise to God. ✣

GOD'S PROMISE TO ME

- Through a relationship with me you can understand how to live a pure and blameless life.
- I receive glory and praise when fruit grows and ripens in your life.

MY PRAYER TO GOD

Lord, please help me and those for whom I am praying to grow spiritually and understand what really matters in life. I pray I not will chase after what doesn't matter but instead will focus on my relationship with you and on growing to be more like you.

day114

april 24

YOU CAN LIVE BY FAITH

For through the law I died to the law so that I might live for God. I have been crucified with Christ and I no longer live, but Christ lives in me. The life I now live in the body, I live by faith in the Son of God, who loved me and gave himself for me.

GALATIANS 2:19–20

These verses have a mystical wonder to them. When we try to wrap our minds around these concepts, we can't figure them out: We have been crucified, yet we live. We died, and yet we are alive. We are still ourselves living our lives, but Christ is living in and through us. In these words we find the breathless wonder of our intimate relationship with Jesus Christ. He is not a god "out there" somewhere nor a stone-cold idol. He is a person who lived, died and rose again. Jesus is God himself, brought into focus before our eyes. When we accept him as our Savior, his crucifixion becomes our own, for he was crucified in our place. Now, through his Holy Spirit, he lives in us, and we live our lives by faith in him, trusting the One who loved us and gave himself for us.

Let's pray that we will sense the wonder of what Christ has done for us. May we sense the glory of being crucified and raised with Christ and resolve to live out our faith in him. ✤

GOD'S PROMISE TO ME

- I died so you can be made new.
- You share in my death.

MY PRAYER TO GOD

I have been crucified with Christ, and so I no longer live, but you live in me. What a wonder it is, Lord, that you would take up residence in my life. Set me free to serve you with all my heart and soul. May I live joyously because of my faith in you.

YOU ARE CHRIST'S WITNESS

Go and make disciples of all nations, baptizing them in the name of the Father and of the Son and of the Holy Spirit, and teaching them to obey everything I have commanded you.
MATTHEW 28:19–20

There's no doubt about the job Jesus left for us to do. He did not say, "Go hide away from this evil world and keep clear of its influence." He didn't say, "Don't get near those nasty unbelievers who do such sinful things!" He said, "Go and make disciples of all the nations." That means stepping out of our comfort zones—whether across the street or around the world—to find people who need to know Christ. They are the ones who need to hear the message.

In this life we will encounter plenty of unbelievers who need to be reached. Whether God calls us to live on the other side of the globe or to have an impact at our local school or in the workplace, we need to gain a heart for the lost so that we can do as Christ commands and "make disciples." We also can be an example to others in our concern for the lost and our witness to the people God has placed in our sphere of influence. ❖

GOD'S PROMISE TO ME

- Through my power you can help make disciples of all nations.
- I am with you always.

MY PRAYER TO GOD

Jesus, help me to be a good example in my concern for the lost. In words, deeds and attitudes may I stand out in the crowd as one who has found the answer to life! Thank you for the promise of your presence.

day116

april 26

YOUR THOUGHT PATTERNS CAN CHANGE

Finally, brothers and sisters, whatever is true, whatever is noble, whatever is right, whatever is pure, whatever is lovely, whatever is admirable—if anything is excellent or praiseworthy—think about such things. Whatever you have learned or received or heard from me, or seen in me—put it into practice. And the God of peace will be with you.

PHILIPPIANS 4:8−9

Do you have days when you feel completely out of control? Perhaps your mind focuses on everything that could be improved in your life: job, house, body, abilities.

On those days in particular these verses from Philippians come in handy. We can fix our thoughts on what is true and noble and right, not on what is false, undignified or unrighteous.

How easy it can be to fall into the haze of self-pity. Instead, we can think about *what* we think about. We can meditate on Scripture and put into practice what the Bible commands.

This passage reminds us to monitor our thoughts. With God's help, we can think about things that are "excellent or praiseworthy." ❖

GOD'S PROMISE TO ME

• When you fix your thoughts on positive things, you can avoid much sin.

MY PRAYER TO GOD

You have told us, Jesus, that sin begins with thoughts. Give me the ability to think as you think, so that I will be able to dwell on what is true, noble and right. Help me to focus on what is pure, lovely and admirable.

YOU CAN HAVE JOY IN TROUBLES

Consider it pure joy, my brothers and sisters, whenever you face trials of many kinds, because you know that the testing of your faith produces perseverance. Let perseverance finish its work so that you may be mature and complete, not lacking anything.

JAMES 1:2−4

Believers should be identified as people with an amazing outlook on their troubles. Think about it. We ...

- Have the Holy Spirit in our hearts.
- Know that God promises to work all things together for good.
- Know that anything that happens to us is allowed by God for a purpose.
- Know that God wants us to grow to maturity.

The troubles that come into our lives should not surprise us, make us doubt God's love for us or put us into a tailspin. Instead, our response should be joy. No, we don't have to be happy about the trouble, but we can graciously accept what God has allowed to happen because we know that he has a good purpose for it. And yes, troubles test our faith, but tested faith results in endurance. And as endurance grows, we gain spiritual maturity.

Troubles are inevitable. How we handle them shows our true colors. God enables us to face troubles with joy and so gain endurance and strong character. ❖

GOD'S PROMISE TO ME

- Troubles and trials can be opportunities for joy.
- When your faith is tested, I will teach you endurance and produce maturity and strength of character.

MY PRAYER TO GOD

Lord, one hallmark of my faith should be my ability to face troubles with your perspective in mind. Give me the ability to face troubles with your grace. Help me to hold on to your promise so that when my faith is tested, endurance has a chance to grow.

YOU HAVE POWER

For the Spirit God gave us does not make us timid, but gives us power, love and self-discipline.   2 TIMOTHY 1:7

Paul wrote the words in today's verse to Timothy, a young man with a big responsibility as pastor of the church in Ephesus. God has not called Christians to be fearful, cowering doormats waiting to let the world step on our faith and wipe its feet on our principles. With the God of the universe in our hearts, we have a spirit of power, love and self-discipline.

People in leadership need God's help. Wherever we lead, God promises power—boldness to speak the truth. We don't have this power in order to lord it over others but to empower them, to give them boldness in their faith. God promises love, a fruit of the Spirit. We have power to speak the truth, but love for our listeners tempers that power so it does not become prideful. God also promises self-discipline, or self-control, which gives us a cool head and a sound perspective in the hazards of leadership.

God has given us a great gift—power—instead of fear or timidity. How will you exercise this gift? ♣

GOD'S PROMISE TO ME

- When I place you in a position of leadership, I will be with you.
- I can give you a spirit of power, love and self-discipline in order to lead effectively.

MY PRAYER TO GOD

Leadership is a big responsibility, Lord. No leader can please everyone, and every leader eventually needs to take a stand on important issues. I pray that I will be strong in faith and able to stand on my principles. Give me power and boldness without pride.

day119

YOU CAN CONFESS YOUR SINS AND RECEIVE MERCY

Whoever conceals their sins does not prosper, but the one who confesses and renounces them finds mercy.   PROVERBS 28:13

More than likely you know someone who always blames their problems on someone else. It is difficult to admit our mistakes; it's hard to say we're wrong; it's very hard to say we're sorry. Yet we need to be people who do not constantly attempt to cover our sins.

Here in the Old Testament, the Bible tells us that concealing sin doesn't move us ahead. Instead, we'll spend so much time trying to remember what we said to whom that eventually we will get caught. How much better it is to be honest right from the start. How much better to confess and forsake wrongdoing. This verse from Proverbs says that we will find mercy when we confess and renounce our sins. The New Testament promises, "If we confess our sins, he is faithful and just and will forgive us our sins and purify us from all unrighteousness" (1 John 1:9). ❖

GOD'S PROMISE TO ME

- When you confess and forsake your sin, you will receive mercy.

MY PRAYER TO GOD

Lord, give me strength of character to take responsibility for my actions and not to blame others. Please forgive me when I am wrong. You promise that when I confess my sins to you, you will forgive me and cleanse me. Thank you for your faithful mercy.

day120

GOD EMPOWERS YOU TO DO GOOD WORKS

For it is by grace you have been saved, through faith—and this is not from yourselves, it is the gift of God ... For we are God's handiwork, created in Christ Jesus to do good works, which God prepared in advance for us to do.   EPHESIANS 2:8,10

Our Christian lives should be characterized by good deeds. The Bible makes it clear that good deeds cannot earn our salvation. Salvation is a gift. But salvation makes us new people and gives us new lives. God sees us as his masterpieces. As his new people, we embark on a life of adventure. But we don't have to dash around trying to find good things to do for God. Instead, those good things were already planned out for us a long time ago. We simply need to be obedient, and God will make them clear to us.

God will put certain people into our lives, bring us to the right place at the right time, give us special abilities that he will use and give us a heart for meeting a certain need. God calls us to do good works. What those good works will be depends on where God leads us.

We are called to do good things for God. Thus, we can follow him in obedience, knowing that every good deed we do is for his glory. ✤

GOD'S PROMISE TO ME

- I saved you not because you are good but because I choose to show favor to you.
- You are my masterpiece. I make you new so that you can do the good things I planned for you long ago.

MY PRAYER TO GOD

You saved us, Lord! What a glorious gift! We can take no credit for our salvation, for you gave it to us. I pray that I will never be caught in the trap of thinking that I have to do good deeds in order to earn or hold onto your salvation. I am saved by your grace, and good deeds are simply part of your plan for me.

day**121**

GOD CALLS YOU TO USE YOUR GIFTS

There are different kinds of gifts, but the same Spirit distributes them. There are different kinds of service, but the same Lord ... Now to each one the manifestation of the Spirit is given for the common good.　　　　　　　　　　　　1 CORINTHIANS 12:4–7

God graciously gives every believer at least one spiritual gift to use to build up the church. We cannot choose the gift we want; God decides (see 1 Corinthians 12:11). So it follows, then, that we must discover our gift and use it for God's glory.

Paul made it clear that there are different kinds of gifts—different ways the Holy Spirit works through us. The Bible gives some lists of gifts, but these are not meant to be exhaustive (see 1 Corinthians 12:8–10 and Ephesians 4:7–12). We are to use our gifts in harmony with others' gifts so that the entire job of reaching people for Christ and building them up in the faith can be completed.

We can discover our gifts from God as we try out different things and discover what we really love and are good at. This discernment process may take some advice and observations from others. Once we determine our gifting, we can use our gifts for God's glory and to bring others to him. ♣

GOD'S PROMISE TO ME

- I gave you a special gift to use in helping to build my kingdom.

MY PRAYER TO GOD

Lord, your Word says that you give your people special gifts that they can use to build your kingdom. Thank you for the different kinds of gifts that the Spirit has given me. Give me wisdom and discernment and many opportunities to use my gifts.

day122

DO NOT BE JUDGMENTAL

Do not judge, or you too will be judged. For in the same way you judge others, you will be judged, and with the measure you use, it will be measured to you. MATTHEW 7:1–2

Not long ago a celebrity quoted these verses to back up her opinion that people should be tolerant of all kinds of aberrant behavior. Often, when Christians take a stand against sin, others throw these verses back in their faces. "Your own Bible says that you're not supposed to judge," they say with a sneer.

Today's verses do not negate the need for critical thinking or making discerning judgments. Other places in the New Testament tell us to expose false teaching, admonish others when they need it and even exercise church discipline in cases of sinful behavior. Clearly we must make some judgments. The point is that we are not to have an attitude that is consistently condemning and critical, for that is not an attitude of love. We are not to attempt to take God's place as judge. It may seem like a fine line, but believers *can* take a stand against sin without being judgmental toward the sinners. God created them, and he loves them too.

Christ has set us free to serve him with joy. Therefore, we can be discerning about sin without having a critical spirit. ✤

GOD'S PROMISE TO ME

• You can take a stand against sin without being judgmental.

MY PRAYER TO GOD

Lord, you say that we are not to take your place in judging others, for that judgment will be turned back on us. I pray for a discerning spirit, one that is able to see sin for what it is and deal with it honestly and lovingly while not being critical and judgmental.

YOU CAN ENJOY GOD'S GIFTS AND BE THANKFUL

Everything God created is good, and nothing is to be rejected if it is received with thanksgiving.   1 TIMOTHY 4:4

Here's another verse that people love to quote out of context and make it mean what it doesn't mean. Some try to say that "everything God created is good" means that even sinful behavior can be acceptable because, well, God created it, right? Wrong.

Paul was writing in response to false teachers who had added many rules in order for people to be truly saved (specifically, forbidding marriage and abstaining from certain foods, see 1 Timothy 4:3). Paul explained that God created marriage and food and both are good. Of course, people can abuse anything. According to the Bible, God designed marriage to be between one man and one woman. Homosexuality and adultery are not what God planned and, therefore, are not good. God gave us food to enjoy, but gluttony is an abuse of God's gift and not good. Paul clarified that believers do not have to abstain from God's good gifts in order to be saved. We should instead recognize God's hand in all the pleasures of his creation, use them according to his guidelines and be thankful.

God gave us gifts to enjoy. We can have an attitude of thankfulness for all that he has given us. ✤

GOD'S PROMISE TO ME

- Everything I created is good, and you need not reject any of it in order to be saved.
- When you use what I have created within my guidelines, you can receive those pleasures gladly.

MY PRAYER TO GOD

Thank you for all the wonderful pleasures you created for us, Lord. Thank you for your beautiful creation, for wind, rain and sunshine, for the joy of friendship, the intimacy of marriage, the enjoyment of good and nourishing food. Let me never forget to thank you for all these joys.

DO NOT BE TIED TO THE WORLD

Don't you know that friendship with the world means enmity against God? Therefore, anyone who chooses to be a friend of the world becomes an enemy of God.   JAMES 4:4

At first glance this verse seems to completely contradict yesterday's verse (see 1 Timothy 4:4). That verse said to gladly receive everything God created and even to find pleasure in those things. Today's verse says that if we aim to enjoy the world, we can't be God's friends.

The Greek word for *world* here refers to the evil system under Satan's control. This verse is not saying that we cannot enjoy anything in this world. Instead, it is making the point that if we make it our aim—goal, life focus, final destination—to enjoy this world's evil, we cannot be God's friend. Nothing is wrong with enjoying life and God's blessings. Friendship with the world, however, involves seeking pleasure at the expense of others or being involved in sinful practices. Taking pleasure in God and his blessings is good; taking pleasure in the sin of this world is not.

We can enjoy the blessings God gives us in this world because this is where we live. While we can bring light into darkness, we can also pray that we will never become "friends" with that darkness. ❖

GOD'S PROMISE TO ME

- You are my friend as you take pleasure in me.

MY PRAYER TO GOD

Heavenly Father, give me the discernment to know when I'm about to compromise. I want to enjoy your creation without embracing the world system. I don't want to be your enemy. Help me to appreciate my friendship with you.

day125

YOU CAN FIND CONTENTMENT

I know what it is to be in need, and I know what it is to have plenty. I have learned the secret of being content in any and every situation, whether well fed or hungry, whether living in plenty or in want. PHILIPPIANS 4:12

How would you define *contentment*? Paul defined it as the secret of living joyfully in every situation. Paul was able to hold this view because of his fellowship with Christ. He knew that he could do everything with the help of Christ who gave him the strength he needed. And so can we.

Contentment is not some fatalistic acceptance of whatever comes our way. Contentment is peace within that allows us to keep our perspective, our priorities and our faith no matter what happens. It allows us to move beyond and live above bad circumstances; it allows us to keep perspective and be thankful in good times. Whether we have a lot or a little, we trust that God will supply all of our needs "according to the riches of his glory in Christ Jesus" (Philippians 4:19). How can we not be content when we have God's glorious riches at our disposal?

We can ask God for the grace to be content in all situations. ❖

GOD'S PROMISE TO ME

- I will help you be content.

MY PRAYER TO GOD

Lord, whether I have little or much, I pray that I will be able to live joyfully. Thank you for promising that you will give me the strength I need to do your will.

YOU CAN PRAY FOR YOUR COUNTRY

If my people, who are called by my name, will humble themselves and pray and seek my face and turn from their wicked ways, then I will hear from heaven, and I will forgive their sin and will heal their land. 2 CHRONICLES 7:14

No country is perfect. No matter where we live, we know that our leaders are human and have flaws. We know that our society could use some moral grounding. We look around in dismay at the sin that surrounds us. We cry to God when we see terrorism, murder, school shootings or other senseless acts people do to one another.

What can we do? As God told his people Israel to humble themselves and pray, so must we.

For those of us who have wonderful privileges, we also have big responsibilities. If we see problems, we should be willing to work to make a difference. If we live in a country that is democratic, we should educate ourselves about issues and candidates before every election, and we should exercise our right to vote.

No matter where we live, we need to pray for our nation and its leaders. God promises that when his people humble themselves and pray, he will hear from heaven. ✤

GOD'S PROMISE TO ME

- When you pray for your country, I will hear those prayers.

MY PRAYER TO GOD

Thank you, Lord, for the reminder to pray for my country and the leaders who govern. Give them wisdom and a sense of your justice. May I never take my opportunities and the responsibilities I have for granted.

day**127**

GOD GOES BEFORE YOU

The LORD *himself goes before you and will be with you; he will never leave you nor forsake you. Do not be afraid; do not be discouraged.* DEUTERONOMY 31:8

Sometimes life hits us right between the eyes. Sometimes we feel so worried and afraid that we are nearly immobilized. The news we hear is frightening. School shootings. Terrorist bombings. It's easy to wonder, *What next?* It seems that our world is an increasingly fearful place and that horror occurs in what should be safe havens. However, we can take comfort in God's words to his faithful servant Joshua: We do not need to be afraid because God is with us.

God will be with us wherever we go. He's as close as our next prayer. We can pray for divine protection and take to heart God's promises. God will never fail us nor forsake us. ♣

GOD'S PROMISE TO ME

- Don't be worried. I will never fail or forsake you.
- I will go before you and watch over you.

MY PRAYER TO GOD

Lord, you tell us not to be afraid or discouraged because you go before us. Thank you for that promise. As you went before Joshua to handle the huge task of conquering the land, so you go before me today. Help me sense your presence today, and free me from fear and worry.

day128 may 8

GOD IS YOUR REFUGE

God is our refuge and strength, an ever-present help in trouble.　　　　Psalm 46:1

Europe is the home of countless stunning castles. Many are now decaying and moss-covered, but they still proudly remind us of a time when the world was very different. Those castles were places of safety, built on the hilltops. They were places of refuge and strength.

The psalmist describes God as a refuge and strength. As our refuge, he is a place to run to when we need protection in times of trouble. As our strength, he provides what we need to keep on fighting. When life gets the better of us, we can run to the refuge and hide behind its thick walls, knowing we are safe. Then, after we've had a time of rest, God enables us to face the trouble again.

Do you know God as your refuge? When the battle gets thick and trouble surrounds you, God will give you the strength you need to face the trouble at hand. ❖

GOD'S PROMISE TO ME

- I will be a refuge for you in times of trouble.
- I will give you the strength you need.

MY PRAYER TO GOD

Lord, I need a place to run to for safety. Times of trouble are inevitable. Even today I need your strength. Your Word says you are always ready to help in times of trouble. Thank you for that promise.

day**129**

GOD SHIELDS AND SHELTERS YOU

He will cover you with his feathers, and under his wings you will find refuge; his faithfulness will be your shield and rampart.   PSALM 91:4

Many of us struggle with worry. Bills, layoffs at work, health problems—all of these are fodder for anxious thoughts and sleepless nights. We may proclaim our trust in God on Sunday, but come Monday when the bills pile up in the mail or we receive frightening reports from the doctor, trust often takes a backseat to worry. We feel like a person who desperately seeks shelter during a storm.

There is good news: God is a refuge! He promises his protection during the storms of life. Like a mother bird sheltering her offspring under her wings, God will shield and protect us with his strong wings and warm feathers. Since many wild birds pluck their own feathers to make their nests comfortable, warm and safe, this is an image of God's sacrifice, care and love for us.

Ultimate protection is found in God alone. Are you facing a stormy situation? He's greater than any worry you may have. ❖

GOD'S PROMISE TO ME

- I will cover you with my wings and shelter you as a mother bird shelters her young.
- You are safe in my hands.

MY PRAYER TO GOD

Heavenly Father, I'm in the midst of one of life's storms. I could use your protection. Keep me safe. Be a shield and shelter for me. My life is in your hands.

day130

GOD EXCHANGES PEACE FOR WORRY

Do not be anxious about anything, but in every situation, by prayer and petition, with thanksgiving, present your requests to God. And the peace of God, which transcends all understanding, will guard your hearts and your minds in Christ Jesus.

PHILIPPIANS 4:6–7

People spend a lot of money on security systems for their homes. Some businesses even have security guards at the entrances to their buildings.

Even if we're not business owners, we could all use a security guard—one around our heart and mind. Fears and worries come in, attack and overwhelm us sometimes. If our hearts had a guard, the guard would say to worry, "Sorry, you don't have clearance. You'll have to leave." And then worry would simply go on its way. As security guards offer peace to a building's inhabitants, we too would have peace, knowing that no worry or fear could gain entrance.

When worry comes knocking at our heart's door, God promises a way to guard us from it: pray. God promises that he will give us peace, a peace that is far more wonderful than we can ever understand. That peace will guard our hearts and minds from fear and worry. ✤

GOD'S PROMISE TO ME

- You don't have to worry about anything, but instead you can pray about everything.
- When you tell me about your needs, you will experience my peace which passes all human understanding.

MY PRAYER TO GOD

Lord, help me to focus on you so that when worry tries to get in, your peace will send it away. Guard my heart and mind today with your presence.

day131

GOD ALLOWS YOU TO GO THROUGH HARD TIMES

Just as we share abundantly in the sufferings of Christ, so also our comfort abounds through Christ.   2 CORINTHIANS 1:5

How many rousing sermons or best-selling books about "the glory of suffering" have you heard about or read in the last year?

Despite the fact that the Bible speaks in great detail about the certainty of suffering and the undeniable blessing to be found in it, we pretend it doesn't exist. We don't discuss it. We rarely make even the slightest attempt to see God's purposes in it.

The apostle Paul was a man well acquainted with suffering. And Paul came to understand that not only does suffering lead to eventual glory, God uses it to transform us here and now.

Ian McPherson, a wise saint, put it this way, "The bitterest cup with Christ is better than the sweetest cup without him."

You'll never draw a big crowd advocating such an idea, but you will draw near to Jesus. ✣

GOD'S PROMISE TO ME

- You will one day share my glory.
- You must now share my suffering.

MY PRAYER TO GOD

Father, suffering is confusing and painful, and it is something I avoid rather than embrace. Teach me to respond in a godly fashion to suffering. Use difficulty in my life to transform me.

day132

GOD PROTECTS YOU

Pray that we may be delivered from wicked and evil people, for not everyone has faith. But the Lord is faithful, and he will strengthen you and protect you from the evil one.

2 THESSALONIANS 3:2–3

Have you ever run across someone who is truly evil? You might not call him or her "evil"; you might just say that person is "amoral" or "dishonest." But evil people do exist. The world is full of such people, and they will not hesitate to attack believers because of their faith. In reality, they are part of the opposing army in a spiritual battle. As the battle intensifies, it is apparent that there is only one real enemy—the evil one himself, Satan.

In today's verse, Paul asks the Thessalonian Christians to pray for him and his fellow travelers as they spread the gospel. If Paul asked for prayer, how much more should we be praying for others as they seek to live for Christ in a hostile world? Paul came up against his share of evil—and so will we today. But God promises to be faithful to his people, to make them strong and to guard them from Satan's attacks. This doesn't mean we or others close to us won't face difficulties, but it does mean that God is faithful. In the end, that's what we need to hold onto. ✤

GOD'S PROMISE TO ME

- I will be faithful to help you stand against evil.
- I will make you strong and protect you from the evil one.

MY PRAYER TO GOD

Lord, sometimes I'm overwhelmed by the evil I read about or see. Such evil causes me to sometimes doubt your ability to deal with it. Forgive me for doubting. Help me turn to you for protection and strength in the midst of a hostile world. Ultimately, you will triumph and your name will be glorified.

day**133**

GOD COMFORTS YOU

Shout for joy, you heavens; rejoice, you earth; burst into song, you mountains! For the LORD comforts his people and will have compassion on his afflicted ones. ISAIAH 49:13

All of us need comfort once in a while. Maybe it's an illness that sets us on life's sidelines. It might be the pain of hurt or betrayal that causes us to want to withdraw into our shell and never come out. Maybe it's the grief of loss that makes it feel like life is just not worth living anymore.

We search for comfort in all kinds of places — escape into the latest TV sitcom, food, the Internet. Maybe we have some caring friends who listen and try to understand, but we can only lean on them so much, for we know they have their own lives and responsibilities.

So where do we turn for comfort? Today's verse tells us to "shout for joy" for "the LORD comforts his people and will have compassion on afflicted ones." That's you. And that promise is for you. The Lord will give the comfort you need. Turn to him and pour out your hurt in prayer. He is always there for you. ❖

GOD'S PROMISE TO ME

- I am there for you in your time of need.
- I will give you comfort.
- I will comfort you and have compassion on you.

MY PRAYER TO GOD

I need your comfort today, Lord. The hurt goes deep. I need to know that there is purpose for this pain; I need to know that it will not be wasted. I need to feel the comfort that only you can give.

day134

GOD RESCUES YOU

The righteous cry out, and the LORD hears them; he delivers them from all their troubles ... The righteous person may have many troubles, but the LORD delivers him from them all.   PSALM 34:17,19

It's easy to believe that the righteous face many troubles; our daily experiences bear that out. But when we or those close to us face huge, ongoing difficulties, we might question the last part of today's promise: "the LORD delivers him from them all." We may wonder that especially if our prayers for deliverance have not been answered.

God promises that he hears us when we call to him for help. Sometimes his answer is years in coming, but God promises to rescue us from every trouble and give us strength to endure. He can take our troubles and use them for his good purposes—and for our own growth.

God doesn't promise smooth sailing, but he does promise rescue. He doesn't say when or how, he just says he *will*. God knows a life without troubles would make us spiritually immature. We need to face difficulty in order to grow. But God also knows when it is enough, and he will rescue. We can be confident that God will rescue us from trouble in his way, in his time. ✤

GOD'S PROMISE TO ME

- I will hear you when you call for help.
- I will rescue you from trouble.

MY PRAYER TO GOD

Dear Lord, you promise to rescue your people from all their troubles. Rescue me today. When other trials arise and cause me pain and difficulty, I claim your promise of rescue.

day135

GOD GOES WITH YOU THROUGH TRIALS

When you pass through the waters, I will be with you; and when you pass through the rivers, they will not sweep over you. When you walk through the fire, you will not be burned; the flames will not set you ablaze. ISAIAH 43:2

These are God's gracious words to the nation of Israel. What vivid pictures of God's protection in trials!

Deep waters can be frightening. There's an awesome power to water — whether it is a still lake or a restless ocean. In deep waters we have very little strength. When we face a painful trial, we can feel as if we're alone in the ocean with no rescue in sight, ready to give up. Then there are rivers of difficulty, perhaps not deep but moving with swift currents. Sometimes the difficulty threatens to sweep us away and smash us on the rocks below. We cannot swim against it. The fight seems useless.

As frightening as water is, fire is even more so. A tiny spark flashes into a huge conflagration, and nothing will stop it.

Humanly speaking, we have no hope in these situations. But with God, we have an option — to trust him. God promises to be with us in the deep waters of great trouble — in the rivers of difficulty and the fire of oppression. ✣

GOD'S PROMISE TO ME

- When you face deep waters of trouble, rivers of difficulty or fires of oppression, I will go with you. You will not be harmed.

MY PRAYER TO GOD

Heavenly Father, I feel up to my neck in deep waters and don't know how to get out. I need your strong hand. Please protect and guide me through this trial.

day**136**

THE HOLY SPIRIT HELPS IN YOUR DISTRESS

The Spirit helps us in our weakness. We do not know what we ought to pray for, but the Spirit himself intercedes for us through wordless groans. And he who searches our hearts knows the mind of the Spirit, because the Spirit intercedes for God's people in accordance with the will of God. And we know that in all things God works for the good of those who love him, who have been called according to his purpose. ROMANS 8:26–28

The Holy Spirit helps us in our difficult times. In the middle of great pain, we often can't pray. We don't know what to say; we don't have the strength to muster the right words. So the precious Holy Spirit, who lives within us because we are believers in Christ, intercedes for us with God. He expresses our deepest pain and pleads for us in line with God's will because he knows God's will.

Not only are we promised the Spirit's help in our distress, we are also promised that everything that happens to us will work together for good. The things that happen to us might not be "good," but God will make them work to our ultimate benefit, to help us become what he wants us to become—mature, Christlike and prepared for heaven. There may be suffering, pain and trials, but under God's control, even these will be for our good.

The Holy Spirit will intercede for us when our trials become so intense that we cannot find words to pray. God promises that his Spirit will plead in harmony with his will. God also promises that he will work all things together for our good. That's how much God loves us. ✤

GOD'S PROMISE TO ME

- My Spirit can help you in your distress. He can pray when you can't.
- I cause everything in your life to work together for your greatest good.

MY PRAYER TO GOD

Lord, thank you for the Spirit's intercession for me when I am overwhelmed by trouble. I trust you to take my distress and work it out for my good.

GOD STRENGTHENS YOUR FAITH THROUGH TRIALS

In all this you greatly rejoice, though now for a little while you may have had to suffer grief in all kinds of trials. These have come so that the proven genuineness of your faith — of greater worth than gold, which perishes even though refined by fire — may result in praise, glory and honor when Jesus Christ is revealed. 1 PETER 1:6–7

Peter says that we can be truly glad as we endure trials because of what we look forward to in heaven. Trials are not haphazard potshots that we're supposed to dodge; instead, they are opportunities for spiritual growth. They test our faith to see how strong it is. Do we hold on to our faith, without doubting, in the midst of trials? Do we seek God's guidance? Do we follow his instructions? Do we wait patiently for God to move, without whining and complaining? Do we stay close to God through it all?

Sometimes we pass with flying colors; at other times, we need to fall on our knees in repentance. But in the end, as God strengthens our faith through our trials.

We can rejoice no matter what trials may be occurring in our lives. We don't need to be happy about the trials, but we can learn to be joyful in spite of them. ❖

GOD'S PROMISE TO ME

- You can rejoice even in trials, for trials can strengthen your faith.
- Your faith is more precious to me than gold.

MY PRAYER TO GOD

Lord, during times of trial help me rejoice, not in the trial, but in you. Help me to hold on to what you promise for the future. As I face trials, I pray that my faith will be strong and pure.

GOD HELPS YOU TO STAND FIRM

Therefore put on the full armor of God, so that when the day of evil comes, you may be able to stand your ground, and after you have done everything, to stand.   EPHESIANS 6:13

A battle is raging—a battle we can't see. There are powers beyond our senses, beyond what we can see and hear. The Bible tells us that "our struggle is not against flesh and blood, but against the rulers, against the authorities, against the powers of this dark world and against the spiritual forces of evil in the heavenly realms" (Ephesians 6:12). Pretty heavy stuff, huh? But it is true. The battles we wage in our lives are but part of a huge cosmic battle that has been going on since Satan's fall. This battle will not end until he is destroyed.

In the meantime, God promises that if we wear his armor, we can stand firm. As we pray God's promises for ourselves or for others, we need to pray for strength in the unseen spiritual battles. Over the next few days we will pray for each item of God's armor that he supplies. ✤

GOD'S PROMISE TO ME

- I will provide you with armor so that you can stand firm and resist the enemy in times of evil.

MY PRAYER TO GOD

Heavenly Father, I acknowledge that there is a spiritual battle being waged, a battle far beyond the scope of my senses. I claim your promise that as I wear the armor you provide, I will be able to resist the enemy in the time of evil and still be standing firm after the battle. Thank you for providing this armor.

day139

GOD GIVES YOU THE BELT OF TRUTH

Stand firm then, with the belt of truth buckled around your waist.   Ephesians 6:14

God promises that we can stand firm even in the heat of battle, but we need his armor. The first piece is the belt of truth.

A Roman soldier's belt was about six inches wide; it held together his clothing and provided a holding place for some of the other pieces of armor and weapons. The belt was the foundation of the soldier's armor.

The foundation of our armor is the belt of truth. The truth of the gospel is the foundation of the Christian life. As we strap on the belt of truth, we are making the truth of God our foundation, the standard by which we measure everything else. We are also stating our conviction of the truth of our faith, the certainty that Jesus is "the truth" (see John 14:6).

Knowing and believing in the truth will help us stand strong against the enemy in any battle. ❖

GOD'S PROMISE TO ME

- You will be able to stand your ground when you are wearing the sturdy belt of truth.

MY PRAYER TO GOD

Lord, you promise that we can stand strong in any battle if we wear your armor. I choose to wear your sturdy belt of truth. May it help me stand firm against false doctrines.

day140

GOD GIVES YOU THE BREASTPLATE OF RIGHTEOUSNESS

Stand firm then ... with the breastplate of righteousness in place.   Ephesians 6:14

The next piece of armor is called "the breastplate of righteousness." The breastplate protected the body from the neck to the thighs, often in the front and the back. It may have been made of leather, bronze or chain mail. This piece protected the vital organs. No soldier went into battle without his breastplate. Isaiah describes God as putting on "righteousness as his breastplate" (see Isaiah 59:15 – 17).

No Christian soldier should go into battle without wearing righteousness. As we don this piece of body armor, we are reminded that this righteousness is not our own but Christ's. As believers, we have been made righteous in God's eyes — in other words, right with God. This "rightness" gives us the ability to stand up to Satan's attacks when he tries to say we're not really Christians or that we're not "good enough" Christians. We can stand strong knowing that we have been saved by God's grace alone and that Satan is incapable of inflicting any damage on our "right standing" with God. ❖

GOD'S PROMISE TO ME

- You will be able to stand your ground when you wear the breastplate of my righteousness.

MY PRAYER TO GOD

Lord, you promise strength for the battle when I wear your armor. Help me hold on to the truth that you died for me and thus I have your righteousness. Satan cannot damage my right standing with you. May the breastplate of righteousness protect my faith and help me stand strong when the battle rages.

day141

GOD GIVES YOU THE SHOES OF PEACE

Stand firm then ... with your feet fitted with the readiness that comes from the gospel of peace.   EPHESIANS 6:14–15

No armor is complete without the right shoes. Roman soldiers had special shoes that allowed ease of motion and protection for long marches.

Believers need special shoes too, the shoes Paul described as "the readiness that comes from the gospel of peace." When we put on these shoes, we are ready for any battle because we are completely at peace, knowing that we are already on the winning side. This is "the peace of God, which transcends all understanding" (Philippians 4:7).

When Satan tries to disturb our peace with his temptations, troubles, trials or accusations, we must have on the shoes of peace. We must trust in the Good News. That peace can override whatever Satan throws our way. ✤

GOD'S PROMISE TO ME

- You will be able to stand firm and be fully prepared when you wear shoes that are the gospel of peace.

MY PRAYER TO GOD

You have promised, Lord, that we can stand firm if we wear the right armor. Today I choose to have my feet "fitted with the readiness that comes from the gospel of peace." I praise you for giving your people the gift of peace. I know that I can be fully prepared for battle, being assured that victory will always be mine in Christ.

day142

GOD GIVES YOU THE SHIELD OF FAITH

In addition to all this, take up the shield of faith, with which you can extinguish all the flaming arrows of the evil one. EPHESIANS 6:16

In combat, a soldier's shield was invaluable. It protected him from blows in hand-to-hand combat and shielded him when flaming arrows flew down from enemy lines. Whatever came his way, the soldier could hold up his shield and protect himself.

Believers need the shield of faith. Faith means total dependence on God. Hebrews 11:1 says, "Faith is confidence in what we hope for and assurance about what we do not see." We need the shield of faith because Satan will shoot his fiery arrows of temptation, doubt, fear, despair, accusation or problems. Strong faith can deflect these arrows. With faith we trust that God is in control, that he loves us, and that he is working out everything for our good. Such faith can deflect Satan's flaming arrows.

We're not expected to have faith in our *faith*; faith in *God* is the key to victory. ✤

GOD'S PROMISE TO ME

- You will be able to resist the enemy and stop the fiery arrows of Satan with the shield of faith.

MY PRAYER TO GOD

Thank you, Lord, for the shield of faith to deflect Satan's fiery arrows. I know that I will face a constant barrage of attacks throughout my life. May I use the shield of faith to provide protection.

day143

GOD GIVES YOU THE HELMET OF SALVATION

Take the helmet of salvation.   EPHESIANS 6:17

With many active sports, a helmet is a necessary piece of equipment to protect the head—the most vulnerable spot on the body. For a soldier on active duty, a helmet is even more vital. God says that his people are to include in their armor the helmet of salvation. The prophet Isaiah describes God as placing "the helmet of salvation on his head" (Isaiah 59:17).

God saves us when we trust Christ as our Savior. We are rescued from the bondage of sin and from an eternity separated from God. "This righteousness is given through faith in Jesus Christ to all who believe. There is no difference between Jew and Gentile" (Romans 3:22). The helmet of salvation protects our minds from the doubts that can so easily creep in and undermine our faith. Doubt can deal death blows to those not protected by an assurance of salvation. When we know, beyond a doubt, that we are saved, we can handle any adversity, question or difficulty. That knowledge will protect us like a helmet protects the head. ❖

GOD'S PROMISE TO ME

- You will be able to stand firm in battle when you wear the helmet of salvation.

MY PRAYER TO GOD

Lord, I'm especially grateful for the helmet of salvation and the protection it offers. I pray that the assurance of salvation will guard my thoughts and mind even as difficulties come and doubts attempt to creep in.

day 144

GOD GIVES YOU THE SWORD OF THE SPIRIT

Take ... the sword of the Spirit, which is the word of God.　　　　Ephesians 6:17

The soldier goes into battle well protected from attack, but since his job is also to do his share of attacking, he needs a weapon. Roman soldiers carried swords, most likely short double-edged swords designed for hand-to-hand combat. A soldier's sword was a deadly weapon.

Believers also need an offensive weapon, and God gives it. He tells us to take up the sword of the Spirit, his Word. When we know God's Word, we are prepared to answer Satan's attacks as well as other people's doubts and questions.

Satan tried to tempt Jesus by misusing God's Word, but Jesus replied to Satan by using God's Word correctly and defeated him (see Matthew 4:1–11). Likewise, the Holy Spirit will help us understand what we read in the Bible and enable us to apply it correctly in our lives. When we build the habit of studying God's Word, we become prepared for battle or to share our faith. ✤

GOD'S PROMISE TO ME

- You will be able to stand firm in the heat of the battle when you carry the sword of the Spirit, my Word, in your mind and heart.

MY PRAYER TO GOD

Lord, thank you for the Bible. Please allow your Holy Spirit to enlighten my mind to understand what I read and how it applies to my life. May that sword be drawn and ready when Satan attacks with a lie. Give me the wisdom to use your Word correctly.

day145

YOU CAN TRUST GOD'S STRENGTH IN YOUR WEAKNESS

He said to me, "My grace is sufficient for you, for my power is made perfect in weakness." Therefore I will boast all the more gladly about my weaknesses, so that Christ's power may rest on me.   2 CORINTHIANS 12:9

Paul was suffering. He had some kind of debilitation or chronic illness that he felt was hindering his effectiveness in ministry. He figured he could be more effective, share the Good News with more energy and travel more places if God would take away the problem.

Makes sense, right?

So Paul pleaded with God: "Three times I pleaded with the Lord to take it away from me" (2 Corinthians 12:8). But each time God's answer was no. In fact, God said that his power worked best through Paul's weakness. God's grace was enough to make Paul's ministry effective.

We don't like to hear that the answer is no. We prefer the promises of healing—and God can indeed heal; nothing is impossible with God. But sometimes, for reasons unknown to us, God chooses to say no. He only says, "I can do more with you this way." And then, we simply have to trust. ❖

GOD'S PROMISE TO ME

- My gracious favor is all you need.
- I can use your weaknesses for my glory.

MY PRAYER TO GOD

You promise, Lord, that your power works best in my weakness. Work in and through me. I'm thankful that I don't have to be perfect in order to be useful to you. Help me trust in your strength.

day146

may 26

YOU CAN TRUST GOD'S STRENGTH
IN YOUR WEARINESS

The LORD is the everlasting God, the Creator of the ends of the earth. He will not grow tired or weary, and his understanding no one can fathom ... Even youths grow tired and weary, and young men stumble and fall; but those who hope in the LORD will renew their strength. They will soar on wings like eagles; they will run and not grow weary, they will walk and not be faint.　　　　　　　　　　　　　　　　　ISAIAH 40:28,30–31

Ever seen an eagle in flight? They're able to reach great heights because of their ability to soar on the updrafts. Because they've learned to use the wind, they don't have to work as hard, pumping their wings in order to get anywhere. As they coast on the wind, they renew their strength.

Isaiah said those who wait on the Lord will be like the eagle—discovering renewed strength. At times we feel spiritually battered and emotionally drained; we are tired and weary. But it is during those times when we face physical, spiritual or emotional exhaustion that God offers us his strength.

If you're feeling tired and weary, take Isaiah's advice: "Hope in the LORD," for he promises strength. ✤

GOD'S PROMISE TO ME

- When you are weak or worn out, I will give you strength.
- When you hope in me, you will find new strength.

MY PRAYER TO GOD

Lord, I feel weary. You promise that those who hope in you will find new strength. Help me trust that you will give me the strength to run and not grow weary, to walk and not faint.

YOU CAN TRUST IN GOD'S FORGIVENESS

If we claim to be without sin, we deceive ourselves and the truth is not in us. If we confess our sins, he is faithful and just and will forgive us our sins and purify us from all unrighteousness. 1 JOHN 1:8–9

Is anything more precious than forgiveness? What a blessing when, after we've really blown it with someone, we apologize and hear that person say, "I forgive you." A weight is lifted from us, and our relationship is restored.

Today's verses acknowledge the reality of sin. We have sin—that's the truth. And at times we yield to our sinful nature. Beyond our comprehension is the fact that God sees us as righteous because of his Son's death on our behalf, yet he knows that we will not be truly righteous until we get to heaven. So in the interim, God offers forgiveness. If we confess our sins, he is faithful and just to forgive and to cleanse us.

We don't need to live our lives attempting to attain some fashion of "sinlessness," for we only fool ourselves in the attempt. Jesus has already paid for our sin. Instead, we can live to please God. When we mess up, we can own up to our wrongs. God promises forgiveness and cleansing. His justice provides for the promise; his faithfulness guarantees it. ✤

GOD'S PROMISE TO ME

- When you confess your sins, I will be faithful and just and will forgive those sins and cleanse you from every wrong.

MY PRAYER TO GOD

Lord, you say that if we claim to be sinless we're only fooling ourselves. Our old nature still exists. Give me an attitude of discernment and humility, so that when I sin I will know it and desire to be cleansed of it. Thank you for your forgiveness, which removes sins as far as the east is from the west.

day148

may 28

YOU CAN TRUST IN GOD'S PROVISION

Do not worry, saying, "What shall we eat?" or "What shall we drink?" or "What shall we wear?" For the pagans run after all these things, and your heavenly Father knows that you need them. But seek first his kingdom and his righteousness, and all these things will be given to you as well.   MATTHEW 6:31–33

Food, drink and clothing are important. Add shelter to the list, and you have the basics for survival. In this passage, God is not advocating homelessness; we must take care of the necessities of life. The key word here is "worry." We are expected to provide the basics for ourselves and our families, but we should not *worry* about them. God will provide what we need. We often worry because we get in over our heads trying to get what we want instead of simply what we need.

In the midst of providing for ourselves and our families, we can infuse all of our pursuits and responsibilities with concern for God's kingdom. When that is our primary concern, even as we work at our jobs, tend our homes or shop for clothing, we will have the right perspective. We can honor God at all times. And when the going gets tough for a time, we don't need to worry; we can trust God to provide everything we need. ✤

GOD'S PROMISE TO ME

- You don't need to worry about your basic needs, for I already know them and will provide them for you.
- You can live a bountiful life—even in day-to-day activities—when you keep the honor and glory of my kingdom as your primary concern.

MY PRAYER TO GOD

Heavenly Father, I confess to worrying over issues beyond my control. Give me the right perspective on this, Lord. Help me see the difference between needs and wants. Please transform my life.

day149

YOU CAN TRUST IN GOD'S GRACE

Come to me, all you who are weary and burdened, and I will give you rest. Take my yoke upon you and learn from me, for I am gentle and humble in heart, and you will find rest for your souls. For my yoke is easy and my burden is light. MATTHEW 11:28–30

The pious religious leaders of Jesus' day had burdened the Jewish people with many rules for living an "acceptable" life. Then along came Jesus, setting people free from the burdens of trying to be good enough for God. Jesus told the people to take off those burdens and pick up his yoke. There is still a yoke—following Jesus means commitment and sacrifice—but his yoke yields joy, fruitful service and fulfillment.

There are a couple of extremes in the world today. Some believers want to take away other believers' freedom in Christ and replace it with a list of rules for how to live acceptably. These people are modern-day Pharisees. Others claim to be Christians but throw out all of the Bible's clear commands. The first group ignores grace; the second abuses it. In between stands Jesus, having set us free from bondage in order to take up his yoke of righteousness.

We can live the joyous life of grace. Jesus's yoke is not meant to drag us down into shame or guilt but to make us contagious, thankful, joyous believers. ❖

GOD'S PROMISE TO ME

- You can come to me with your weariness and heavy burdens, and I will give you rest.
- Take up my yoke, for it fits perfectly and is light.

MY PRAYER TO GOD

Thank you, Jesus, for setting me free from my burden of sin and my attempts at trying to be good enough for you. You paid the price—for me to try to do more is to say that your death wasn't sufficient. Your yoke fits perfectly.

day150

YOU CAN TRUST IN THE POWER OF PRAYER

The prayer of a righteous person is powerful and effective. JAMES 5:16

Does prayer really make a difference? If God knows everything that's going to happen, why pray? Can we really change God's mind?

We might be tempted to live as though everything happens by chance, and we must sit back and watch it all unfold. We have no control, so why try to do anything?

We know that God knows everything, that all our days are in his book and the hairs of our head are numbered. But it's important to remember that while *we* don't know everything, our lives on this earth are a continuous quest of getting to know God better. *He* knows everything. So we talk to him, asking for guidance and help or protection.

Does prayer change anything? Perhaps a better question is how does prayer change us? The Bible promises that our earnest prayers have great power and wonderful results. Prayer changes things—but most of all, it changes us. ❖

GOD'S PROMISE TO ME

• Your prayers can have great power and wonderful results.

MY PRAYER TO GOD

Heavenly Father, you say that the earnest prayer of a righteous person has great power. I realize this doesn't mean you answer every prayer with an unequivocal yes. I want to experience that power today. I trust that you hear my prayers and that you will answer.

day151

GOD DISCIPLINES YOU BECAUSE HE DELIGHTS IN YOU

My son, do not despise the LORD's discipline, and do not resent his rebuke, because the LORD disciplines those he loves, as a father the son he delights in.   PROVERBS 3:11–12

"This will hurt me more than it hurts you." Have you heard those words? They're usually spoken in regard to discipline. We give the advice in these verses to our precious children when we discipline them. We certainly train them never to ignore us, and we also hope that they will not be discouraged by our discipline.

Loving discipline teaches our children what is right while showing them that we discipline them because we love them. So it is with God. Like a loving father he disciplines us because he wants us to mature and to act correctly and responsibly. He disciplines us because he delights in us.

Holding on to this truth isn't always easy, especially when we are in the middle of being disciplined by God. We typically get angry or discouraged. Yet discipline, like pruning, is necessary and beneficial. We need to pray that we will not be discouraged but, instead, see God's discipline as evidence that he delights in us. ✤

GOD'S PROMISE TO ME

- I may discipline you at times, but only because I am a loving Father who corrects the child in whom I delight.

MY PRAYER TO GOD

Lord, you say that you correct me because you love me and delight in me. I admit that I don't always see your discipline this way. Help me to grasp the truth that you are disciplining me because you delight in me. Thank you for being a loving Father who cares enough to teach me what is right.

day**152**

june 1

GOD'S DISCIPLINE LEADS TO HOLINESS

They disciplined us for a little while as they thought best; but God disciplines us for our good, in order that we may share in his holiness. No discipline seems pleasant at the time, but painful. Later on, however, it produces a harvest of righteousness and peace for those who have been trained by it.   HEBREWS 12:10–11

Our fathers and mothers disciplined us, and now we discipline our own children. Often, however, our discipline is not perfect, especially when we offer discipline out of irritation or when we are exhausted. God's discipline, however, is always right—and always good for us.

Today's promise is that God's discipline means we will share in his holiness. We already share in God's holiness because of our faith, but God is preparing us to be truly perfect in heaven.

Of course, discipline is not enjoyable—in fact, it can be downright painful. Precisely because it is painful, we want to avoid it, and so we try to learn what God wants to avoid further pain. That's what the writer of Hebrews meant when he said that afterward there would be a quiet harvest of right living. As we become holy, we are being prepared for heaven. ✤

GOD'S PROMISE TO ME

- When I discipline you, it is always right and good for you, for I am preparing you to share in my holiness.
- My discipline will result in a quiet harvest of right living in your life.

MY PRAYER TO GOD

God, you promise that your discipline is always right and good and that I will share in your holiness. Thank you for that promise. I pray that I will learn the lessons you have for me and that I will move on to maturity.

day153

GOD WILL BRING YOU OUT OF THE DARKNESS

Do not gloat over me, my enemy! Though I have fallen, I will rise. Though I sit in darkness, the LORD will be my light. Because I have sinned against him, I will bear the LORD's wrath, until he pleads my case and upholds my cause. He will bring me out into the light; I will see his righteousness. MICAH 7:8–9

Micah served as a prophet to both the northern kingdom of Israel and the southern kingdom of Judah. During Micah's time the northern kingdom was taken into captivity by Assyria. As the northern kingdom endured the oppression of Assyria, King Hezekiah of Judah returned his nation to the worship of God — perhaps on Micah's advice. The reign of good King Hezekiah bought more time for Judah.

Micah spoke the words above to the northern kingdom. He proclaimed that though the people had been punished severely for their sin, God would still be with them. In the darkness he would be their light. They needed to be patient through punishment because eventually God would bring them out of the darkness. When that time came, God would punish their enemies.

When we sin, we can expect God's punishment. But we need to be patient, for God promises that he will be our light in the darkness. It may take some time, but God has not given up on us. He promises that we will see his righteousness. ❖

GOD'S PROMISE TO ME

- Though you sit in darkness, I will be your light.
- I will bring you out of the darkness and into the light. You will see my righteousness.

MY PRAYER TO GOD

Heavenly Father, bring me out of the darkness and into your light. Show me your righteousness and give me victory, Lord, nothing less.

NOTHING IS IMPOSSIBLE WITH FAITH IN GOD

[Jesus] replied, "Because you have so little faith. Truly I tell you, if you have faith as small as a mustard seed, you can say to this mountain, 'Move from here to there,' and it will move. Nothing will be impossible for you." MATTHEW 17:20

In this verse Jesus wasn't pointing to a measurement of faith, as though we could check our faith by stepping on a scale and claiming that the extra weight comes from extra faith. (Wouldn't that would be nice?) Immediately after saying the disciples didn't have enough faith, Jesus told them that even faith as small as a tiny mustard seed would be enough to move a mountain. Obviously it was not the *amount* of faith but the *focus* of the faith.

Earlier in Matthew 17 the disciples had tried to cast out a demon without success. Perhaps they had tried to cast it out depending on what they considered their own power. Whatever occurred, their faith must have been in the wrong place. When they put their faith in the right place—in the all-powerful God—then even a tiny grain of faith would be enough. Nothing is impossible when our faith is in God.

This kind of faith moves mountains and makes all things possible. At times we may feel that we have great faith; at other times we may feel that our faith is suffering. In the end, however, if even that suffering faith is in God, then it is enough to do the impossible! ❖

GOD'S PROMISE TO ME

- If you have faith in me as small as a mustard seed, then it is enough to move mountains and do the impossible.

MY PRAYER TO GOD

You promise, Lord, that with faith in you nothing is impossible. Thank you for being the God of the possible. Help me to remember that my faith, even small and weak, can do great things for you.

TREASURE A TIMELY REBUKE

Like an earring of gold or an ornament of fine gold is the rebuke of a wise judge to a listening ear.   PROVERBS 25:12

Criticism is so easy to give and so hard to receive. While we don't want to be around people who have critical spirits, we do want to surround ourselves with people who aren't afraid to tell us the truth. We need friends who can give us a timely rebuke—people whom we know and trust, people who love us. When they offer a rebuke, we can trust their words and be thankful they care enough to tell us the truth. Such friends help us to avoid being embarrassed and from being criticized by people who don't care about us.

If we don't have these kinds of friendships, we can pray for them. We can also pray that we will be able to receive criticism graciously and be humble enough to make changes where needed. We can also be the kind of friend who rebukes others in love. ✤

GOD'S PROMISE TO ME

- You can learn to graciously heed a wise rebuke. When you do, you will have found great treasure.

MY PRAYER TO GOD

Lord God, you say that people who heed a rebuke have found a real treasure. Give me true friends, the kind who will be honest. I also ask you to make me humble enough to heed a rebuke and then do what needs to be done to make a change.

GOD CARES WHEN YOU NEED COURAGE

Have I not commanded you? Be strong and courageous. Do not be afraid; do not be discouraged, for the LORD your God will be with you wherever you go.   JOSHUA 1:9

Joshua needed courage—after all, Moses was going to be a hard act to follow. Joshua's task was to take over the promised land, fulfilling God's promise to Abraham hundreds of years earlier: "Look around from where you are, to the north and south, to the east and west. All the land that you see I will give to you and your offspring forever" (Genesis 13:14–15). The promise was already in place, yet God helped his servant Joshua when he needed it most. God promised his presence with Joshua, and as a result, Joshua was able to be strong and courageous.

We face many days when we could use a little bit of courage. A tough task at work, a difficult conversation, a medical procedure, fear of the unknown, taking a stand for what's right. God says to us as he said to Joshua, "Do not be afraid; do not be discouraged, for the LORD your God will be with you wherever you go." ✤

GOD'S PROMISE TO ME

- You can be strong and courageous, rather than afraid and discouraged, because I will be with you wherever you go.
- I will give you the courage you need.

MY PRAYER TO GOD

I know that every day is a training ground, Lord. I pray that you will help me to be an example of daily courage to others. I need courage to face the day ahead. Make your presence very real to me today.

day157

GOD CARES WHEN YOU PRAY

This is the confidence we have in approaching God: that if we ask anything according to his will, he hears us. And if we know that he hears us — whatever we ask — we know that we have what we asked of him. 1 JOHN 5:14–15

It's hard to imagine a more precious promise than this one — that God listens to us and answers our requests. Imagine — the sovereign God of the universe listens to *every* prayer of *every* believer on the planet and promises to answer. Our faith in that promise can cause us to boldly come before God, knowing that he will listen and answer those prayers.

We can pray for others to have this same confidence. So many people doubt God's existence and his ability to listen to our prayers. But this passage, written by the apostle John, provides God's guarantee that God does listen to our prayers, and when requests are in line with his will, he gives what is requested.

Our requests will be in line with God's will if we stay in a close relationship with him. As John recorded in his Gospel, Jesus promised his disciples that "if you remain in me and my words remain in you, ask whatever you wish, and it will be done for you" (John 15:7). So we need to stay close to God so that our requests will be in line with his will. God hears and answers prayer. ❖

GOD'S PROMISE TO ME

- You can be confident that whenever you ask me for anything in line with my will, I will listen and answer.

MY PRAYER TO GOD

Oh Lord, help me hold on to your promise that you hear me when I pray. When I bring requests to you, I pray that they will be in line with your will.

day158

june 7

GOD CARES WHEN YOU FEEL LONELY

Where can I go from your Spirit? Where can I flee from your presence? If I go up to the heavens, you are there; if I make my bed in the depths, you are there. If I rise on the wings of the dawn, if I settle on the far side of the sea, even there your hand will guide me, your right hand will hold me fast. PSALM 139:7–10

In a world with billions of people, it's amazing how many people feel lonely. Some of the biggest cities in the world harbor some of the loneliest people. It's not about proximity, they would say, it's about connection. When we don't feel a connection to anyone, when we feel cast adrift from anyone who might care about us, loneliness sets in.

Yet these precious words from this psalm give us the answer for our feelings of loneliness. Want someone who understands? Who loves? Who connects? Who never ever leaves? That someone is God. In fact, if you try to get away from him, you can't.

Sure, you still need a human connection, but when that fails at times, remember that God is always there for you. He says, "Never will I leave you; never will I forsake you" (Hebrews 13:5). ❖

GOD'S PROMISE TO ME

- You can never escape from my presence.
- No matter where you go, my hand will guide you, and my strength will support you.

MY PRAYER TO GOD

Lord, your plans are perfect. You promise that I can never escape from your spirit, never get away from your presence. Wherever you take me, your hand will guide me, and your strength will support me. Guide me today and support me with your strength.

GOD CARES WHEN YOU FEEL WORTHLESS

Your eyes saw my unformed body; all the days ordained for me were written in your book before one of them came to be. How precious to me are your thoughts, God! How vast is the sum of them!   PSALM 139:16–17

How precious children are to us. Modern technology allows us to see those little feet and tiny hands and beating heart while the baby is still in the womb. But we also see with our mind's eye as we dream about what God has in store for these little people. We don't know the future, but what a precious promise it is to know that God does. As we walk day by day with them, guiding them, protecting them and watching with wonder as they grow, we entrust them to God who knows every moment. We don't know where our children will go in life, but he does. We don't know how God will use them, but he does. We don't know what they will accomplish for God's kingdom, but he does.

We can also understand how precious we are to God. What value he places on each of us. God knew us before we were born. He knew every day of our lives before our lives even began. May we understand the promise of God's knowledge of the future and take comfort in it. ✤

GOD'S PROMISE TO ME

- I knew you before you were born. Every day of your life is known to me.
- I think about you more than you know. Don't worry; you are safe in my hands.

MY PRAYER TO GOD

Lord, you created me for a purpose. Every day of my life was recorded in your book and laid out before my life even began. I choose to take comfort in this knowledge. May I understand the depth of your love for me all the days of my life.

WE'RE CHOSEN AND WE CHOOSE

Those God foreknew he also predestined to be conformed to the image of his Son, that he might be the firstborn among many brothers and sisters. And those he predestined, he also called; those he called, he also justified; those he justified, he also glorified.

ROMANS 8:29–30

There are Christians who love to get into a debate about whether we choose Christ or he chooses us. Besides being quite an exercise for the mind, the question is probably beyond the ability of humans to completely answer. The Arminians and the Calvinists will never fully agree on this—and maybe they don't need to.

God gave us verses that make it sound as if we are chosen and do nothing whatsoever; and he gave us verses that make it sound as if we need to make a choice. What a gift! As believers, we have the peace of knowing that we have been chosen by God and called to him. He has given us right standing with him and has promised us his glory. Yet from our perspective, we don't know if we're chosen until we choose. We need to say the words and confess Jesus as our Lord. We have been chosen, so we choose; we choose, so we have been chosen. ❖

GOD'S PROMISE TO ME

- I call you to be my own.
- I promise my glory to those who have right standing with me.

MY PRAYER TO GOD

You know your people in advance, Lord, and you choose us to become like your Son. Thank you for choosing me and making me a part of your family. You have given me right standing with yourself, and you have promised me your glory. I look forward to the day when I will be with you forever.

day**161**

GOD CARES WHEN YOU NEED HOPE

His compassions never fail. They are new every morning; great is your faithfulness. I say to myself, "The LORD is my portion; therefore I will wait for him." The LORD is good to those whose hope is in him, to the one who seeks him.   LAMENTATIONS 3:22–25

Have you ever known that feeling deep in the pit of your stomach when you thought a situation was hopeless? The pain of hopelessness is almost visible.

God understands that pain. He feels along with us the awful ache of hurt, sorrow and fear. Believers are not immune to pain, that's obvious. Yet quite often we get into those painful situations and feel that somehow this shouldn't be happening to us. Did we do something sinful to deserve this? Has God left us? Where is God when we feel so hopeless?

The reality of these situations is that God is right there with us. "His compassions never fail. They are new every morning; great is your faithfulness." We need to place our hope in him alone.

When we experience the pain of hopelessness, we desperately need the assurance of God's daily mercy. We can place our hope in God alone, waiting for him and seeking him. As we wait for God's salvation, hope will carry us through. ✤

GOD'S PROMISE TO ME

- My faithfulness is great; my mercy begins afresh each day.
- You can hope in me because I am good to those who wait for me and seek me.

MY PRAYER TO GOD

Lord, show me that there is hope in you. You promise that you are wonderfully good to those who wait for you and seek you. Reveal your great faithfulness to me.

GOD CARES ABOUT YOUR DEEPEST DESIRES

*Take delight in the L*ORD*, and he will give you the desires of your heart.*   PSALM 37:4

Deep down at the bottom of your heart, what does your heart desire?

God promises that if we take delight in him, he will give us our heart's desires. To "delight" in God—what does that mean? When we delight in someone, we long to be with them, we love having them around, we love talking and laughing with them. So it is with God. To delight in him means that we long to be with him; we love his continual presence in our lives, and we love communicating with him.

We long for many things in our lives. Will God grant those? Perhaps. But more importantly, he grants us himself. When we have a relationship with the Lord that is based totally on his presence and not on what he will do for us, perhaps we have already found our heart's true deepest desire. Do you delight in the Lord? ✤

GOD'S PROMISE TO ME

• As you delight in me, I will give you the desires of your heart.

MY PRAYER TO GOD

Lord, I delight in your presence and your love. I pray that I will always desire your presence and always enjoy communicating with you.

GOD IS GOOD

Good and upright is the LORD; therefore he instructs sinners in his ways.   PSALM 25:8

What do we mean when we say that the Lord is good? In Mark 10:17–18 Jesus has an interesting exchange with a man. When the young man came running up to Jesus and called him "Good teacher," he heard this response: "'Why do you call me good?' Jesus answered. 'No one is good—except God alone.'"

God's goodness is expressed in showing the proper path to those who go astray. Who goes astray? Everyone! "For all have sinned and fall short of the glory of God" (Romans 3:23). And what did God do? "God demonstrates his own love for us in this: While we were still sinners, Christ died for us" (Romans 5:8). We do not need to be good enough for God; God's goodness is good enough for us. Because God is good, he sent his Son to a sinful world and took on sin itself so that we might become God's children.

Today let's revel in the truth that God is good and we don't have to be good enough for him. His goodness has provided everything we need. ✤

GOD'S PROMISE TO ME

- I am perfectly good. Everything I do is good and right.
- When you go astray, I will show you the proper path.

MY PRAYER TO GOD

Thank you, Lord, for your goodness. Because you are good, you came to a sinful world to die for me. Because you are good, you show the proper path to those who go astray. Because you are good, I don't have to strive to be "good enough" in order to be acceptable to you.

day164 june 13

GOD IS SOVEREIGN

Yours, LORD, is the greatness and the power and the glory and the majesty and the splendor, for everything in heaven and earth is yours. Yours, LORD, is the kingdom; you are exalted as head over all.   1 CHRONICLES 29:11

Sovereignty means complete authority. So if God is sovereign, do human beings really have any choice? The truth is that God is sovereign and yet somehow he also gives us freedom to choose. That's what the two trees in the garden of Eden were about (see Genesis 3). God did not need to put the forbidden tree there, but he desired that people would love and obey him because they chose to. Yet God, being sovereign, knows all things. Did he know that Adam and Eve would choose wrongly? Of course. Does he know everything you have done and will do? Of course. Somehow beyond our comprehension is the fact that we have a choice, yet God still knows everything. Both can be true at the same time because God is sovereign.

Many people try to fit God into some kind of box so they can say they understand him. But God is beyond understanding. If he weren't, he wouldn't be God. Can we comprehend his sovereignty? No, but we can praise him for it. God's sovereignty would be frightening if we did not know that God is also loving. His rule is loving and just. That can give us all great peace. ✤

GOD'S PROMISE TO ME

- I am perfectly sovereign.
- You can trust in and take comfort in my sovereignty—for I am also good, loving, faithful and merciful.

MY PRAYER TO GOD

Lord, yours is the greatness, the power, the glory, the victory and the majesty. I adore you as the One who is over all things.

GOD IS FAITHFUL

Know therefore that the LORD your God is God; he is the faithful God, keeping his cove-nant of love to a thousand generations of those who love him and keep his commandments.

DEUTERONOMY 7:9

God is faithful. That's a powerful statement. To be faithful means to keep one's promises, to keep an agreement. God is perfect in all of his characteristics, so he is perfectly faithful. That means that every promise he gives is a promise that he will keep.

God also desires that we be faithful to him. In fact, much of the Old Testament talks about the unfaithfulness of the people of Israel despite God's constant faithfulness to them.

We want to be faithful, and we hope that the people around us are faithful too. But faithfulness is not work that we must do in order to be accepted by God. It is a fruit of the Spirit's work in us.

The prophet Jeremiah reminds us of God's faithfulness: "His compassions never fail. They are new every morning; great is your faithfulness" (Lamentations 3:22–23). ❖

GOD'S PROMISE TO ME

- I am perfectly faithful. I will keep all of my promises to you.
- Faithfulness is the fruit of my Spirit working in you.

MY PRAYER TO GOD

Thank you, Lord, for being faithful. You keep all of your promises for a thousand genera-tions. None of your promises will ever fail. May I exhibit faithfulness in my relationships and interactions with others.

day 166

GOD IS JUST

I will proclaim the name of the LORD. Oh, praise the greatness of our God! He is the Rock, his works are perfect, and all his ways are just. A faithful God who does no wrong, upright and just is he. DEUTERONOMY 32:3–4

God is just. That means he is right, lawful, correct and true and that he gives deserved punishment or reward. But wait a minute! Punishment? Isn't that a bit unfair?

Actually, God's justice requires that at times he punishes. People have a human perspective of right and wrong, fair and unfair. They try to impose that concept on God, thinking that he is bound to what they think is fair and just. The reality, however, is that God himself is the standard of justice. He is morally perfect, so he cannot be unfair or unjust.

The Bible is the story of God's justice. God created a perfect world. People sinned. God is merciful and loving, and so he set into motion a plan of salvation. A God of impersonal justice would have simply left us without hope. A God of grandfatherly love would have overlooked our sin, but that would deny his holiness. So God justly dealt with sin. Sin required death, and so God sent his Son to die in our place. Christ's death satisfied God's justice, and love and mercy were extended to sinners. God's justice is our salvation. "Upright and just is he." ♣

GOD'S PROMISE TO ME

- I am perfectly just. Everything I do is right and fair.
- You can trust in my justice, knowing that I am also merciful and loving.

MY PRAYER TO GOD

How glorious you are, God. You are my Rock and your work is perfect. You promise that everything you do is just and fair. Thank you for giving me a clear standard for living in your Word, a standard in which to trust.

day167

GOD IS MERCIFUL

He saved us, not because of righteous things we had done, but because of his mercy. He saved us through the washing of rebirth and renewal by the Holy Spirit. TITUS 3:5

God is merciful. Mercy means undeserved kindness. God saved us by sending his Son to die on the cross for us. Was it because we are so deserving, wonderful or good? Certainly not. We are undeserving sinners, but in his mercy, God washes away our sins and gives us a new life through the Holy Spirit.

Because God is merciful, we too need to be merciful. In Matthew 18 Jesus told a parable about a man who owed a king a lot of money. The man asked the king for mercy, and the king kindly canceled his debt and let him go. The man left and found someone who owed him a small amount of money. That man begged for mercy, but received none and was thrown into prison. When the king heard about it, he said to the man whose debt he had forgiven, "Shouldn't you have had mercy on your fellow servant just as I had on you?" (Matthew 18:33). And the king threw that man into prison.

God has shown us much mercy, so we should show mercy to others. They may not deserve it, but then again, neither did we. ❖

GOD'S PROMISE TO ME

- I am perfectly merciful.
- I saved you because of my mercy.

MY PRAYER TO GOD

Thank you, Lord, for your mercies. I could not have been saved otherwise. Help me extend mercy to others, even when they don't deserve it.

day168 june 17

GOD IS HOLY

Be holy because I, the LORD your God, am holy. LEVITICUS 19:2

God is holy. His holiness separates him completely from sin. The Bible tells us that we must be holy. But how can we be holy when we still have our sinful nature?

Some people would have us think that we must try really hard, live a certain way or do or not do certain things, and then we can be classified as "holy." However, to try to attain holiness is an impossible task. Instead, the Bible tells us that we become holy in God's eyes because of what Christ has done. "Those sanctified in Christ Jesus and called to be his holy people" (1 Corinthians 1:2). "For he chose us in him before the creation of the world to be holy and blameless in his sight" (Ephesians 1:4). "He has reconciled you by Christ's physical body through death to present you holy in his sight, without blemish and free from accusation" (Colossians 1:22). "God chose you as firstfruits to be saved through the sanctifying work of the Spirit and through belief in the truth" (2 Thessalonians 2:13).

We mustn't get caught up in thinking that we must work hard to be holy. God has made us holy through Christ. ✣

GOD'S PROMISE TO ME

- I am perfectly holy.
- Everything I do is holy.
- You are already holy in my eyes because of your faith in Christ.
- I will help you live a holy life.

MY PRAYER TO GOD

Thank you, Lord, for your holiness. You are perfect! That fact gives me great peace. I choose to trust that you already see me as holy and that your work in my life will help me mature in holiness.

GOD EMPOWERS YOU TO BUILD HIS KINGDOM

Rather, as servants of God we commend ourselves in every way: in great endurance; in troubles, hardships and distresses ... in truthful speech and in the power of God; with weapons of righteousness in the right hand and in the left.   2 CORINTHIANS 6:4,7

All Christians have a responsibility both to practice and to proclaim their faith. Evangelism is not optional. But what about when hard times come? Don't we get a break? Aren't we exempt from the "Great Commission"—at least until our lives calm down?

Not really. Trials aren't an excuse for not sharing our faith; on the contrary, they are an opportunity to speak out for God. The apostle Paul says as much in the passage above. It is during these times that God gives us the strength to endure in order to keep going in our task of kingdom building. In fact our endurance fuels our message.

Trials didn't stop Paul from announcing the Good News; they should not deter us either. ❖

GOD'S PROMISE TO ME

- I have forgiven your sin and reconciled you to myself.
- I have given you Good News to share with others.

MY PRAYER TO GOD

God, you have given the gospel to me so that I might show it and share it. Help me to see beyond my problems today, to my real purpose—building your kingdom. Give me creativity in using my struggles to speak for you.

JESUS IS THE WAY, TRUTH AND LIFE

Jesus answered, "I am the way and the truth and the life. No one comes to the Father except through me."   JOHN 14:6

People who say that Jesus was just a good man or a great teacher have certainly not read the Bible. Jesus was pretty unmistakable in his claims.

Jesus is *the way*. When people show us the "way," they give us directions or show us the path to our desired destination. If we are seeking God, then Jesus is the way—the only way. We cannot get to the Father except through Jesus. In other words, to have a relationship with God, we must believe in his Son, who accepted the punishment for our sin so that we could approach our holy God.

Jesus is *the truth*. When something is true, it is dependable, reliable, trustworthy and right. Jesus himself *is* truth; everything he says and does is true, right and trustworthy. Our trust is in the right place when we place it in the truth.

Jesus is *the life*. Sure, everyone is alive, but true "life," a life of complete and total satisfaction, joy and fulfillment can be found in only in Christ. ✤

GOD'S PROMISE TO ME

- I am way, the truth and the life.
- I am the only way you can gain eternal life and total satisfaction.

MY PRAYER TO GOD

Thank you for being the way to salvation, Lord. You are the truth and the life. Nothing this world can offer satisfies; nothing gives total fulfillment or contentment except you.

day171

GOD IS LOVE

We know and rely on the love God has for us. God is love. Whoever lives in love lives in God, and God in them. This is how love is made complete among us so that we will have confidence on the day of judgment: In this world we are like Jesus. There is no fear in love. But perfect love drives out fear. 1 JOHN 4:16-18

God *is* love. Everything about his character is perfectly loving. He cannot be otherwise. We know how much God loves us because he sent his Son to die for us.

Is there any better feeling than being loved? To know that someone loves us gives us a sense of assurance, a sense of being special. That feeling can be ours every day because of God's love for us. God has taken up residence in our lives through his Holy Spirit; therefore, love has taken up residence in our lives. We literally "live in love." We are surrounded by it, filled with it. Love envelops us every moment of every day. Such love fills us and then overflows to other people, like water from a fountain. The result of such love? We will not be afraid on the day of judgment. God promises that we will be able to face him with confidence because we know that our salvation is sure.

We can trust in this God who is love. We can also pray for others to sense God's love and know their salvation is certain. ✢

GOD'S PROMISE TO ME

- I love you.
- As I live in you, your love will grow more perfect.
- Because of my love, you need not fear the day of judgment but can be confident in your salvation.

MY PRAYER TO GOD

Fill me with your love, O God. May it overflow on others like a fountain of refreshment.

day**172**

GOD SHOWED HIS LOVE THROUGH HIS SON

God demonstrates his own love for us in this: While we were still sinners, Christ died for us. Since we have now been justified by his blood, how much more shall we be saved from God's wrath through him! ROMANS 5:8–9

"God loves you? How do you know that?" someone may challenge us. Well, we have a ready answer that comes straight from the Bible: "God demonstrates his own love for us in this: While we were still sinners, Christ died for us."

God sent his Son to die not because we deserved it or because it appeared that we might improve and be good enough for him. He sent his Son to die knowing full well that we were sinners without hope, unable to ever be good enough. To those who accept his sacrifice, he gives forgiveness and eternal life. Christ's death on the cross makes us right in God's sight, saves us from God's judgment and assures us of eternal life. John 3:16 tells us, "God so loved the world that he gave his one and only Son, that whoever believes in him shall not perish but have eternal life."

That's the greatness of God's love. Would we give our child or spouse or other loved one to save others? We cannot imagine it, yet that's what God did for us. ✤

GOD'S PROMISE TO ME

- I showed my great love for you by dying for you while you were still a sinner.
- My blood will make you right, save you from judgment and give you eternal life with me.

MY PRAYER TO GOD

You showed your great love for me by sending your Son to die for me while I was still a sinner. What great love, Lord. I cannot imagine such an act. Help me share that love with others. May it make a difference in my life today and every day.

NOTHING CAN SEPARATE YOU FROM GOD'S LOVE

I am convinced that neither death nor life, neither angels nor demons, neither the present nor the future, nor any powers, neither height nor depth, nor anything else in all creation, will be able to separate us from the love of God that is in Christ Jesus our Lord.

ROMANS 8:38–39

Believers are secure in Christ. Paul presents a remarkable argument in these verses. He asks, "If God is for us, who can be against us?" (8:31). If God gave up his only Son for us, won't he also give us everything else? Is God going to accuse us? No, because our right standing comes from God. Is Christ going to condemn us? No, because Christ died for us and is now at God's right hand interceding for us. Can anything separate us from God's love? No. Will we face lots of difficulties? Yes, but no matter what we face, "in all these things we are more than conquerors through him who loved us" (8:37).

Paul was convinced that nothing can separate us from God's love. Whether our bodies are alive or dead, we are with God. The unseen spiritual forces cannot separate us from him. No matter where we go, God's love is there.

Once we belong to God, we cannot ever be separated from him. Christ's death proved that. No matter where we go, how we feel or what battles we face, we are never separated from God's love. His presence and his love hold us securely—forever. ❖

GOD'S PROMISE TO ME

- Nothing can ever separate you from my love.
- In my love you are secure.

MY PRAYER TO GOD

Heavenly Father, you promise that nothing can ever separate me from your love. Thank you for that promise and the assurance of my security in you.

day174 june 23

GOD'S LOVE NEVER FAILS

The LORD is compassionate and gracious, slow to anger, abounding in love. He will not always accuse, nor will he harbor his anger forever ... For as high as the heavens are above the earth, so great is his love for those who fear him; as far as the east is from the west, so far has he removed our transgressions from us. PSALM 103:8 – 9,11 – 12

God is full of unfailing love. It is seen in his mercy and grace toward us. Just as he got angry with his people the Israelites, so he gets angry with us today when we turn away from him. Yet he is slow to anger and does not remain angry forever.

The psalmist knew that God was merciful and forgiving. God's love is as high as the heavens and his forgiveness is boundless. Only a God so loving would not punish us as we deserve but instead take our sins and remove them as far as the east is from the west. In other words, our sins are completely separated from us and are remembered no more.

God's love never falters or fails. We may make him angry; we may face punishment, but we can always count on his forgiveness, mercy and love. Even in his anger God does not stop loving us. ✤

GOD'S PROMISE TO ME

- I am merciful, gracious, slow to anger and full of unfailing love.
- My love for you is greater than the height of the heavens.
- I take your rebellious acts and remove them as far as the east is from the west.

MY PRAYER TO GOD

Thank you for your love and mercy, Lord. Even when I am rebellious, I can return to you and find forgiveness and love. Your love is greater than I can comprehend.

GOD'S LOVE ENDURES FOREVER

Give thanks to the LORD, for he is good. His love endures forever.   PSALM 136:1

Every other line in Psalm 136 has the words, *"His love endures forever."* As the psalmist briefly recites parts of Israel's history, each act is followed by these words. God showed his love in creation (136:1–9); in bringing his people out of Egypt (136:10–15), in protecting them in the wilderness (136:16–22) and in providing for them (136:23–26).

When you look back over your life, what choices, changes, trials or great joys come to mind? Perhaps you didn't always sense God's love, but the perspective of time shows that God's faithful love was in each situation. That means that the situations of today are bound up in God's faithful love as well. You can trust him today because you have experienced his loving hand in the past.

Make a list of key times across the span of your life. Then, after each, write *"His love endures forever."* God is at work. His love endures forever. ✣

GOD'S PROMISE TO ME

• My faithful love for you endures forever.

MY PRAYER TO GOD

Nothing can stop you from loving me, Lord. Your love works through every situation today just as your faithful love carried your people Israel. I can trust your love today, tomorrow and for the rest of my life. Thank you that your love endures forever.

day176

THE HOLY SPIRIT GUARANTEES FUTURE PROMISES

You also were included in Christ when you heard the message of truth, the gospel of your salvation. When you believed, you were marked in him with a seal, the promised Holy Spirit, who is a deposit guaranteeing our inheritance until the redemption of those who are God's possession—to the praise of his glory. EPHESIANS 1:13–14

Who are the "you also" to whom Paul referred? This meant all non-Jews who had become believers. Christ came to die for everyone—not just Jews, but Gentiles too. God had promised that through one of Abraham's descendants, "all peoples on earth will be blessed" (Genesis 12:3). Jesus fulfilled that promise when he opened the way of salvation to everyone. When we believe the Good News, God saves us. In that moment God gives us his Holy Spirit, who is like a security deposit. The fact that we have the Holy Spirit means that all the rest of God's promises will come true.

God's promises about eternity are as certain as our salvation. There is no need to doubt what God says. While we may not understand everything in our lives or even agree on how the future will play out, we can agree that Jesus is coming back to take us to heaven to be with him forever.

We can have confidence in God's promises for the future. The Holy Spirit testifies daily to the fact that all of God's promises will come true "to the praise of his glory." ✤

GOD'S PROMISE TO ME

- I gave you my Spirit as a guarantee that I will give you everything else I promised.
- You can be confident in all of my promises for the future.

MY PRAYER TO GOD

God, thank you for giving me your Holy Spirit and for identifying me as your child. Thank you for the glorious future you have in store for me.

GOD PROMISES RESURRECTION

Christ has indeed been raised from the dead, the firstfruits of those who have fallen asleep.
1 CORINTHIANS 15:20

Jesus rose from the dead. People may deny it, but it is a fact recorded in God's Word and verified by many people who saw him. It is a fact for which the disciples — and many believers across the centuries — gave their lives.

The promise for us is that because Christ was raised from the dead, so we will be raised. Jesus said to a weeping Martha at the tomb of Lazarus, "I am the resurrection and the life. The one who believes in me will live, even though they die; and whoever lives by believing in me will never die" (John 11:25 – 26).

Eternal life begins the moment we trust Jesus as our Savior, and it carries us through our physical death into our resurrected life in heaven with God. Death is not the end; it is merely the transition from this life into the glorious promised eternity.

When we know Christ, we need not fear death. We may experience the sadness of losing loved ones or our own mortality through sickness. But we can take comfort in the promise that as children of God, we will be raised from the dead to be with Christ forever. ❖

GOD'S PROMISE TO ME

- I rose from the dead.
- I am the resurrection and the life.
- When you believe in me, you will not perish but will have everlasting life.

MY PRAYER TO GOD

You were raised from the dead, Jesus, the first of many who will be raised. Death comes to everyone, but you are the resurrection and the life. One day all believers will be raised to live in a glorious eternity with you. Thank you for that amazing gift!

GOD PROMISES A PRICELESS INHERITANCE

Praise be to the God and Father of our Lord Jesus Christ! In his great mercy he has given us new birth into a living hope through the resurrection of Jesus Christ from the dead, and into an inheritance that can never perish, spoil or fade. This inheritance is kept in heaven for you. 1 PETER 1:3–4

You've seen it in the movies—an expectant family gathers around to hear the reading of the will. Family members are especially interested if the recently-deceased loved one (or maybe even not-so-loved one) had a lot of money. Everyone wants a piece of the pie. They all expect a windfall of money or stuff. And too often, that little session in the lawyer's office doesn't end well for everyone involved. And frequently those who do receive a large inheritance find a way to blow it.

Inheritances aren't always what they're made out to be.

But not so with God. He who owns everything, who gave it all up to save you, and then returned to heaven to prepare a place for you, also has an inheritance waiting for you. It can never perish, spoil or fade. And it lasts forever. ❖

GOD'S PROMISE TO ME

- I have reserved a priceless inheritance in heaven for my children.
- When you believe in me, you are promised that inheritance.
- I will protect you until you receive that inheritance.

MY PRAYER TO GOD

Lord, it is because of your boundless mercy that I have the privilege of being born again. Thank you for giving your Son to die for me so that I could become your child. You promise that I can look forward to a priceless inheritance with you, an inheritance that "can never perish, spoil or fade."

day179

GOD PROMISES THAT YOU WILL BE LIKE HIM

Dear friends, now we are children of God, and what we will be has not yet been made known. But we know that when Christ appears, we shall be like him, for we shall see him as he is.   1 JOHN 3:2

We are *already* God's children—not when we're good enough, not sometime in the future, not if we prove ourselves—*now*. Yet there's something more to come, something we cannot even imagine. When Christ returns, "we shall be like him, for we shall see him as he is." We not only share in his family, his blessings and his inheritance, we will also share in his glory.

This is a vision of what awaits us. We may not understand fully, but we do know that it is what we strive for. Even as we live our lives seeking to obey God and become more Christlike, we know that we cannot do it in this life. We will not be perfect until we see him as he is. When he returns, we will look into the face of our Savior and become like him in his glory. Think of it: Christ will share his glory with us!

We can trust in this glorious future. No matter how many times we may trip and fall as we seek to grow in Christ, when we belong to him, our future is secure. One day we will be like him, "for we shall see him as he is." ✤

GOD'S PROMISE TO ME

- One day you will share in my glory.
- When you see me, you will be like me.

MY PRAYER TO GOD

You say that I am your child, Lord. Thank you for that amazing privilege. I trust that one day I will be like you, for I will see you as you are. Help me to await that day with eager anticipation.

GOD PROMISES TO MAKE ALL THINGS NEW

He who was seated on the throne said, "I am making everything new!" Then he said, "Write this down, for these words are trustworthy and true." REVELATION 21:5

Have you ever heard people talk about what they imagine about heaven? Perhaps they spoke of living in the clouds or people lying around playing the harp all day, every day, for *eternity*. Sounds boring, right?

This kind of perception does not take into account an infinite God with the power to totally change everything, to make every day a new and glorious experience.

So, what will it *really* be like to live with God? John tried his best to describe what apparently was indescribable. We may not understand it completely, but we can trust that heaven will be a place of perfect joy. The old world and its evils will be gone forever. God promises to make all things new. Not just *some* things—all things.

When we're tempted to fear that life in heaven will be as exciting as watching grass grow, we can take comfort in this glorious promise. A God who has no limits can be counted on to keep that promise. ❖

GOD'S PROMISE TO ME

• I will make all things new!

MY PRAYER TO GOD

Lord God, you are worthy of my praise. Thank you for the promise of making everything new, of making heaven a place of infinite joy.

GOD CALMS YOUR TROUBLED MIND

Peace I leave with you; my peace I give you. I do not give to you as the world gives. Do not let your hearts be troubled and do not be afraid. JOHN 14:27

In a fallen world, what we have most is trouble. What we have precious little of is peace. Peace of mind so that we can turn off all the nagging worries and "what ifs?" and find true rest. Peace of heart so that we are not forever paralyzed by crippling emotions. Peace of soul so that we can face the future with confidence.

Temporary distractions and short-term pleasures are the best our world can offer. These provide a brief respite from our concerns, but they do not fill our souls with peace. Though we escape our pain or medicate it, we must eventually come back to reality. And there we are again: face to face with our external and internal storms.

What we really need is what Jesus offers. Not the promise that we'll escape from trouble but the promise of peace in the midst of our tough times. Real peace. Otherworldly peace. Enduring peace. Who wouldn't want such a gift? ✤

GOD'S PROMISE TO ME

- I offer you peace of mind and heart.
- My peace is totally different than the world's version of peace.

MY PRAYER TO GOD

Lord Jesus, I want to know your peace firsthand. Keep me from chasing after counterfeits. I don't want worldly distractions or pleasurable diversions. I want the blessedness of resting in you.

GOD IS GOOD

The LORD is good, a refuge in times of trouble. He cares for those who trust in him.

NAHUM 1:7

It has been said that one of the greatest struggles in life is believing that God is good.

In the garden of Eden, Adam and Eve doubted the goodness of God—apparently thinking that he was withholding something wonderful from them. As a result they sampled the forbidden fruit and plunged the human race into sin (see Genesis 3).

We wrestle with the same doubt. Why else would we refuse to do what a good God tells us to do or do the very things he forbids? When trouble comes, do we run to God for refuge, or do we run away from him and try to solve our problems on our own, believing that if God really loved us, he wouldn't have allowed this thing, whatever it is, to happen to us.

The truth you can take to heart today is the reality that God *is* good. So are his plans and purposes for you. He wants only the best for those he loves. Ask him to make that truth real to you today. ✤

GOD'S PROMISE TO ME

- I am good.
- I am a strong refuge.
- I am intimate with those who trust me.

MY PRAYER TO GOD

You are absolutely good, Lord. Teach me to trust wholeheartedly in this most basic of truths. When I am in trouble, help me to run to you and experience your goodness. Keep me from the foolish mistake of believing that life and help can be found outside of you.

GOD IS YOUR SHEPHERD

The LORD is my shepherd, I lack nothing.   PSALM 23:1

Psalm 23 is probably the most beloved chapter in the Bible. And for good reason. It contains beautiful imagery of God's care and concern for his people.

In David's picture, we are sheep—implying we are helpless, not too bright, skittish and prone to wander off and get into trouble. And for many of us, that's a fairly accurate description.

The Lord, however, is depicted as our shepherd (see also John 10:11–14). He's watching. Leading. Feeding. Protecting. Caring. As long as we stay close to him, we have no worries whatsoever.

That's the timeless message of the Bible's most well-known psalm. Can you think of any promise more relevant for busy Christians in a bustling age? ✢

GOD'S PROMISE TO ME

- I am your shepherd.
- I will provide all that you need.

MY PRAYER TO GOD

Shepherd of my soul, I praise you and thank you for your care. You are not just my Creator or my God. You are not just the King or the Judge of the universe. You are my Shepherd. I am so blessed! Because of you, I lack nothing. Keep me from complaining. Help me not to worry. Let me rest in the promise that as I go where you lead, you will meet all my needs.

day184

july 3

GOD IS YOUR FATHER

Yet to all who did receive him, to those who believed in his name, he gave the right to become children of God.   JOHN 1:12

There's a scene in the classic Christmas movie *It's a Wonderful Life* where a delivery boy named George Bailey is told to take some diphtheria medicine to the Blaine family. He hesitates. He's pretty sure the druggist, despondent over the death of his own son, has inadvertently put poison powder in the capsules. Frozen in indecision George looks up to see a Sweet Caporal advertising sign on the wall, which reads simply, "Ask Dad. He Knows." He grabs the box of pills and dashes out the door to his father's office.

What a great picture of the privilege we have as Christians. When we acknowledge Christ as our Savior, he not only forgives our sin, he makes us children of God. This means in the confusing busyness of everyday life, we have a perfect Father who is always glad to help and guide us. ✤

GOD'S PROMISE TO ME

• You are my child if you believe and accept my Son.

MY PRAYER TO GOD

Lord Jesus, I do believe in you. I have accepted you as my Savior and Lord. Thank you for revealing yourself to me. Thank you for saving me. Because of your grace and my faith, I am a child of the living God. I praise you! What a privilege! What joy to know that in every situation I have a loving, wise and good heavenly Father to counsel me.

GOD FREES YOU FROM SIN

This righteousness is given through faith in Jesus Christ to all who believe. There is no difference between Jew and Gentile, for all have sinned and fall short of the glory of God, and all are justified freely by his grace through the redemption that came by Christ Jesus.

ROMANS 3:22–24

What a glorious promise! God loves us so much that he wanted to make us right with him. Because he is a just God, he could not simply overlook our sin. His justice required that someone pay the penalty for it. And someone did. God sent his only Son as the perfect sacrifice to take the punishment our sins required.

God promises that when we trust in what Jesus did for us, he will take away our sins—no matter who we are or what we have done. No sin is so great that God cannot wipe it away. Because of Jesus' death, God declares us not guilty and sets us free. Of course, we will never be completely without sin until we get to heaven, but in the meantime, God looks at us and sees Christ's righteousness instead of our sin.

Today, declare your independence. God has freed you. ❖

GOD'S PROMISE TO ME

- You are made right in my sight when you trust my Son to take away your sins.
- I declare you not guilty.

MY PRAYER TO GOD

Heavenly Father, thank you for sending Jesus to declare me "not guilty" by his death on the cross. I trust you, Lord.

day186

GOD EXALTS HIS SERVANTS

Whoever wants to become great among you must be your servant, and whoever wants to be first must be your slave. MATTHEW 20:26–27

The world has it all backwards. The world ascribes greatness to those who are excessively ambitious. The world applauds the proud who are willing to do almost anything to climb to the top of the heap. To the world's way of thinking, such obsession for glory is the true measure of success.

Jesus has other ideas. He tells his followers that the way up is down. If we want to be great from heaven's perspective, we must be willing to take the place of a lowly servant.

Today as you move out into a world that has embraced values that are diametrically opposed to the teachings of Jesus, remember that the arrogant and self-serving face eventual humiliation. Only the humble will be honored in the end, when the stakes are eternal. ✣

GOD'S PROMISE TO ME

• I honor those who serve.

MY PRAYER TO GOD

Lord, give me the grace to choose the way of servanthood. I want to imitate you. Help me to put others' needs and desires before my own. Your Word teaches that true reward awaits those who humble themselves in loving service. Keep me from the tendency to be busy, to be driven, to step on others and to exalt myself.

GOD REWARDS YOUR HARD WORK

Lazy hands make for poverty, but diligent hands bring wealth.   PROVERBS 10:4

The book of Proverbs is Hebrew wisdom literature—meaning it is a collection of wise sayings written in poetic form. Essentially these verses of wisdom are the universal observations of those (mostly King Solomon) with vast experience and skill in living.

Modern-day readers are mistaken if we see these pithy maxims as absolute promises; technically, they are general principles—things that are normally true. Even so we are wise to read and heed what we find in these 31 chapters.

The proverb above contrasts laziness and diligence. Typically, the lazy person ends up suffering while the hard worker eventually enjoys a measure of prosperity. It's not a guarantee, but success is much more likely for the diligent person (see Ephesians 6:7–8).

What about you? Are you doing your best and going the extra mile? Remember: Excellence usually results in a handsome payoff. ❖

GOD'S PROMISE TO ME

• I reward the diligent.

MY PRAYER TO GOD

Heavenly Father, you honor the diligent. I want to do my work with enthusiasm and for your glory. Keep me from a lazy spirit. Even though many around me expect something for nothing, help me to be willing to labor. Please honor my efforts.

GOD DIRECTS YOUR WAYS

Trust in the LORD with all your heart and lean not on your own understanding; in all your ways submit to him, and he will make your paths straight. PROVERBS 3:5−6

Here's an exercise for the next time you find yourself up to your neck in question marks. Whenever you're wondering which path to go down, and perhaps feeling pressured by the fast pace of life to make a quick choice, ask yourself: Am I looking to and leaning on God?

Do I put more stock in God's counsel than in my own ideas or the opinions of others? Am I open to the idea that God may very well ask me to do something that everyone else thinks is crazy?

Do I honestly want what God wants—in every part of my life? Am I willing to wait until I have a clear sense of his leading?

If you can answer "yes" to these questions, God promises to direct you. How good is that? ♣

GOD'S PROMISE TO ME

• If you trust me and seek me, I will show you the way to go.

MY PRAYER TO GOD

You want me to trust you, Lord, with all my heart, and I want to do that. You're worthy of my trust. Forgive me for the times I doubt. In times of uncertainty I know I need more than mere human understanding. I need you! I want your will, God. Please show me which way to go.

day189

GOD IS MOST CONCERNED WITH YOUR HEART

The LORD does not look at the things people look at. People look at the outward appearance, but the LORD looks at the heart.   1 SAMUEL 16:7

When does concern over one's appearance cross the line between healthy and unhealthy?

Is it wrong, for instance, to work out every day? What about cosmetic surgery? Or spending time and effort searching for the "perfect" haircut, suntan, makeup or wardrobe?

There are no simple answers to these questions, but the promise above reminds us that God is far more interested in what's going on inside us than how we look on the outside.

The apostle Paul's words fit well here: "Train yourself to be godly. For physical training is of some value, but godliness has value for all things, holding promise for both the present life and the life to come" (1 Timothy 4:7–8). ❖

GOD'S PROMISE TO ME

- I don't evaluate people by looking at their outward appearance.
- I judge people by their thoughts and intentions.

MY PRAYER TO GOD

Lord, it's true that our world thinks external image is everything. Forgive me for the times I am overly concerned with my appearance. Grant me the wisdom and discipline to expend the necessary time and energy to care for my soul. May you be pleased more and more as you examine my thoughts and intentions.

GOD IS TENDER TOWARD YOU

[The LORD] tends his flock like a shepherd: He gathers the lambs in his arms and carries them close to his heart; he gently leads those that have young. ISAIAH 40:11

Some of the Bible's verbal pictures of God provoke healthy awe and reverence: Creator (see Isaiah 40:28 and Ephesians 3:9); Ruler (see 2 Chronicles 20:6); Lord (see Exodus 3:14–20); Ruler (see Psalm 22:28 and Isaiah 6:5); Judge (see Psalm 94:2).

Other Biblical portraits provide a strong sense of hope and safety: Redeemer (see Isaiah 44:24); Father (see Psalm 103:13).

But perhaps one of the most comforting and familiar descriptions of God is that of Shepherd, the metaphor used by the prophet Isaiah in the promise above.

The overall meaning is clear. God is protective and alert. He is proactive on our behalf, always seeking our best and providing for us. But notice also the words and phrases "close to his heart," and "gently." Can you think of a more comforting description of God anywhere in the Bible?

The Good Shepherd shows great tenderness to his lambs—which means you. You are close to his heart. ✤

GOD'S PROMISE TO ME

- I will feed you and lead you.
- I will carry you in my arms.
- I will hold you close to my heart.

MY PRAYER TO GOD

Shepherd of heaven, you faithfully feed and guide your flock. Thank you for your protection and provision. You are gentle, and you hold me in your arms. What an amazing promise! When I am afraid, worried or tired, remind me that you desire to carry me with all tenderness.

GOD HAS RESCUED YOU FROM SIN AND DEATH

It is by grace you have been saved, through faith—and this is not from yourselves, it is the gift of God. EPHESIANS 2:8

"Not seeing the forest for the trees" is the phrase often used to describe a person who has lost perspective. It's when you get so immersed in countless little details, that you no longer see the big picture. In the spiritual realm, if you lose this over-arching sense of "Why?" you also lose the important element of "Wow!" Weariness and a loss of motivation are sure to follow.

One solution for this common condition is to push the pause button on your hectic life and spend some time reflecting on the great salvation you have in Christ. Imagine being an enemy of God (see Romans 5:10 and Colossians 1:21). You once were! Consider the awful thought of your sins being counted against you. They once did! But now, because of Christ, everything is changed. You are clean, forgiven, accepted.

That is God's amazing gift to you. ✤

GOD'S PROMISE TO ME

- I have saved you.
- My salvation is a gift.

MY PRAYER TO GOD

God, you have saved me from an empty existence now and an awful existence in eternity. Thank you for this wonderful, undeserved gift. Keep me from losing sight of what you've done for me. Even in the midst of a crazy, busy day, remind me of the big picture—that I am your beloved child.

GOD SHOWS MERCY TO THE MERCIFUL

Blessed are the merciful, for they will be shown mercy.　　　　MATTHEW 5:7

Someone has described mercy as "not getting what we deserve."

That's not a bad explanation. Spiritually, the Bible says we deserve to be eternally separated from our holy God (see Romans 6:23) because of our great rebellion against him (see Romans 3:23). But God, in the ultimate act of mercy, offers us a full pardon and the riches of heaven. We deserve the worst. In Christ we get the very best.

In his famous Sermon on the Mount, Jesus mentioned mercy (see Matthew 5:7). His point is that if we're truly right with God, we will extend mercy to the undeserving people in our lives. The more mercy we show, the more of mercy we will know.

Who in your life needs to be shown mercy? ✤

GOD'S PROMISE TO ME

- I bless those who are merciful.

MY PRAYER TO GOD

God, you are merciful. Thank you for not giving me the eternal death I deserve. Instead, I have life in Christ. Teach me to be wild and lavish in my willingness to overlook wrongs and to bless those who don't deserve blessing.

day193

GOD GIVES US THE WILL TO KEEP DOING RIGHT

For the Spirit God gave us does not make us timid, but gives us power, love and self-discipline.   2 TIMOTHY 1:7

Ever meet a Christian who is motivated, tireless and fearless? This is the ultimate "get it done" person, the poster child for spiritual accomplishment. Think "the apostle Paul." Think "rare."

Most believers can't relate to such faith and courage. We identify more with Timothy, Paul's young friend and protégé who struggled with fear, feelings of inadequacy and complacency.

In the last letter he ever wrote, Paul reminded Timothy that God had supplied all the resources necessary to do his will—the strength, the motivation and the ability to stay focused on the task.

That promise is good for you too. ✣

GOD'S PROMISE TO ME

- I have supplied you with power.
- I have given you love.
- I have provided you the resource of self-discipline.

MY PRAYER TO GOD

What a shocking promise, Lord! You give me your power. When I turn to you, I can find the right motivation (love), the necessary strength (power) and the self-discipline I need to do your will in a way that brings you glory.

day194

THE JOY OF THE LORD IS YOUR STRENGTH

Do not grieve, for the joy of the LORD is your strength.   NEHEMIAH 8:10

The returned exiles had just completed rebuilding the wall around their beloved city of Jerusalem. They gathered to hear the reading of God's Law, and they wept with sorrow for how far they had strayed from their Lord. Nehemiah told them not to grieve, but to move forward in the joy of the Lord. God had brought them back from exile and kept his promises to them—and as they returned to him, he would return to them.

Sadly, a lot of people get stuck. They feel that they have strayed so far away from God that there's no use coming back. Unlike the prodigal son who finally realized that returning home in humility was better than living with the pigs (see Luke 15), they simply keep trying to make it on their own—and made a worse mess of their lives.

Are you a prodigal? Do you know one? It's never too late to come back to God. Do not grieve. The joy of the Lord is your strength. ♣

GOD'S PROMISE TO ME

- It's never too late to come back to me.
- My joy will give you strength to move ahead no matter what your past has been like.

MY PRAYER TO GOD

Thank you, God, that it's never too late to come back to you. The past is difficult to let go of, but with your joy helping me, I can move forward into what you have for me.

day195

THE SON OF GOD PRAYS FOR YOU

Because Jesus lives forever, he has a permanent priesthood. Therefore he is able to save completely those who come to God through him, because he always lives to intercede for them.   HEBREWS 7:24–25

If you have people who pray for you regularly, you are blessed—and rightly so. If one or two of those praying people happen to be godly, respected saints, you probably feel an added comfort.

How much more wonderful is the news that Jesus Christ prays for us continually before the throne of God?

It's true. Hebrews 7 says it. The Greek word translated "to intercede for them" was often used in ancient times to refer to the practice of petitioning a king on behalf of someone else. This is known as interceding.

This is what Jesus does for us—stationed at the right hand of God, he intercedes for us nonstop, probably in much the same manner we find him praying for his disciples in John 17.

Such a guarantee can't help but give us confidence as we live in chaotic, uncertain times. ♣

GOD'S PROMISE TO ME

- I am your great High Priest.
- I am the one who saves you.
- I am your representative.

MY PRAYER TO GOD

I praise you, Lord, for your wonderful salvation and constant care. Thank you for praying for me continually before the throne of God. I ask you to make my life and actions conform to your will.

day196

july 15

GOD STRENGTHENS THOSE WHO LOOK TO HIM

This is what the Sovereign LORD, the Holy One of Israel, says: "In repentance and rest is your salvation, in quietness and trust is your strength." ISAIAH 30:15

In 739 BC, the Jewish nation of Judah was in a mess. Rather than trusting in the Lord during tough times, the rebellious nation had instead called on Egypt for help. The prophet Isaiah was sent by God to confront the Israelites, and his wasn't a very "user-friendly" message. Isaiah used scary words and phrases like *brought low, humbled* and *lament*. Many people dismissed him as an overly religious kook. But Isaiah spoke with heaven's authority, and his words and manner must have caused a few sleepless nights—at least for some.

The details vary, but the principles and promise are still valid today. To experience all that God desires for us, we must turn to him—and walk with him—in trust. If we ignore him, or trust in other people or other things, we do so at our own peril. Our tough times will only multiply. ❖

GOD'S PROMISE TO ME

- Return to me and wait for me, and I will deliver you from trouble.
- You will find strength when you quietly trust me.

MY PRAYER TO GOD

Forgive me, Lord, for acting at times as though I am in charge of my own life. Forgive me for trusting in anyone or anything but you. Give me the wisdom to see that a rich, full, satisfying life is possible only when I look to you and wait for you.

day**197**

GOD GAVE HIS SON FOR YOU

For God so loved the world that he gave his one and only Son, that whoever believes in him shall not perish but have eternal life. JOHN 3:16

"John 3:16."

Christians write this Bible reference on signs and hold them up for the TV cameras at big sporting events. Christ-following football stars scribble it in their eye black and sometimes on their shoes. Why the obsession with this particular verse? Because as much as (or more than) any other passage of Scripture, this one sentence summarizes the message of the Bible.

This verse speaks of God's breathtaking, proactive, lavish, sacrificial love for a rebellious human race. God couldn't bear to see people perish, so he sent a Savior, Jesus Christ, his one and only Son. The verse promises that anyone—anyone at all—can have new life, eternal life, through faith alone in Christ alone.

Here's something to consider. *You* are part of the world. That means God loves *you*. Christ died for *you*. Christ offers eternal life to *you*.

Can you think of a message more worth pondering ... or embracing ... or sharing? ❖

GOD'S PROMISE TO ME

- I love you.
- If you believe in my Son, you will have eternal life.

MY PRAYER TO GOD

God, this is an amazing verse about an amazing truth, and it comes with an amazing promise. Please cause that promise to take root in my heart in a deep, new way.

day198

GOD IS FAITHFUL TO YOU

Your faithfulness continues through all generations; you established the earth, and it endures. PSALM 119:90

Asked to list their favorite words, respondents in one poll cited *mother*, *home*, *Christmas*, *free* and *vacation*.

A word that didn't make the list is *faithful*. Faithful means reliable, loyal or trustworthy. A faithful person is one you can count on, one who will be there till the bitter end ... and beyond. Such dependability is a rare commodity these days. Maybe that explains why *faithful* didn't make the list.

But get this, the Bible claims—repeatedly—that God is forever faithful. He doesn't give up on us, even when we're faithless (see 2 Timothy 2:13). His love is solid rock. That's a promise we can count on. ♣

GOD'S PROMISE TO ME

• I am forever faithful.

MY PRAYER TO GOD

God, your faithfulness is eternal. Thank you for being eternally devoted to me. When I can't sense your presence or see you at work, help me to remember that you are still there, and you will never let me go.

GOD IS FAIR WITH YOU

The LORD is righteous in all his ways and faithful in all he does.   PSALM 145:17

The first complete sentence uttered by most children is "That's not fair!" Kids say this a lot. And, truth be told, grown-ups think it a lot. It's not hard to see why. We live in a world filled with inequity and injustice. The undeserving seem to get all the breaks. Nice guys, as the saying goes, finish last.

What's important to remember is that even though life is unfair, God never is (see Hebrews 6:10). Because he is righteous (see Psalm 71:16), everything he does is just (see Psalm 111:7). Furthermore, he loves righteousness and justice (see Psalm 33:5).

The next time you are faced with an unfair situation, turn to the one who is righteous in everything he does. ✤

GOD'S PROMISE TO ME

- I am always righteous.
- I am faithful in all that I do.

MY PRAYER TO GOD

I struggle, God, with living in a world where evil seems to be rewarded and good is ignored or punished. Help me to keep me eyes on you and on the truth of your word. You are righteous in all you do. When I am being treated unfairly, help me to resist the urge to respond in kind.

day**200**

GOD BRINGS LIGHT TO YOUR DARKNESS

If I say, "Surely the darkness will hide me and the light become night around me," even the darkness will not be dark to you; the night will shine like the day, for darkness is as light to you. PSALM 139:11–12

Psalm 139 is widely regarded as one of the most beautiful and beloved passages in the Bible.

David reflects first on the fact that God knows, not just all things (see verses 1–6), but all things *about him*. This sobering truth seems to make David uneasy. It's as if he wants to run from God and hide. But quickly David realizes there's nowhere he can go where God is not (see verses 7–12).

Even overwhelming darkness cannot separate us from God, David says, because he is by nature light. There is no such thing as darkness where God is concerned.

This theological truth is comforting whether the darkness in which we find ourselves is self-chosen or the result of hard, painful circumstances beyond our control. Either way, God's very presence brings light—clarifying, guiding light. In God's light, we see light (see Psalm 36:9).

You may not be able to "see" God, but without question, he sees you (see Psalm 139:16–18). So why stumble in the darkness when almighty God stands ready to lead you out into the light? ❖

GOD'S PROMISE TO ME

- Darkness is not dark to me.
- I am light, and those who walk with me live in the light.

MY PRAYER TO GOD

Heavenly Father, may your Word and your truth be a lamp to my feet and a light to my path.

day201

GOD SHOWERS YOU WITH BLESSINGS

Praise the LORD, my soul, and forget not all his benefits—who forgives all your sins and heals all your diseases ... who satisfies your desires with good things so that your youth is renewed like the eagle's.   PSALM 103:2–3,5

Many busy, high-energy people are list makers. They have lists for everything—letters/emails to write, home improvement projects (in order of priority), presents to buy, sights to see on their next vacation, and on and on the lists go. But how many times do people take time to stop and list all the good things God has done?

David did this in Psalm 103, and the result was spectacular. He erupted in praise as he recited the long list of amazing blessings he'd received from God.

Guess what? This is not just David's list, it's also God's list of promises to you. Which of these blessings do you need most today? ✤

GOD'S PROMISE TO ME

- I forgive your sin.
- I heal your diseases.
- I surround you with love and mercy.
- I fill your life with good things.

MY PRAYER TO GOD

You are worthy of praise, Lord, for you do countless good things for your children. Forgive me for the times I fail to acknowledge your blessings in my life. Forgiveness, healing, rescue, love, mercy—you fill my life with undeserved blessings. Teach me the wonderful habit of counting my blessings.

day**202**

GOD DELIVERS YOU FROM CONDEMNATION

There is now no condemnation for those who are in Christ Jesus. ROMANS 8:1

One of the most destructive types of busyness is practiced by professing Christians. Though they proclaim a gospel that promises a new standing with God as his beloved children, these individuals privately practice a different belief.

They busy themselves with thoughts of unworthiness and guilt. They live under a self-imposed cloud of condemnation. And they do this despite the promise that followers of Jesus are free—forever—from the threat of divine retribution.

The New Testament is clear: Christ took the awful punishment we deserved because of our sin. This action cannot be undone. So if we are going to busy ourselves, it should be with continual praise to God for his amazing grace. ✤

GOD'S PROMISE TO ME

- As my child, you do not have to fear punishment.

MY PRAYER TO GOD

Lord, forgive me for the times I wrongly think you want to punish me for my failures. Jesus took my punishment and gave me his righteousness. Because of that you see me as perfect and precious. Help me to better understand your grace and mercy so that I might be more gracious and merciful.

day203

WHEN YOU GIVE, GOD BLESSES

"Bring the whole tithe into the storehouse, that there may be food in my house. Test me in this," says the LORD Almighty, "and see if I will not throw open the floodgates of heaven and pour out so much blessing that there will not be room enough to store it."

MALACHI 3:10

When events don't live up to our expectations, we experience disappointment. And if that disappointment continues long-term, we can subtly descend into discouragement and despair. And when that happens, we can be tempted to disregard our beliefs and develop unhealthy — even sinful — habits.

That's essentially the scenario for God's people at the time of the prophet Malachi. The Israelites were back in their homeland after the Babylonian exile, but they were still under Persian domination, and they faced hard times. Harvests were meager. Hope was in short supply. And so the people began to cut corners. Among other things, they stopped giving to God.

Through Malachi God declared his faithfulness and instructed his covenant people to be faithful, too. They needed to keep trusting God and keep doing right even when obedience didn't seem to make sense.

The promise? In so many words: "Watch how I will bless you when you are generous with the material blessings I give you."

Will we trust that promise today? Will we give gladly and sacrificially to the work of God? ❖

GOD'S PROMISE TO ME

- If you obey me in the area of giving, I will more than meet your needs.

MY PRAYER TO GOD

God, all that I have comes from you. All that I have belongs to you. Develop my faith and make me generous. I am never more like you than when I give.

YOU DON'T NEED MIGHT AND POWER — YOU NEED HIS SPIRIT

"This is the word of the LORD to Zerubbabel: 'Not by might nor by power, but by my Spirit,' says the LORD Almighty."   ZECHARIAH 4:6

The noted author A. W. Tozer once observed, "If the Holy Spirit was withdrawn from the church today, 95 percent of what we do would go on and no one would know the difference."

Ouch! We may not completely agree with his percentage, but his point is valid. How easy it is, even for the people of God, to depend on human strength, man-made solutions, and/or worldly strategies.

When the Jewish exiles returned from Babylonian captivity, they set about the project of rebuilding the temple. The foundation was quickly laid under the able leadership of Governor Zerubbabel. But then the workers tired, and the work languished.

God raised up the prophet Zechariah to motivate the people. His timeless reminder? Great works of God and for God are always empowered by God. If we are not dependent on God's Spirit, then our efforts, no matter how noble they may appear, will not accomplish what God has in mind.

What important work or needed task looms in front of you? Will you yield yourself to the control of God's all-powerful Spirit? ♣

GOD'S PROMISE TO ME

- You accomplish my work by trusting in my Spirit.

MY PRAYER TO GOD

Father, forgive me for the times when I try to do your work in my way and by my power. I yield myself now to you. Fill me with your Spirit. Do immeasurably more than all I ask or imagine.

GOD OFFERS YOU HIS PERFECT INSIGHT

The fear of the LORD is the beginning of wisdom; all who follow his precepts have good understanding. To him belongs eternal praise. PSALM 111:10

"Eat out or stay in?"

"Smoking or non-smoking?"

"Would you like fries with that?"

You can easily make these decisions. But what about those trying life situations where the choices are harder and the stakes are higher?

Thankfully, God has pledged to give wisdom to the humble soul who looks to him. How do we distinguish his counsel from the chorus of other voices in our busy lives? God's wisdom will always square with Scripture—though it may come to us from other sources. It will always result in God's glory. It will always be practical and down-to-earth.

Need clarity in a tough situation? Ask in faith for guidance, and then listen for the God's response. ✤

GOD'S PROMISE TO ME

- I will give you wisdom.
- I will gladly show you what to do.
- I will never be annoyed by your request for wisdom.

MY PRAYER TO GOD

O Lord, my life is so full, and I face so many hard decisions. I need insight from above. I praise you for being the source of all wisdom. You do not resent my requests. Help me to remember your willingness to help in my times of trial. You promise to tell me what to do. What wonderful assurance!

GOD LONGS TO BE CLOSE TO YOU

Here I am! I stand at the door and knock. If anyone hears my voice and opens the door, I will come in and eat with that person, and they with me.   REVELATION 3:20

These words of Jesus are often used in sharing the gospel. Those who are not yet followers of Christ are urged to open the door of their hearts and let Jesus come in.

But if we look at the context of this verse, we find that Jesus is actually speaking to believers. The book of Revelation was written by John to Christians. Apparently, they had somehow gotten so busy or sidetracked that Jesus had been excluded from their lives.

Perhaps this is an apt description of your current situation. Is Christ on the outside of your life (or at least your thoughts and plans), looking in? But he knocks. He waits. All that is required for you to once again enjoy his company is to hear him and swing open the door of your heart. There he will be—your faithful, loving Savior, Guide and Friend. ✤

GOD'S PROMISE TO ME

- I am near you.
- I want your attention.
- If you let me, I will be your intimate friend

MY PRAYER TO GOD

O, Lord, you are always near and always desirous of my attention. Forgive me for the times I ignore you or push you to the edges of my life. You deserve the central place. Whenever I hear you calling and knocking, help me to open myself to you so that we can enjoy rich intimacy together.

GOD'S TRUTH BRINGS ULTIMATE SATISFACTION

Blessed are those whose ways are blameless, who walk according to the law of the LORD. Blessed are those who keep his statutes and seek him with all their heart.   PSALM 119:1–2

"Don't worry. Be happy!" Bobby McFerrin's chart-topping pop song counseled. The problem is everyone seems to have a different opinion about how and where to find happiness. Thus the frenetic desperation of modern life—everyone is scrambling to find the kind of soul satisfaction that lasts.

This is why many people go from relationship to relationship; from expensive toy to expensive toy; from job to job; seeking—in vain—that elusive satisfaction.

The psalmist understood that deep satisfaction is bound up in understanding and obeying God's truth. Those who are focused on the Lord, and who build their lives on his unchanging Word, experience a wholeness of soul that leads to enduring satisfaction in life. ❖

GOD'S PROMISE TO ME

- True satisfaction is yours when you seek me and do what I say.

MY PRAYER TO GOD

O, Lord, stir up within me a deep hunger for your Word. You want me to seek you with all my heart. Reveal yourself and your will to me. Satisfy me with your truth. I know that I will find true, lasting happiness when I consistently live according to what is true and right. I want to be a person of integrity. I want to follow you and keep your commands.

THE LORD IS YOUR STRENGTH

The Sovereign LORD is my strength; he makes my feet like the feet of a deer, he enables me to tread on the heights.   HABAKKUK 3:19

"Out of gas." "Nothing left to give." "Bone tired." These are the common confessions of the weary.

Perhaps you've lived through hard, uncertain circumstances for long periods of time. If so, you know all too well the deepest meanings of the word "exhaustion." Sometimes even when your body can still go, your soul just can't.

The prophet Habakkuk experienced this kind of emotional, spiritual weariness. He was deeply troubled by Israel's sin. He called on God to act. Then he was even more shocked by God's announced intention to use the evil Chaldeans to discipline the people of God.

But the more time Habakkuk spent in God's presence, the more his fear turned into faith, and the more his despair turned into determination.

Where did the beleaguered prophet find the strength to carry on? In God himself. The "Sovereign LORD," the one who is the ultimate source of all power, is the one who "enables" us to keep going.

Need a new burst of power? Strengthen yourself in the Lord your God (see 1 Samuel 30:6). ❖

GOD'S PROMISE TO ME

- I am your strength.
- I enable you to live as I command.

MY PRAYER TO GOD

Sovereign Lord, I need you. My strength is limited; your strength is endless. Fill me and empower me. Right now, enable me to do all that you've called me to do.

day209

GOD ORDERS YOUR STEPS

The LORD makes firm the steps of the one who delights in him; though he may stumble, he will not fall, for the LORD upholds him with his hand. PSALM 37:23–24

Be honest. Doesn't talk of heaven and eternity seem a bit unreal? Doesn't it seem sensible to focus on the things of this world? When you do, doesn't it seem as though evil has the upper hand? Don't you wonder on occasion if God really sees or cares? Sometimes he seems so distant, perhaps even disinterested?

The thirty-seventh psalm was penned by David to urge the people of God to trust their Creator and not be shaken by the seeming good life of the godless. No matter how desperate things may appear, the truth is that God watches over his precious children. Like a caring father, he longs to walk with us, hold our hands and steer us through trouble (see Psalm 145:14; Proverbs 24:16; Micah 7:8).

No matter how you feel or how things seem, the reality is that God is there. Will you take his hand? ✤

GOD'S PROMISE TO ME

- I direct your steps.
- I delight in the details of your life.
- I will not let you fall.
- I am holding your hand.

MY PRAYER TO GOD

As I walk with you, Lord, my steps are directed by you. Thank you for not leaving me to fend for myself. Your Word says you delight in every detail of my life. Thank you for the assurance that you care, that you see — even when it seems you are far away. O God, I may stumble in this life, but you promise to keep me from ultimate harm.

day210

GOD RESPONDS TO YOUR CRIES

He will deliver the needy who cry out, the afflicted who have no one to help.

PSALM 72:12

Prayer is a topic shrouded in myth. Reports of ancient saints like Martin Luther praying for two hours a day intimidate us. The eloquent prayers of mature, modern-day believers often leave us questioning our own faith.

Memo to twenty-first century believers: God isn't monitoring our prayers with a celestial stopwatch. Neither is he impressed by flowery terminology.

According to the promise above, the person God hears is the person who simply cries out to him. He knows every need before we utter it.

Swamped? Overwhelmed? The simple heartfelt cry, "Help!" may be the most genuine, God-honoring prayer you've got. And it may actually be the one that brings the best and quickest answer. ♣

GOD'S PROMISE TO ME

- I hear those who are right with me.
- I do big things in response to honest prayer.

MY PRAYER TO GOD

Lord, teach me to pray honestly from a heart that wants, above all else, to be right with you. Show me any wrong thoughts or actions that I need to turn away from, that might hinder my communication with you.

GOD TAKES CARE OF TOMORROW

Your heavenly Father knows that you need them. But seek first his kingdom and his righteousness, and all these things will be given to you as well. Therefore do not worry about tomorrow, for tomorrow will worry about itself. MATTHEW 6:32–34

Listen to Claire. See if her words (and worries) sound familiar:

"I don't know what to do. My car needs work and my daughter really needs braces. But we're already just barely living paycheck to paycheck. I guess I could get a second job—maybe as a sales clerk at the mall on weekends? I don't know. I just know I'm waking up—wide awake—every morning at, like, four. And I can't seem to go back to sleep."

If it's not financial worries for you, it may be concerns of another kind. Jesus' promise? God sees. He knows. He cares. And, best of all, he comes to the aid of those who live for him.

Instead of panicking or fretting, instead of "pre-living" a dark future that may never come, roll your burdens onto the one who cares for you ✤

GOD'S PROMISE TO ME

- I know all your needs.
- I will meet all your daily needs as you live for me.

MY PRAYER TO GOD

O God, you know all of my needs. I praise you for knowing all things, including every detail of my situation. Nothing surprises you—ever. Thank you for caring so much and being so good. Help me to seek you first, to trust your gracious promise and to keep from worrying about the future.

day212

GOD HAS MOVED INTO YOUR LIFE

Now it is God who makes both us and you stand firm in Christ. He anointed us, set his seal of ownership on us, and put his Spirit in our hearts as a deposit, guaranteeing what is to come. I call God as my witness—and I stake my life on it. 2 CORINTHIANS 1:21–23

Could any living soul pen a theatrical masterpiece to rival the works of Shakespeare? Most folks don't even know what "iambic pentameter" is! But what if "the spirit of William Shakespeare" could somehow reside in you and write through you? Suddenly the impossible would become possible.

The same principle is true in the Christian life. Can we balance our lives? Can we live as we should? Can we exhibit godly qualities when life goes haywire? Not a chance, unless God lives within us.

Guess what? He does! At the moment we put our faith in Christ, God places his Holy Spirit inside us to give us the power to live as we should.

Are you confused? Frustrated? Tired? Ready to throw in the towel? God's Spirit is in you. He will help you when you turn to him for help. ❖

GOD'S PROMISE TO ME

- The ability to stand firm comes from me.
- I have commissioned you.
- I have identified you as my own by placing my Spirit in your heart.

MY PRAYER TO GOD

Father, most of the time I feel weak and overwhelmed. But you are the one who gives me the ability to stand firm for Christ. You created me for yourself and called me to yourself. I want to yield to you and follow your lead. I want your power to flow through me today. Fill me with your Holy Spirit.

day213

GOD HAS GIVEN YOU ALL YOU NEED

Praise be to the God and Father of our Lord Jesus Christ, who has blessed us in the heavenly realms with every spiritual blessing in Christ. EPHESIANS 1:3

When life gets chaotic, we are prone to daydream: "If only I could stop the clock for two weeks, I could catch up." "If only I could win a million bucks, my life would be simplified." "If only I ..."

If only. If only.

In stressful times, whether self-induced or externally imposed, we are quick to look for relief through physical or material means. This is unfortunate since what we really need most in hard times are immaterial realities like peace, patience, joy, endurance, inner strength, faithfulness and humility.

The good news is that all those priceless qualities are available to us now—in limitless quantities. The lesson? We are to stop wishing for superficial things that don't really help and start taking advantage of the spiritual blessings that can and will make a real difference in our lives. ♣

GOD'S PROMISE TO ME

- I am the God who blesses.
- I have already prospered you with every spiritual blessing that you need to live in a fallen world.

MY PRAYER TO GOD

O God, I praise you! You are the God who blesses. How easy it is to forget that you are the source of every good thing and that you yourself are good. Your goodness to me is not because of any goodness on my part. It is all because of Christ, all because of grace.

day214

GOD COMES TO THOSE WHO WAIT

You are my strength, I watch for you; you, God, are my fortress, my God on whom I can rely. God will go before me and will let me gloat over those who slander me.

PSALM 59:9–10

Feeling overwhelmed is an experience for some people all the time, and for all people some of the time. The details may vary, but the result is the same—thick dread, perhaps even fear, a spirit of helplessness and hopelessness.

For David in Psalm 59, the crisis was the paranoid Saul and a murderous band of assassins. Our overwhelming situation—hopefully not hit men—may be a calendar filled to overflowing. One more event or one more pressure and we feel sure we'll come unglued.

Whatever your predicament, David's example is wise to follow. He placed his full confidence in God's strength. He believed with all his heart that God would come through.

God proved himself reliable to David. He's ready to do that for you, too. ❖

GOD'S PROMISE TO ME

- I am your strength, your safety, your help.
- I will rescue you.
- My love never fails.

MY PRAYER TO GOD

God, you are my strength, my place of safety, my help. Instead of depending on my own strength or concocting a human solution, I will call on you and wait on you. Your love is unfailing. Give me the grace to keep trusting you to work in your way, in your time.

day**215**

GOD SUSTAINS YOU

Praise be to the Lord, to God our Savior, who daily bears our burdens.   PSALM 68:19

"Count your blessings" urges the old hymn. "Name them one by one."

It's good counsel. Try it. Pull back from your busy life for a few minutes and ponder all that God has done for you and in you. You may be surprised and encouraged by what you discover.

Psalm 68 is a record of one occasion when King David counted Israel's blessings. In the hymn, David cites God's power and his fatherly compassion. Then, in verse 19, David erupts in praise.

The reason for such celebration? God's promise that he "daily bears our burdens."

God is the one who enables us to keep going. Today (and every day) you can be confident of his concern and powerful care. ❖

GOD'S PROMISE TO ME

- I am the Lord.
- I am your Savior.
- I daily bear your burdens.

MY PRAYER TO GOD

O Lord, I praise you! You are the one who delivers. You are in control of my life and all things. Thank you for going before me and going with me. Thank you for saving me in numerous tough situations. I choose to believe that you will sustain me today, through whatever comes.

day**216**

GOD ENCOURAGES THE DISCOURAGED

When we came into Macedonia, we had no rest, but we were harassed at every turn —
conflicts on the outside, fears within. But God, who comforts the downcast, comforted us
by the coming of Titus. 2 CORINTHIANS 7:5 – 6

A discouraged person is one who is without courage. The person is so downcast
that they lose heart, see all things as negative and have no confidence in the future.

The apostle Paul occasionally was overcome by this same pessimistic mindset.
Nonstop traveling, financial shortages, ministry pressures, personal frailties, bitter
opposition, concern for his converts and colleagues — add it all together and it's no
wonder even the great apostle sometimes felt overwhelmed.

But look again at the passage above. God encouraged the deflated apostle with
the arrival of a beloved friend.

That's God's nature. He encourages those who are discouraged. Could you use
a shot of courage and renewed confidence today? ❖

GOD'S PROMISE TO ME

  • I encourage the discouraged.

MY PRAYER TO GOD

Father, thank you for the portions of your Word that give me insight into the saints of old.
They were regular people just like me, in need of grace and strength and help. Like Paul,
I battle discouragement. I praise you for being the encourager of those who are discouraged.
Help me find a renewed sense of confidence today.

day217

GOD GRANTS YOU PERSEVERING POWER

I can do all this through him who gives me strength. PHILIPPIANS 4:13

A bumper sticker seen on a worn-out car, sputtering and smoking up a long mountain road: "I'm peddling as fast as I can!"

Ever feel like that? You're giving it all you've got, but still moving at what seems like a glacial pace. Those are the stressful times when we want to pull over and quit. Those are the times we need today's promise.

The apostle Paul learned the lesson that we need to know: Even in the most trying times, Christ is enough. He gives us the help and strength we need to persevere. That means life doesn't have to seem like an uphill battle. We have the strength—God's—to make it through even the most trying of circumstances. ✤

GOD'S PROMISE TO ME

- I will give you the strength you need.
- You will be able to do whatever is necessary.

MY PRAYER TO GOD

I need help, Lord. I feel so weary and tired. Without your power, I don't feel like I can continue. With your help and strength I know I can do whatever you ask of me. Give me a second wind. I look to you in trust because I know you are faithful.

day218

august 6

GOD SETS YOU FREE FROM FEAR

I sought the LORD, and he answered me; he delivered me from all my fears. PSALM 34:4

Fear encompasses a wide spectrum. It runs the gamut from terror to disquiet, from rare, all-consuming phobias to everyday, nagging trepidations. "How are we going to pay for that?" "Does this mole look funny to you?" "What if no one shows up?" "What if I miss my connecting flight?"

Psalm 34 tells us that the best remedy for our apprehensive moments is prayer. Not mouthing pious, rehearsed words, but honestly pouring out our hearts to the living God. When we seek God in fearful times, we will find him. In his presence, fear must flee. In its place comes unearthly joy. ✤

GOD'S PROMISE TO ME

- I will answer your cries for help.
- I will free you from fear.

MY PRAYER TO GOD

God, there are a million and one "fearful" things in this world. Too often I take my eyes off you, and I allow my mind to play the "What if?" game. You have promised to hear me, to answer me, to help me. Thank you for being so attentive.

GOD WILL USE YOU TO HELP OTHERS KNOW HIM

Thanks be to God, who always leads us as captives in Christ's triumphal procession and uses us to spread the aroma of the knowledge of him everywhere.   2 CORINTHIANS 2:14

The urgent and unceasing demands of a busy life have a way of altering our perspective. We can feel defeated and discouraged. We can begin to lose sight of what matters most in life.

Today's promise uses imagery from ancient Roman victory processions. Typically, a conquering general would return to the capital city with his captives in tow. The smell of incense and crushed flowers would fill the air.

The apostle Paul is saying that in the ultimate victory celebration, Christ is at the head of the parade. He has captured us with his kindness and now leads us in triumph. He wants to use us to fill the world with the sweet smell of his love.

Is that your focus today? ✤

GOD'S PROMISE TO ME

- I have captured you.
- I lead you in victory.
- I use you to spread the Good News.

MY PRAYER TO GOD

You have captured my heart with your love, Lord. Thank you for changing my life by giving me life. You are the victor in the great spiritual conflict of the ages. You deserve all praise and honor and glory. Help me open my mouth and speak powerfully and effectively for you.

day**220**

GOD WELCOMES YOU INTO HIS PRESENCE

The LORD detests the sacrifice of the wicked, but the prayer of the upright pleases him.

PROVERBS 15:8

Projection is the term used to describe our tendency to assume that others think and act the same ways that we think and act—and for the same reasons. For example, we are busily trying to accomplish a long list of urgent tasks. We are focused and do not want to bothered. But inevitably our children interrupt us, a friend calls or we get an urgent email, and we become annoyed.

Because this is our common reaction, we often assume God operates in the same way. "Running the universe is a big job," we reason. "And God has more important issues to address than my silly old problems. No sense bothering him."

This is wrong thinking—projection at its worst. God welcomes us into his presence. In fact he invites us to come boldly to him. Our prayers are his delight! ✤

GOD'S PROMISE TO ME

- Your prayers please me.
- I want you to come into my presence.

MY PRAYER TO GOD

You understand me, Lord, and my situation. I am in awe that you delight in me. Thank you for welcoming me into your presence.

day**221**

GOD LIFTS YOU UP

You, LORD, are a shield around me, my glory, the One who lifts my head high.

PSALM 3:3

As you survey your life, what situation seems most hopeless to you?

Now consider this: When Absalom tried to steal the throne from his father, David may have thought his reign was over. But rather than surrender to his enemies or listen to all the naysayers, David threw himself into the strong arms of God. In his prayer recorded in Psalm 3, David acknowledged the Lord as the ultimate source of protection, honor and restoration.

It's not just a neat historical anecdote. It's a promise. God wants to meet us in the depths and raise us to the heights.

Trust him to be your shield. ❖

GOD'S PROMISE TO ME

- I am your shield.
- I am your glory.
- I am the one who lifts your head high.

MY PRAYER TO GOD

You are a shield about me, Lord. Keep me from faithlessly and foolishly thinking that my life or my future is in jeopardy. You are my glory and the one who lifts my head.

GOD BRINGS YOU THROUGH TROUBLE

He is my loving God and my fortress, my stronghold and my deliverer, my shield, in whom I take refuge.　　　　　　　　　　　　　　　　　　　　　　　Psalm 144:2

Some of Ireland's ancient castles feature secret rooms accessible only by tiny door-ways and extremely narrow staircases. Historians note that in times of enemy attack, children were able to flee to these hiding places and find safety because armor-clad invaders could not fit through the small openings.

What a great picture of the kind of protection God promises to provide his children. He provides a way of escape and surrounds us with his love. He shields us from ultimate harm. He is a fortress and tower of safety. All that is necessary is for us to run to him and take refuge.

This should prompt us to say with the psalmist: "The Lord is with me; I will not be afraid. What can mere mortals do to me?" (Psalm 118:6). ✣

GOD'S PROMISE TO ME

- I am your ally.
- I am your fortress and your tower of safety.
- I will shield you when you take refuge in me.

MY PRAYER TO GOD

Lord, you are my loving ally. Nothing can separate me from your love. I am your child. You are my impregnable fortress, my unconquerable tower of safety.

day223

THE LORD WILL BE GLORIFIED

For the earth will be filled with the knowledge of the glory of the Lord as the waters cover the sea. HABAKKUK 2:14

Go online and check out the reader comments at the end of almost any news story that has a religious angle. You will be stunned at the venom and vitriol spewed by those who profess to be skeptics and atheists. Mocking, taunting, blasphemous comments for pages on end.

Is godlessness growing? Perhaps. Are the forces of unbelief winning the day? Not a chance!

In an extremely bleak and dark time in Israel's history, God spoke to and through the prophet Habakkuk. His message? Don't fret over the mighty and much-feared Babylonians. Their opposition to God, his plan and his people was in vain. In fact, they were mere tools in the Lord's hands. He would sovereignly use them for divine purposes. And in the end, all their efforts would amount to nothing.

The promise? Ultimately, God will receive glory from all the peoples of the earth. Everything and everybody everywhere will bring honor to God.

So certain is this fact, so sure is this promise, that it's repeated in Psalm 72:19, Isaiah 6:3 and 11:9.

Pause a moment right now and praise God for the promise that he will be exalted ... guaranteed. ✤

GOD'S PROMISE TO ME

- Nothing can keep me from receiving the honor due to me.

MY PRAYER TO GOD

Jesus, I bow my knee and my will, and say, "You are Lord!" You WILL be honored. You will receive the glory you deserve. May that be true in my life today.

GOD GIVES YOU REAL POWER OVER SIN

We were therefore buried with him through baptism into death in order that, just as Christ was raised from the dead through the glory of the Father, we too may live a new life. ROMANS 6:4

At the end of *The Wizard of Oz*, after Dorothy has endured all kinds of scary adventures trying to get back to Kansas, Glinda the Good Witch casually tells her she's always had the power to go home.

This is a good, if imperfect, picture of the Christian life. We put our faith in Christ and determine to follow him. But still we struggle with old sinful habits and fleshly desires. Perhaps we go off on a busy search for some kind of "magical" answer to our dilemma. All the time the real solution is within us.

How so? Through salvation God has changed our essential nature and linked us permanently to his Son (see Colossians 3:3–4). God has also implanted his Holy Spirit within us to give us the power to live as we should.

None of this is meant to suggest that our living holy lives is as simple as Dorothy clicking her ruby slippers together. But there is great and mysterious power in the promise of new life in Christ. ❖

GOD'S PROMISE TO ME

- I have joined you to Christ.
- Your old sinful nature has no power over you.
- I have given you the capacity to live a brand-new life.

MY PRAYER TO GOD

O Lord, help me to better understand the monumental blessings and changes that salvation brings. The same power that raised Christ from the dead is available to me to live as I should. Give me eyes to see and ears to hear. Give me the faith to believe this amazing promise: As a brand-new creature, I do not have to yield to sin.

day225

GOD IS CONCERNED FOR YOU

Look at the birds of the air; they do not sow or reap or store away in barns, and yet your heavenly Father feeds them. Are you not much more valuable than they? Can any one of you by worrying add a single hour to your life?   MATTHEW 6:26–27

Why do we worry? It doesn't help a thing. In fact, researchers know that people with high levels of anxiety are much more susceptible to long-term health problems than those with lower levels.

It seems we think that if we get worked up and stressed out over a problem, our situation will somehow improve. So we bite off all our nails, wring our hands, pace around. But nothing changes, except maybe our blood pressure.

A better solution is rolling our problems over onto the shoulders of God. Only he is big enough to deal with them. And only he promises to care for us in perfect ways.

Worrying never solves anything. Why not give your troubles to the only one who can solve them, and soothe your worried heart at the same time? ❖

GOD'S PROMISE TO ME

- You can trust me with your worries.
- You are valuable to me.

MY PRAYER TO GOD

Lord, forgive me for the foolish habit of fretting over things I can't control. I don't have to burden myself trying to take care of myself. Teach me to trust your promise—to believe that you have my best interests at heart.

day226

THE LORD WILL BRING WORLD PEACE

He will judge between many peoples and will settle disputes for strong nations far and wide. They will beat their swords into plowshares and their spears into pruning hooks. Nation will not take up sword against nation, nor will they train for war anymore.

MICAH 4:3

Scholars tell us that in all of recorded human history, there have only been a scant few years of worldwide peace.

That's a depressing fact, a very grim reality. On planet Earth, war is the norm. Armed conflict is the rule. Even as fighting begins to die down in one place, new hostilities erupt in another.

And the cost of all this warfare, all this terrible bloodshed? Impossible to tabulate.

Thus the beauty of the prophet's promise of permanent peace. The day is coming, Micah declared, when God's Messiah will rule over every nation, over the whole earth as King. When that happens—and it will happen!—war will become a distant memory, a relic of the time before Love reigned.

As you watch the nightly news or read reports from war zones, as you observe all the saber-rattling between nations, remember that the Prince of Peace, when he comes again, will bring global, eternal peace. He will. It's just a matter of time. ❖

GOD'S PROMISE TO ME

• When I return, I will bring ultimate, permanent peace to the earth.

MY PRAYER TO GOD

O God, thank you for the certainty that the world is destined for true peace. In the meanwhile, give us leaders who are committed to the Biblical value of peacemaking.

GOD IS ABSOLUTELY RELIABLE

So this is what the Sovereign LORD *says: "See, I lay a stone in Zion, a tested stone, a precious cornerstone for a sure foundation; the one who relies on it will never be stricken with panic."* ISAIAH 28:16

Ever feel so panicked by a situation that you felt you couldn't move? Or perhaps you were afraid that if you took a step, it would be in the wrong direction.

Indebtedness, a sudden loss of income, divorce, illness — these are the circumstances that tempt us toward panic. Panic indicates that we're at the end of our resources. Fear beckons and causes us to flail about.

When you feel like you're in an impossible situation, this is the time to stop, take a deep breath, and bring your circumstances to God. Even in your most panic-stricken moments, you can rely on God. It's a process. But you can believe he's with you, that he cares enough and is big enough to help. ❖

GOD'S PROMISE TO ME

- If you rely on me, you won't be panic stricken.

MY PRAYER TO GOD

O Lord, I desperately need your help. Instead of trying to solve my dilemmas myself, I want to let you guide. Show me the way to go.

GOD GIVES PEACE TO PEOPLE OF FAITH

You will keep in perfect peace those whose minds are steadfast, because they trust in you. Trust in the LORD forever, for the LORD, the LORD himself, is the Rock eternal.

ISAIAH 26:3–4

Turmoil, conflict, restlessness—these are the opposites of peace. They're also accurate descriptions of our own hearts much of the time.

Why do we churn with worry? What makes us so restless? More importantly, what is the solution to an anxious, stirred-up soul?

The prophet Isaiah revealed that perfect peace comes only to those who trust the Lord. He goes on to say that this trusting process involves fixing our thoughts on God—on who he is, what he has done and what he is able to do. This isn't just an Old Testament idea; we find such counsel in the New Testament too (see Colossians 3:2 and Hebrews 12:1–2).

In the midst of your busy life, where's your mind fixed? ✤

GOD'S PROMISE TO ME

- I will give you perfect peace when you focus on me and trust in me.
- I am the eternal Rock.

MY PRAYER TO GOD

You promise peace to those who trust in you and set their minds on you, Lord. You are solid and dependable. You are worthy of my full trust. I love you. You are my rock. As long as I look to you, I cannot be shaken.

GOD NEVER CHANGES

I the LORD do not change.   MALACHI 3:6

Sometimes we do it to ourselves—foolishly taking on too much and getting in over our heads. At other times we are doing right but still find ourselves inundated by a tidal wave of events beyond our control.

Whatever the reason, in moments of excessive stress and uncertainty, it is good to remember we have an anchor in the storm: the constancy of God.

Theologians call this *immutability*—a fancy word for the fact that God is unchanging. He is not moody or unpredictable. His affection and care for us do not waver. God's eternal plans are not altered by time, nor are they foiled by human choices.

Memorize today's concise promise and meditate on it the next time you feel overwhelmed by personal upheaval or professional chaos. ❖

GOD'S PROMISE TO ME

- I am the Lord.
- I do not change.

MY PRAYER TO GOD

O Lord, you are God! Help me to remember today that I can rest in the truth that you control all things. You never change—you are the same yesterday, today and forever. When my life is like a whirlwind, and I begin to lose my bearings, give me the wisdom to anchor myself to your unchanging character.

day230

GOD BLESSES YOU WHEN YOU TRUST

Commit your way to the LORD; trust in him and he will do this.   PSALM 37:5

God helps those who help themselves, right? That's in the Bible, right? Wrong. God helps those who trust him. That's the promise in the verse above. The verb *commit* means to "roll it over on." It's a synonym for trust.

Trusting requires stillness of soul and an ongoing willingness to listen. "What is the Lord saying? How and where does he want to lead me?" Trusting also requires us to wait. This is perhaps the most despised four-letter word of our generation.

Trying, on the other hand, feeds our ego and helps us fit in. We go to bed late and get up early because everybody else does, and because our culture applauds and rewards the productive, get-it-done person.

Today when you feel the pressure to get busy, to make it happen, to push ahead, to knock down doors, make sure you first look to and listen to God. Without his perspective, leading and help, you cannot find true blessing or ultimate success. ❖

GOD'S PROMISE TO ME

- I help those who trust me.

MY PRAYER TO GOD

You promise to help me, Lord, if I will trust you. It goes against my old sinful nature to wait on your leading and to rely on your strength. My tendency is to get busy in my own strength. Forgive me. Change me. Increase my faith.

GOD PROMISES TO BUILD HIS CHURCH

So Christ himself gave the apostles, the prophets, the evangelists, the pastors and teachers, to equip his people for works of service, so that the body of Christ may be built up until we all reach unity in the faith.   EPHESIANS 4:11 – 13

The Thompson family is like so many other Christian families — they juggle a long list of obligations and just as many opportunities. Last weekend was typical: a soccer tournament, a recital, yard work, a dinner party, church, plus an invitation to go with friends up to the lake.

Why in situations like this do many Christians make the same choice the Thompsons made — to drop church from the weekend schedule of events? What does that say about our priorities and beliefs?

The New Testament is clear that the church — for all its faults — is God's primary tool for growing us up in the faith. We need the church. It's only as we gather regularly with other believers (see Hebrews 10:24 – 26) in study and worship that we are challenged to grow deeper.

The church also needs us. When we skip an opportunity to gather with other believers, they miss out on the unique gifts we have to offer. ❖

GOD'S PROMISE TO ME

- I give you spiritual leaders to equip you.
- I want to use you to help others grow, and use them to help you reach spiritual maturity.

MY PRAYER TO GOD

The church is your plan, Lord, for accomplishing your will on earth. Forgive me for the times I'm critical of my own church. It's not perfect, but neither am I. Help me to have a deeper appreciation for the way you have designed the body of Christ to work together.

day**232**

august 20

GOD HELPS YOU FACE YOUR FEARS

When you pass through the waters, I will be with you; and when you pass through the rivers, they will not sweep over you ... Since you are precious and honored in my sight, and because I love you, I will give people in exchange for you, nations in exchange for your life.
ISAIAH 43:2,4

Let's be clear. God spoke the words of Isaiah 43 for the benefit of the Jews who would one day be living in exile in Babylon. This future generation, far from their homeland, and suffering discipline at the hands of God, would need comfort and courage. They would need a strong reminder in the midst of their mess that God still cared for them and that he had not given up on them.

Modern-day Christians can't technically say this Old Testament prophecy is a promise to us. But we can use the passage as a window into the very heart and character of God. Reading Isaiah 43, we are reminded that God is always with us, that he is our Savior (see also Titus 3:4), and that he loves us with an affection that we cannot begin to fathom (see also Ephesians 3:19).

Such assurances can give us the courage to face whatever troubles life brings. ✤

GOD'S PROMISE TO ME

- I am with you in times of trouble.
- I am your God and Savior.
- You are precious to me.
- I love you!

MY PRAYER TO GOD

You are always with me in times of great trouble. Thank you, Lord, for your constant protection and care. You are the one true God, and the only one who can save. I have confidence and peace when I remember your power and might.

GOD WILL REWARD YOUR FAITHFULNESS

I consider that our present sufferings are not worth comparing with the glory that will be revealed in us.
ROMANS 8:18

If this existence is all we get, why *not* embrace a frantic lifestyle of trying to have it all and do it all? Why not embark on an all-out quest for earthly possessions and pleasures? Such is the mindset of many who have embraced the "busyness" lie.

But there are those who don't believe this lie. They are the faithful few who see the temporal nature of this world. Struck by the piercing reality of the world to come, they embrace a different lifestyle. Like Moses of old (see Hebrews 11:24–26), they say "yes" to God, which simultaneously means they say "no" to most of what is prized and pursued by culture. For this, they are mocked and derided. For this, they suffer — sometimes greatly.

But look at the promise. God rewards the faithful, those with the guts to cling to their convictions even when the cost is great suffering. ✤

GOD'S PROMISE TO ME

- I will give glory to those who have suffered for doing right.

MY PRAYER TO GOD

You promise future glory to those who suffer in the present for their faithfulness. God, give me the courage to stand with your people. Protect me from wrong and shallow ways of thinking. I don't want to suffer, but more than that, I don't want to miss your blessing or the chance to bring you honor.

day234

GOD LOOKS OUT FOR YOU

The LORD is gracious and compassionate, slow to anger and rich in love.   PSALM 145:8

In a typical day we encounter people who are grouchy and snippy. That's just life. Get in the way of self-centered people who are rushing about to get things done and you're almost certain to get run over.

Genuine followers of Christ are guilty too. We occasionally succumb to the pressures of busyness and morph into demanding and irritable people with little patience for an elderly driver, a forgetful colleague or a clumsy child.

Aren't you glad God doesn't get cranky or make cutting remarks about us when we err? No rolling eyes. No looks of disgust. *Ever.* Instead, he is compassionate, patient, slow to get angry and "rich in love." ❖

GOD'S PROMISE TO ME

- I am kind and merciful.
- I am slow to get angry.
- I am full of unfailing love.

MY PRAYER TO GOD

O, Lord, you are compassionate. Thank you for not treating me as I deserve. You are slow to get angry and quick to show love. I praise you for never getting upset with me. Help me to treat others the way I've been treated by you.

GOD BLESSES THE RIGHTEOUS

For the LORD God is a sun and shield; the LORD bestows favor and honor; no good thing does he withhold from those whose walk is blameless. PSALM 84:11

Psalm 84 is an ancient hymn that was sung by Israelites who longed to go to Jerusalem and worship at the temple. What made them eager and willing to disrupt their busy lives and take such a pilgrimage?

The temple was where God had promised to meet his people. It was where the devout prayed, offered animal sacrifices and found God's forgiveness and favor. In short, it was the place of grace.

Today there is no need for daily sacrifices. Christ has made the final payment for our sins. And God, rather than dwelling behind thick curtains in an ornate temple, lives within the hearts of his children.

Yet the promise above still applies. As we long for God and draw near to him (see James 4:7), we experience the full riches of his grace (see Ephesians 1). Because he is good, he delights in giving us good things. ✣

GOD'S PROMISE TO ME

- I am your sun and shield.
- I give favor and honor.
- I give good things to those who do what is right.

MY PRAYER TO GOD

You are my God, the one who provides for me and protects me. Thank you for your glorious grace. Thank you for Christ who died for my sins and who makes it possible for me to experience your presence in my life. You shower me with good things!

GOD'S WORD WILL LAST FOREVER

Your word, LORD, is eternal; it stands firm in the heavens.   PSALM 119:89

A popular statement among Christians not so long ago was "God said it, I believe it and that settles it." Before long some believers had modified the slogan to say: "God said it, and that settles it — whether we believe it or not."

They were pointing out the utter reliability of God. His Word is sure — even when our faith is shaky. And because he himself is one hundred percent faithful, he is worthy of our complete trust.

The goal is not to clutch at a few Bible promises like a desperate mountain climber might grasp a series of dangling ropes. We need, rather, to come to see God's Word as a mighty mountain under our feet — strong, stable and eternal. ✤

GOD'S PROMISE TO ME

- My Word is eternal and firm.
- My faithfulness to you is forever.

MY PRAYER TO GOD

Your Word stands firm forever, O Lord. I praise you for the permanence of your Word. Heaven and earth may pass away but your Word never will. It is reliable because you are trustworthy. You extend your enduring faithfulness to every generation. Thank you for showering your faithfulness on me day after day.

day**237**

GOD SUSTAINS YOU THROUGH ROUGH TIMES

Even to your old age and gray hairs I am he, I am he who will sustain you. I have made you and I will carry you; I will sustain you and I will rescue you.   ISAIAH 46:4

What can we learn from that white-haired couple celebrating their sixtieth wedding anniversary? How about selflessness and commitment? Or forgiveness and stubborn, God-honoring tenacity?

Those are the obvious lessons. But there's a deeper mystery at work here too. Behind the tender devotion of these two octogenarians we catch a glimpse of the Author of love. God is the one who made them. Ask them. They'll tell you. In the rough and stormy times of life when they had nothing left, it was the Lord who sustained them and provided for them.

The same God who brought Israel out of foreign exile is the same God who pledges to care for you today and carry you all your days. ❖

GOD'S PROMISE TO ME

- I will always be your God.
- I made you.
- I will care for you.
- I will carry you through hard times.

MY PRAYER TO GOD

God, you are always with me. No matter what, I have the assurance that you are near. I cannot flee from your presence, not even if I want to. You are my maker and caretaker — the one who saves and sustains me.

GOD USES YOUR TROUBLES FOR GOOD

We know that in all things God works for the good of those who love him, who have been called according to his purpose.   ROMANS 8:28

Viewed from below, the weaving project looks like a disastrous mess of tangled, knotted thread. A peek from above, however, reveals a tapestry of stunning beauty. It is perspective that makes all the difference.

That's the message of Romans 8:28. God promises to cause everything to work together for good in the lives of those who love him and are seeking to live for him. Your suffering, your disappointments, your temptations, your failures — God has pledged to take all that's bad and transform it — somehow — into good.

If your life looks messy from your vantage point, just remember God is still weaving, and the view is quite different from where he sits. ❖

GOD'S PROMISE TO ME

- I cause everything to work for good in the lives of those who love and serve me.

MY PRAYER TO GOD

God, nothing can thwart your plans for me. I praise you for the way you orchestrate all the events of life. You are weaving a masterpiece. I trust you even though the process is painful. Help me to cling to you in the darkest times of trouble.

GOD LETS YOU REAP WHAT YOU SOW

Do not be deceived: God cannot be mocked. A man reaps what he sows. GALATIANS 6:7

We prefer "positive promises," don't we? Verses that guarantee God's blessing or assure our happiness—those are the ones we tend to memorize and needlepoint for display on the living room wall. So what's with the passage above? Why concentrate on such a somber Scripture?

Because Galatians 6:7 is a promise—a troubling one to be sure, but a divine guarantee nevertheless. Here is a warning of dire consequences if we opt for an existence that excludes God and his will.

How easy it is in our culture to get swept up into thinking that we don't need God. How natural it feels to go about our daily activities—many of them good things—and then if we happen to think of it, to try to fit God in around the edges.

God must have the central place. If we ignore him and neglect what he says is important in life, we will one day find ourselves reaping a bitter harvest. And that's a promise. ✤

GOD'S PROMISE TO ME

- You can't ignore me and get away with it.
- You will reap what you sow.

MY PRAYER TO GOD

O Lord, I am prone to self-deception. Keep me from buying into the culture's attractive and popular lies. I cannot ignore you without severe consequences. Give me the desire to make you supreme in my life.

GOD GUARANTEES YOU A WONDERFUL FUTURE

I pray that the eyes of your heart may be enlightened in order that you may know the hope to which he has called you, the riches of his glorious inheritance in his holy people.

EPHESIANS 1:18

Many people are uncertain about the future. Some worry. Some listen to a daily parade of "experts" on radio or TV. Still others read voraciously and surf the Internet religiously in an attempt to spot trends. More than a few confused souls consult astrologers and other similar scam artists.

Christians should not be among these who fret about what's to come. Not that we know what tomorrow holds, much less next year. In a fallen world terrible things happen. Life can turn ugly quickly and even the righteous are not immune to times of darkness and suffering.

However, God has promised us, in the ultimate sense, a wonderful future. Read Revelation 21 and 22 if you want to know what's ahead. Seriously, read those chapters and then try not to feel hopeful. It's hard to do. ❖

GOD'S PROMISE TO ME

• I have a wonderful future planned for you.

MY PRAYER TO GOD

Help me to see, God, not just my present troubles, but the future you have planned for me. Flood my heart with your light. You assure me that a wonderful future awaits. I need to take the long-term view. Keep me from impatience and faithlessness.

day**241**

GOD HAS AN ETERNAL PLACE PREPARED FOR YOU

My Father's house has many rooms; if that were not so, would I have told you that I am going there to prepare a place for you? And if I go and prepare a place for you, I will come back and take you to be with me that you also may be where I am. JOHN 14:2–3

"There's no place like home!" Dorothy admits at the climax of *The Wizard of Oz*, prompting us to brush the tears away. Why do we feel such powerful yearnings for "home"?

Something in us longs for a place where we are safe, secure and comfortable. Home, ideally, is where we don't have to put on a front. It's where those who love and accept us unconditionally await us and welcome us with glad hearts and open arms.

While it's not wrong to love going home, whether it's our childhood home or the place we live now, it is vital that we remember our ultimate home is in the world to come. Jesus is building a heavenly residence for us the likes of which we cannot imagine. ✤

GOD'S PROMISE TO ME

- I am preparing a heavenly home for you.
- I will come for you.
- You will be with me forever.

MY PRAYER TO GOD

O Lord, the most magnificent mansion on earth pales in comparison to the home you are building for me in heaven. I will live with you in a perfect place for all eternity. Thank you for the promise that you will send Jesus to get me and escort me to my true home.

GOD CARES ABOUT YOU

Cast all your anxiety on him because he cares for you.   1 PETER 5:7

If you give a present to someone, do you immediately take it back? Sounds ridiculous, doesn't it? Yet when we give our worries and cares to God, we often end up taking them back. How can we give our worries to God and leave them in his hands?

Consider the case of Hannah in the Old Testament book of 1 Samuel. Struggling with the heartbreak of infertility and the taunting of her husband's other wife, Hannah poured out her heart to God. After she did, "she went her way and ate something, and her face was no longer downcast" (1 Samuel 1:18). Now there's a woman who knew how to give her worries to God.

Think about how great it feels to shed a heavy burden. Just watch the face of the average kid who casts his or her heavy backpack to the floor. That look of relief says it all. We can toss our worries to God. He can handle the load. He's waiting for your face to take on that look of relief. ✤

GOD'S PROMISE TO ME

- You can give your worries to me because I care about what happens to you—even more than you do.

MY PRAYER TO GOD

Lord, I'm guilty of taking back the worries I claim to give you. Forgive me and help me rest the full weight of my worry in your capable hands. Thank you for the peace you give in return.

day**243**

GOD CHANGES YOUR MINDSET

This is the covenant I will make with them after that time, says the Lord. I will put my laws in their hearts, and I will write them on their minds. HEBREWS 10:16

"How can I change?" is one of the great questions of the ages.

Modern "experts" propose all sorts of solutions but many of the more popular answers are nothing more than slick self-help plans. As one frustrated soul put it, "I'm convinced the problem is me, so I'm not really motivated to look within myself for answers."

In many ways, this is the message of the Bible. We are messed-up people in need of rescue (see Jeremiah 17:9).

The help comes in the form of God's new covenant—not a list of external rules, but radical transformation at the heart level. When we trust Christ, and his Spirit takes up residence in our lives, we are fundamentally and forever changed. He gives us new desires and a new way of thinking (see Romans 12:2). Together that equals a new way of living. ✤

GOD'S PROMISE TO ME

- I will give you a new heart and mindset.
- I will change your desires.

MY PRAYER TO GOD

Thank you, God, for your new covenant. Guide me according to the truth that you have written on my heart. I want to obey you. Make me willing to do your will today.

day244

GOD WILL HELP YOU STAND IN TROUBLING TIMES

My help comes from the LORD, the Maker of heaven and earth. He will not let your foot slip—he who watches over you will not slumber. PSALM 121:2–3

When busy people have problems, they often look for "the quick fix." Identify the problem. Think of a solution. Implement it. Move on. That's our preference.

We might opt to phone a trusted friend—or two or three. Buy and read a recommended book. Listen to a tape series while commuting. Or attend a highly regarded seminar or conference.

While none of these things are wrong—and all may actually prove beneficial—it's important to remember that our ultimate help comes from above. God is the one we should rely upon and turn to first.

It's also essential that we keep in mind that God may not solve our problems quickly—in fact, he may not "solve" them at all. He only promises to help—which may simply mean he gives us the grace to keep moving forward. ❖

GOD'S PROMISE TO ME

- I will help you.
- I will not let you stumble or fall.
- I watch over you all the time.

MY PRAYER TO GOD

O Lord, maker of heaven and earth, you alone provide the help I really need. Thank you for watching over me and for caring about my situation. I don't like going through troubles, but I'm grateful for your constant presence.

THE LORD WILL RETURN AND BRING REWARDS

Look, I am coming soon! My reward is with me, and I will give to each person according to what they have done. REVELATION 22:12

"That's not fair!" is one of the most common complaints of children—even very young ones. And why? Because there seems to be within every soul an innate hunger for justice.

The book of Revelation grants us a sneak peek at heaven and earth at the end of human history. One of its most reassuring promises is the pledge by Christ himself to render perfect justice.

In 2 Corinthians 5:10, the apostle Paul tells believers: "For we must all appear before the judgment seat of Christ, so that each of us may receive what is due us for the things done while in the body, whether good or bad."

On that day—and forever after—everything will be absolutely fair. Followers of Jesus who have lived by faith, who've heard and heeded the words of Christ can expect good things. Rewards. Crowns. Commendations. Unimaginable opportunities to serve God in the life to come.

The promise is clear. And so is the principle. Be faithful. Do right. Listen to the words of Christ. Then, in the power of the Spirit, obey them. ❖

GOD'S PROMISE TO ME

- I am coming again.
- I will reward you according to how faithfully you have followed me.

MY PRAYER TO GOD

Lord Jesus, thank you for the certainty that you reign over the affairs of this world. Thank you for being a perfect and wise judge. Grant me the grace to walk faithfully with you and to trust that whatever injustice I experience here and now will be made right there and then.

day246

GOD WILL HUMBLE THE PROUD AND EXALT THE HUMBLE

He gives us more grace. That is why Scripture says: "God opposes the proud but shows favor to the humble." JAMES 4:6

What important person do you know whose cell phone doesn't ring constantly? What powerful individual have you ever heard of who has an empty appointment book or blank calendar?

No, the fact of the matter is that almost all prominent people lead hectic lives. They are sought out, consulted, included and invited — all the things that most of us aspire to be.

The result is that if we are not careful, our desires to achieve and acquire, to do more and have more than others — in short, to be successful and in demand — can seduce us to embrace a lifestyle of busyness.

This is nothing more than human pride — a quality that provokes God's displeasure. It is far better for us to seek out a life that goes against the flow than to let pride rule us. ❖

GOD'S PROMISE TO ME

- I oppose the proud.
- I show favor to the humble.

MY PRAYER TO GOD

Lord, keep me from exalting myself, from being full of myself and thinking myself better than or more important than others. You show favor to the humble. Help me not to worry about keeping up with my friends and family.

day247

GOD UNDERSTANDS YOUR TEMPTATIONS

Lead us not into temptation, but deliver us from the evil one. MATTHEW 6:13

You've taken on too many responsibilities and now you're scrambling to get it all done. People are not cooperating. Your stress level is rising even as your mood is deteriorating. Success looks doubtful. Ever been in this place?

To make matters worse, because of your busyness you haven't taken time out to make sure you're approaching the situation with God's perspective. Just when the external pressure is greatest your inner strength is waning. There's a lesson here: People have a tendency to lower their spiritual guards in stressful situations.

The good news is that when we find ourselves in tempting places—no matter what the source—we have someone to whom we can turn. He understands our weaknesses and promises to help us if we'll cling to him. God is the ultimate preventive measure against falling into temptation. ♣

GOD'S PROMISE TO ME

• You can pray for my help to avoid temptation.

MY PRAYER TO GOD

Lord, I'm grateful that I can turn to you to avoid temptation. Help me trust your leading and learn from your roadblocks.

GOD CAN MAKE YOU HAPPY WITH LESS

Godliness with contentment is great gain. For we brought nothing into the world, and we can take nothing out of it. But if we have food and clothing, we will be content with that.
1 Timothy 6:6–8

We sometimes let our lives be driven by discontent. We feel something vital is missing. We must do whatever it takes to find or get that missing something.

Contentment is the opposite of a driven lifestyle. When we allow ourselves to rest and be content, our attitude says, "I have everything I need. Things are good. I'm satisfied. I will relax and enjoy my lot in life." Contented people don't typically become workaholics, overfill their appointment books or get deeply in debt. For the contented, less is more — or at least it's enough.

Today's promise reminds us that we have never seen a hearse pulling a U-Haul® trailer. Ultimate contentment isn't found in the stuff of this world.

When we get right down to it, if we know God and have our basic needs met, what complaints do we have? ❖

GOD'S PROMISE TO ME

- True wealth is being content with knowing me.
- You can't take your riches and things into the life to come.
- I can help you be content with the basics of life.

MY PRAYER TO GOD

Contentment is your goal for me, Lord. Forgive me for the times I get discontented. Teach me to focus on all I do have, rather than on the things I lack. Make relationships — with you and others — my top priority.

day249

GOD LIBERATES YOU FROM TROUBLE

This poor man called, and the LORD heard him; he saved him out of all his troubles.

PSALM 34:6

If you have a child, can you imagine ever ignoring your child's cry for help? Seems inconceivable, right? Yet we sometimes think the Lord turns a deaf ear to *our* cries. Our desperate prayers seem to bounce weakly off the ceiling. Or so we think. But don't be fooled. He hears.

We sometimes imagine God chooses not to help us when we are in trouble. Maybe he's angry with us, we reason. But that is not true. He is at work.

No matter what we think or how we feel, God is a compassionate Father. He may not solve our problems in the way we'd like. He doesn't always work according to our timetable. But the promise above assures us that those who turn to him will find help—and courage—in times of trouble. ❖

GOD'S PROMISE TO ME

- I hear your cries when you are in trouble.
- I will set you free from your fears.

MY PRAYER TO GOD

Lord, you hear my cries when I'm in trouble. What a blessing to know you care for me! Thank you for being a loving God. Thank you for listening to my pleas. Teach me to cast my cares on you and leave them there.

THE LORD WILL DRY YOUR TEARS

"'He will wipe every tear from their eyes. There will be no more death' or mourning or crying or pain, for the old order of things has passed away."   REVELATION 21:4

"Life is a vale of tears," the old saying goes, and it's doubtful if a truer phrase has ever been spoken.

We are surrounded on all sides by sadness and sorrow. Try as we might we cannot evade grief or loss in this broken world. As a result, we often find ourselves misty-eyed or crying, weeping or sobbing—sometimes even wailing inconsolably. What can we say? Tears of sadness are a regular part of our human experience.

There's a fascinating verse in the book of Psalms that seems to suggest that God keeps a record of our tears (see Psalm 56:8). Another passage (see Psalm 30:5) comforts us with the reminder that most of our sorrows will be short-lived.

But the most encouraging verse of all is today's promise that tells of the coming day when all tears will cease. God will personally bring ultimate and final comfort to his people. He will wipe away every tear. No more crying. Only realized hope and lasting joy.

As you battle life's sorrows and griefs, that's a good promise to tuck away: No more crying. ❖

GOD'S PROMISE TO ME

- I will wipe away your tears.
- I will reverse the curse and all its painful effects.

MY PRAYER TO GOD

Father God, when I am sad, keep me from despair. Instead, remind me by your Spirit that Christ has defeated sin and death. The day is coming when the world will be put right and all sorrow will cease. Praise your holy name!

GOD GIVES SUCCESS IN FIGHTING SATAN

Submit yourselves, then, to God. Resist the devil, and he will flee from you. James 4:7

Someone has quipped that temptations are like stray cats: if you treat one nice, it'll be back shortly with a whole bunch of its friends. There's a lot of truth in that old joke. The more we yield to sin, the more enticements to sin we seem to encounter.

But the opposite is also true. The more firmly and consistently we resist temptation, the stronger our resolve becomes. Sin becomes less attractive. Holiness becomes more desirable.

It's worth noting that when Jesus bluntly rejected Satan's overtures in the wilderness (see Luke 4:1–13), the devil departed in a huff. He didn't leave for good, and he didn't give up his diabolical fight. But Satan did get a small taste of his ultimate defeat and humiliation, which is the same thing he gets whenever we tell him to take a hike (see Romans 16:20). ✤

GOD'S PROMISE TO ME

- If you firmly resist Satan, he will flee from you.

MY PRAYER TO GOD

O God, my enemy is strong and sinister. But you are stronger. Give me the grace to recognize the attacks of the enemy and the strength to spurn his sinful offers.

day252

september 9

GOD WILL PURIFY YOU

May God himself, the God of peace, sanctify you through and through. May your whole spirit, soul and body be kept blameless at the coming of our Lord Jesus Christ.

1 THESSALONIANS 5:23

Some years ago, Charles Swindoll wrote a book about the Christian life entitled *Three Steps Forward, Two Steps Back.*

If you've been a follower of Christ for any length of time, you know that's an apt description of the journey of faith. Our experience is full of stops and starts, hits and misses, ups and downs. We think we're making progress one day, only to encounter some kind of unexpected obstacle the next. When the smoke clears after a day of spiritual setbacks, we feel even further from our goal.

But in the midst of our struggle comes the promise that God is making us holy. He is transforming us from within, bringing the new life of the soul to the surface of our lives. He is fully committed to the process of purification within us. ❖

GOD'S PROMISE TO ME

- I will make you holy.
- I will keep you holy.

MY PRAYER TO GOD

God of peace, do your work of holiness within me. I want to honor you with my life. I want to resist sin today. But at the same time, I confess something within me is often attracted by evil. Keep me blameless. Give me a love for you and a zeal for your glory that far surpasses any impure passion.

september 10   **day253**

GOD NEVER STOPS LOVING YOU

For I am convinced that neither death nor life, neither angels nor demons, neither the present nor the future, nor any powers ... will be able to separate us from the love of God that is in Christ Jesus our Lord.   ROMANS 8:38–39

Most of what our world calls "love" is conditional. You get to be on the receiving end only if or because you are a certain way or if or because you do certain things. Stop being or doing those things and watch how quickly the "love" disappears. Except when it comes to God.

His love is unconditional, permanent, sure. Like sunlight it shines on us no matter what we do or don't do. We can't cause it to burn more brightly. We can't possibly turn it off. It is the great constant in life—the one thing we can't evade.

Sin in our lives might prevent us from the vivid experience of God's love, but it doesn't diminish that love any more than a few clouds can diminish the sun.

Take time today to bask in the warmth of divine love. ✤

GOD'S PROMISE TO ME

• Nothing can separate you from my love.

MY PRAYER TO GOD

Your love is permanent, Lord. Transform me as I understand more deeply your undying affection for me. When I am in situations where I cannot sense your love, give me the faith to trust that you are still there and that I am always in your care.

day254

GOD GIVES PEACE IN CRAZY TIMES

Let the peace of Christ rule in your hearts.　　　　　　　　Colossians 3:15

Few people in this world have ever known true peace. Most live in a state of trepidation. In uneventful times they find plenty about which to be anxious. And when life gets really nerve-wracking, they completely fall apart.

It's not just the irreligious who fit this description. Sadly, God's people are often some of the most worrisome folks around.

But look at the promise of Christ, the one the prophets called the "Prince of Peace" (Isaiah 9:6). Jesus offers us peace in him. If we don't have peace, we need to look at our lives. Are we living in his will and trusting in his Word?

In the darkest times and saddest moments this world can throw at you, take heart. Let the peace of Christ rule your heart. ✤

GOD'S PROMISE TO ME

- You will have troubles in this life.
- During worldly trials and sorrows, you can find peace in me.

MY PRAYER TO GOD

O God, help me learn to rest in you, to draw near to you in good times and bad. Thank you for the promise of victory over my trials. In tough times teach me to look to you and lean on you. Make me an example of your supernatural peace.

GOD MAKES YOU ABLE

Such confidence we have through Christ before God. Not that we are competent in ourselves to claim anything for ourselves, but our competence comes from God.

2 CORINTHIANS 3:4–5

In what situations do you feel incompetent or ineffective? Maybe you lack a certain personality trait. Perhaps you're inexperienced or untrained.

The apostle Paul was familiar with such helpless feelings. Once he was concerned about the young church he had begun in Corinth. The church members were struggling—not always successfully—to live for God in a godless culture. To make matters worse, a band of false teachers had come along and begun to question Paul's motives and attempted to undermine all his ministry efforts.

In the face of such pressure and opposition, Paul might have limped away into the darkness. Instead, he remembered that God gives strength in weakness (see 2 Corinthians 12:9–10). He plowed ahead, relying fully on God and believing that God would somehow work in and through him. And, of course, God did.

There are lessons galore here for us. But the biggest is this simple truth: God is able to make you able. ✤

GOD'S PROMISE TO ME

- I give power and success.
- I give you the ability to have a lasting impact.

MY PRAYER TO GOD

Lord, teach me the art of looking to you instead of at my problems. Remind me that anything of lasting value in my life is because of you, not me. Power and success come from you. Give me eyes of faith that I might press on even when I feel I'm in over my head.

day256

september 13

GOD WANTS TO DO MORE THAN YOU THINK

Now to him who is able to do immeasurably more than all we ask or imagine, according to his power that is at work within us.   EPHESIANS 3:20

The record of God's people is a record of the unthinkable and the unimaginable: A ninety-year-old woman making her first trip to the maternity ward. A nation of slaves conquering the greatest empire in the world. A shepherd boy going one-on-one with the fiercest warrior of his time and winning.

The Bible and history confirm that such hard-to-believe events are commonplace when people of faith dare to believe that God will do all he has said he will do.

Do a little sanctified daydreaming. Given your unique background, abilities, experiences and desires, what do you suppose God could do in your life and through your life if you'd let him have his way?

Considering the promise above, whatever lofty visions you're seeing are probably not grand enough. ✤

GOD'S PROMISE TO ME

- I am at work in you with my limitless power.
- I want to do more in and through you than you can even imagine.

MY PRAYER TO GOD

God, I praise you! You are magnificent, glorious and awesome. You possess all power and wisdom. Forgive me for having such a small view of you and your will. You are able to do amazing things in and through me.

GOD PLEDGES TO TRAIN YOU

Do not make light of the Lord's discipline, and do not lose heart when he rebukes you, because the Lord disciplines the one he loves, and he chastens everyone he accepts as his son.
HEBREWS 12:5–6

Does God "punish" us? If we define "punishment" as making us pay for the wrongs we've committed, then the answer is a resounding "no!"

The Bible records how our ancestors inexplicably rebelled against God (see Genesis 3). Divine justice called for a death sentence for all sinful humanity. Jesus, however, endured the very punishment we deserved. At the cross he took our place. Now, with sin paid for, reconciliation with God is possible. When we trust in Christ, we receive a full pardon and become part of God's family.

As members of God's forever family we don't have to fear punishment, but we are subject to "discipline." Discipline is the corrective action a parent uses to train a child in the right way to go. Discipline is never pleasant, but it is a vivid reminder of God's love. He cares too much to let his children move in destructive directions. ♣

GOD'S PROMISE TO ME

• I discipline you because you are my child and I love you.

MY PRAYER TO GOD

Lord, your discipline is a sign of your love. Help me to have the wisdom to turn away from evil before I have to face stern corrective measures. I don't want to dishonor you or suffer needlessly. Thank you for being a loving Father.

day258

GOD BLESSES THOSE WHO CLING TO HIM

Blessed is the one who trusts in the LORD, whose confidence is in him. They will be like a tree planted by the water that sends out its roots by the stream. It does not fear when heat comes; its leaves are always green. It has no worries in a year of drought and never fails to bear fruit.   JEREMIAH 17:7–8

Sheep and goats. Wheat and weeds. The wise man and the fool. The blessed and the cursed.

Have you ever noticed how the Bible repeatedly divides people into two categories? One bunch consistently looks to God in faith and seeks to serve him. The other group largely ignores God and lives independently of him.

When the prophet Jeremiah was moved by God to contrast these two types of people, he pictured those who rely on God and obey his Word as being vibrant and fruitful—like lush trees blossoming alongside a river. Those who shut God out of their lives were compared by Jeremiah to "a bush in the wastelands" (Jeremiah 17:6).

It's a vivid contrast. In which group are you? ❖

GOD'S PROMISE TO ME

- I bless those who trust me.
- Those who trust me prosper and bear fruit in hard times.

MY PRAYER TO GOD

You are my hope and confidence, Lord. I trust in you. Draw me ever closer to you and give me a passion to seek you. I want to be fruitful even during life's hard times. It is only when I put my roots deep into you and your Word that I am able to endure dry spiritual times.

GOD ASSURES TRIUMPH IF YOU DON'T GIVE UP

Let us not become weary in doing good, for at the proper time we will reap a harvest if we do not give up.   GALATIANS 6:9

Cara is a stay-at-home mom who fills her life caring for a husband, two active children, assorted friends and neighbors, a pet or two, a rose garden and a little brick bungalow. Her days begin early and end late.

Many nights when her weary head hits the pillow Cara doesn't have much to show for all her labors. The house doesn't stay clean very long. The laundry hamper is always overflowing. The needs of loved ones are never ending.

Are my efforts even worth it? she wonders in the darkness. *Why do I feel like I'm spinning my wheels?*

Cara needs the reassurance of today's promise: There is a payoff for long-term faithfulness.

Keep doing right. Press on—even when you feel discouraged. God sees. And one day he will reward your diligent efforts. ✤

GOD'S PROMISE TO ME

- Those who keep doing good will reap a harvest of blessing.

MY PRAYER TO GOD

Sometimes, Lord, I want to give up. Remind me that you see and reward faithfulness. I want to do right. I want to please you. Help me to persevere. May the knowledge of your goodness keep me going when I feel like quitting.

day260

GOD IS LONG-SUFFERING

For that very reason I was shown mercy so that in me, the worst of sinners, Christ Jesus might display his immense patience as an example for those who would believe in him and receive eternal life.   1 TIMOTHY 1:16

Who's the most evil person to ever live? Hitler? Caligula? Jack the Ripper? Charles Manson? Attila the Hun? The apostle Paul?

You read that right. In inspired Scripture, Paul of Tarsus claimed to be the worst of all sinners (see 1 Timothy 1:15).

Apparently Paul viewed himself in this way because of his pre-conversion participation in arresting and killing the followers of Jesus. Unlike a one-time crime of passion, Paul undertook a cold, calculated campaign built on fierce religious hatred.

The memories of this old life always seemed to fill Paul with regret. But they also filled him with wonder at the infinite patience of God.

No sins are too great. No sinner who humbles himself will ever be turned away. God longs to bless, not judge (see 2 Peter 3:9). ❖

GOD'S PROMISE TO ME

- I am patient and merciful.
- I forgive and give eternal life.

MY PRAYER TO GOD

You show mercy, O Lord. Thank you for not treating me as my sins deserve. You are patient toward sinners. Help me use my testimony to encourage others to seek your mercy and grace. I know that what you have done in my life, you will do for others.

GOD SPARES THE FAITHFUL FROM SHAME

In you, LORD my God, I put my trust. I trust in you; do not let me be put to shame, nor let my enemies triumph over me. No one who hopes in you will ever be put to shame, but shame will come on those who are treacherous without cause.   PSALM 25:1–3

A dying father once told his teenage son: "Make sure you are right with God and you have nothing to fear." Wise words.

Others may question our actions, mock us or even spread vicious rumors about us, but if we know in our heart of hearts that we are walking with God and honoring him, we never have to fret over the evil intents of others. This is because disgrace, in the most literal sense, means "without grace." Such a description is never true of the children of God. We are always in his care. We are always loved and favored.

Trust the Lord. Serve him. Then, no matter what happens, you'll be able to hold your head high, knowing that God will vindicate you in the end. ❖

GOD'S PROMISE TO ME

- I will not allow my faithful ones to be disgraced.

MY PRAYER TO GOD

I lift my soul to you, Lord. You are good. I trust you. No one who walks with you will ever be put to shame. As long as I know I am pleasing you, it doesn't matter what others say or do. I believe that you will make all things right in the end.

day262

september 19

GOD PROVIDES SUPERNATURAL STRENGTH

It is God who works in you to will and to act in order to fulfill his good purpose.

PHILIPPIANS 2:13

God wants us to live by faith (see 2 Corinthians 5:7 and Hebrews 11:1). Many times, however, we live by feelings. If we are moved by a rare desire to pray or reach out to a neighbor, we act upon it. But in the absence of such feelings we often confess weakness and choose to do nothing. The result is an unsatisfying, excuse-filled Christian experience.

Now, consider the promise above. It says God is at work within us—giving us the desire to do right, meaning we can never honestly say, "I don't feel like it."

And it's not just new desires. The promise also guarantees the necessary power to do what needs to be done.

Why would we choose to keep riding the "feelings roller coaster" when God offers us a radical new way to live? ❖

GOD'S PROMISE TO ME

- I am at work in you.
- I give you the desire to obey me.
- I provide the power to do what pleases me.

MY PRAYER TO GOD

God, you are at work within me. Teach me to obey—even when I can't sense the desire to do what is right. You give me new desires—and new power to live as I should. Wean me from the inadequate and immature excuse that "I'm too weak." Your strength is sufficient for whatever I'm facing.

day263

GOD KNOWS YOU INTIMATELY

You have searched me, LORD, and you know me. You know when I sit and when I rise; you perceive my thoughts from afar. PSALM 139:1–2

Chances are good as you rush through a typically hectic week you sometimes feel misunderstood. A co-worker gives you a strange look. A family member overreacts to an innocent remark.

Chances are also good that some days you don't even understand yourself. "Why did I do that?" you sigh. Or "What in the world made me say that?"

Well, here's a bit of comfort: God understands you completely. He made you, and he knows what makes you tick. Your thoughts, your whereabouts, your needs — God sees it all.

Next time you — or others — are having trouble getting a handle on you, turn to the one with perfect knowledge and insight. Rest in the knowledge of his absolute acceptance. ✤

GOD'S PROMISE TO ME

- I see your heart.
- I know your thoughts and actions — everything about you.

MY PRAYER TO GOD

Heavenly Father, you have examined my heart. You see me as I truly am — my failings and flaws, as well as my successes. Thank you for accepting me and for choosing to love and care for me. Help me to rest in your love. I want to follow your guidance.

day264

GOD IS YOUR SOURCE

Wealth and honor come from you; you are the ruler of all things. In your hands are strength and power to exalt and give strength to all.   1 CHRONICLES 29:12

There are occasions in life when all our busy labors pay off. The business deal or special event comes together perfectly. A boss notices our hard work, and we get a promotion or a raise. We're able to purchase something that we've worked hard for. These are wonderful moments—wonderful and dangerous. To what or whom will we attribute our success?

At the end of his reign, David commissioned a national offering for the soon-to-be-built temple. The people's response was overwhelming. Looking at the lavish gifts of silver, gold and precious gems, David stood before the people and praised God. The great Hebrew king recognized the same truth we read in the New Testament "Every good and perfect gift is from above" (James 1:17). ❖

GOD'S PROMISE TO ME

- I rule over everything.
- I am the source of all riches and honor.
- I possess all power and might.
- I give strength and make great.

MY PRAYER TO GOD

God you are in control of all things. Help me remember that you rule the universe and my life. You are the source of all good things—wealth, power and honor. What do I have, Lord, that I did not receive from you?

THE LORD WILL ONE DAY BE WITH US

And I heard a loud voice from the throne saying, "Look! God's dwelling place is now among the people, and he will dwell with them. They will be his people, and God himself will be with them and be their God."   REVELATION 21:3

What must it have been like for Adam and Eve to glimpse Eden that final time? Because of their foolish rebellion against God the world had fallen under a great curse. Innocence was lost. Perfection was ruined. Worst of all, their opportunity to live in God's actual presence (see Genesis 3:8,22–24) was long gone. They would spend the rest of their lives remembering what was … and what could have been.

From Genesis to Revelation, the Bible tells the epic story of all God did to reverse Adam's curse and to restore all things.

In Isaiah 7:14, we find the curious promise of Immanuel (which means "God with us"). In John 1:14 we read about Jesus Christ, the eternal Word of God, who came and "made his dwelling among us" so that, in Peter's words, Christ could "bring [us] to God" (1 Peter 3:18).

In Revelation 21, we see the culmination of this divine rescue mission. A holy God once again dwelling with and among sinful but redeemed people. It's a face-to-face relationship (see verse 4). Revelation 22 goes on to describe a place very much like a garden.

Remember that when God seems far away. ✣

GOD'S PROMISE TO ME

- As a believer in my Son Jesus, you are destined to live with me forever.
- You are one of my people. I am your God.

MY PRAYER TO GOD

Lord, despite the promise that you are always with me, sometimes I can't sense your presence. Encourage me and sustain me with the promise that one day I will see you face-to-face. I will dwell with you forever!

day266

GOD'S WORK IN YOUR LIFE IS UNSTOPPABLE

Though outwardly we are wasting away, yet inwardly we are being renewed day by day.
2 CORINTHIANS 4:16

The physical signs are impossible to deny. Perhaps the wrinkles are spreading and deepening. Or your hair is graying. Certain clothes no longer fit. You find yourself unable to physically do what you used to do.

Fact #1: You are getting older.

Fact #2: Your body is wearing out.

Fact #3: You have two choices: You can devote all your waking energies to trying (futilely!) to preserve your temporal body. Or, you can accept the inevitability of physical aging and focus your attention instead on what God is doing in you spiritually.

That's today's promise. In the life to come God will resurrect and renew your body. It'll be the ultimate makeover. But for now his focus is your inner self—changing you, maturing you.

Is that your focus too? ❖

GOD'S PROMISE TO ME

- I am constantly changing you from the inside out.

MY PRAYER TO GOD

My body is breaking down. O Lord, give me a sense of balance. I want to take care of my body, but I do not want to be like so many in our health and beauty-obsessed culture who are looking for some kind of nonexistent fountain of youth. You are renewing my spirit every day. Help me to depend on you.

day267

GOD SEES EVERYTHING ABOUT YOU

For your ways are in full view of the LORD, and he examines all your paths.

PROVERBS 5:21

Would you modify your behavior this week if you knew that your every word and deed were going to be recorded and shown on a big screen to your family, neighbors or fellow church members?

Of course you would. You may even make some major changes. There's nothing like a little accountability to make people "straighten up and fly right."

What we forget is that God does see everything about us. The verse above indicates that he knows our thoughts and motives. He monitors our conversations, plans and behaviors. And one day we will stand before the Lord and give an account for the way we have lived (see 2 Corinthians 5:10).

As you ponder your schedule for the day ahead and the commitments you've made to people and activities, ask yourself: "What do I need to change in light of the fact that I will one day answer to God for the way I chose to live the life he so graciously gave me?" ✤

GOD'S PROMISE TO ME

- I see what you do.
- I examine your actions.

MY PRAYER TO GOD

God, nothing about me is hidden from your sight. What a sobering and convicting thought. Forgive me for the times I have foolishly acted as though you were oblivious to my lifestyle choices.

day**268**

GOD TURNS SORROW INTO JOY

Sing the praises of the LORD, you his faithful people; praise his holy name. For his anger lasts only a moment, but his favor lasts a lifetime; weeping may stay for the night, but rejoicing comes in the morning. PSALM 30:4–5

When life turns ugly and stays ugly, it's easy to become trapped in an emotional vortex. Disappointment, discouragement, disillusionment, devastation, depression—down and down we spin until we may finally believe God hates us, and all hope is lost.

Psalm 30 by King David gives us a different perspective: the promise that hard times do not last forever. Whether our difficulties are trials intended to strengthen and test our faith (see James 1) or divine discipline intended to correct and train us (see 2 Corinthians 12), the fact remains that God is praiseworthy. He can be counted on to shower his people with favor. He will eventually turn your mourning into dancing (see Psalm 30:11; Isaiah 54:7–8; and John 16:20–22) ❧

GOD'S PROMISE TO ME

- My favor endures.
- You will not weep forever.
- I will bring you joy.

MY PRAYER TO GOD

Lord, you are holy and worthy of praise! I want to worship you at all times—when life is good and when it is difficult. Hard and sad times are temporary, but your favor is continually with me. Though I weep and mourn now, I want to believe—really believe—that you are in control.

day269

GOD CAN BE FOUND WHEN YOU SEEK HIM

After he had dismissed them, he went up on a mountainside by himself to pray.

MATTHEW 14:23

Physical busyness is when we rush to and fro, trying to do this and that, and we end up not knowing whether we are coming or going.

Soul busyness is when our minds are spinning with worry or fear, and our hearts are heavy with care. Soul busyness explains how you can be on vacation, lying in a hammock with your eyes closed, and still be physically, emotionally and spiritually exhausted.

What's the prescription for busyness of soul? Jesus provides the answer. After expending energy healing the sick and feeding well over five thousand people, he desperately craved alone time with his Father. He knew that only the Father could provide the energy and counsel he needed. He just needed to be still and seek the Father.

God also desires some alone time with us. He can replenish our depleted energy and provide the wise counsel we need to keep going. When we seek him, he will be found. ✤

GOD'S PROMISE TO ME

- I am here for you.
- I can replenish you.

MY PRAYER TO GOD

God, I sometimes run myself in circles and wind up exhausted. I truly need to be alone with you, to bask in your glory, to lean on your strength. I'm grateful that when I seek you I will find you.

GOD IS THE SOURCE OF YOUR WEALTH

Command those who are rich in this present world not to be arrogant nor to put their hope in wealth, which is so uncertain, but to put their hope in God, who richly provides us with everything for our enjoyment. Command them to do good, to be rich in good deeds, and to be generous and willing to share.　　　　　　　　　　　　　1 TIMOTHY 6:17–18

Beware anyone who says that God promises a financial fortune to his followers. First, the Scriptures don't say that. Second, the experiences of millions of faithful believers through the ages don't back up such an extravagant claim.

What the Bible does assert is that God owns everything (see Psalm 24:1) and sometimes gives his people great material wealth (see Deuteronomy 8:10–18).

For reasons known only to God, those of us in the West have been especially blessed at this time in history. Compared to our brothers and sisters in many other parts of the world, we are rich.

How can we respond? With humility. God is the one who gives us the ability to earn and acquire money and possessions (see Deuteronomy 8:18). With grateful hearts we can enjoy his lavish provision and use those resources to bless others in need. ✣

GOD'S PROMISE TO ME

- Your money will not last forever.
- I give you all you need for your enjoyment.
- I bless you so you can bless others.

MY PRAYER TO GOD

O God, thank you for your material provision. Keep me from being greedy or selfish. Help me find a God-honoring balance in my stewardship of the resources that you have put in my care. Show me practical and creative ways to use my money to do good.

day**271**

GOD IS SLOWLY CHANGING YOU

Being confident of this, that he who began a good work in you will carry it on to completion until the day of Christ Jesus.   PHILIPPIANS 1:6

Busyness not only rears its head in our personal lives and careers, it is also evident in our approach to the spiritual life.

Personal quiet times, small group gatherings, worship services, short-term mission trips, special seminars and conferences, outreach events, prayer meetings, church ministry obligations—the list of "good" activities is long—and exhausting! Some eager-to-grow followers of Christ try to do it all. They attend every church function. They serve on every committee.

Inevitably these well-meaning believers experience deep disappointment. Despite their faithful efforts to change by plunging into a whirlwind of religious activity, they find they still struggle with sinful desires and old habit patterns. They are learning a crucial lesson: Spiritual busyness is not the way to holiness.

God will patiently change us in his way and according to his timetable. We can relax. God is at work. ✤

GOD'S PROMISE TO ME

- I have begun a good work in you.
- I will continue my good work in you.
- I will complete my good work in you.

MY PRAYER TO GOD

O God, I praise you for your great salvation! You not only took away my sin, but you gave me a new nature that longs to please you. I'm glad you do not give up on me. Continue your work in me, Lord. I look forward to the day when your work is complete.

GOD WILL DEAL WITH DEATH—FOREVER

He will swallow up death forever. ISAIAH 25:8

It's easy to forget that caskets and crematoriums were not part of God's original, perfect plan for the world.

So why *do* we have funeral homes? Why *do* we attend graveside ceremonies in cemeteries? The apostle Paul explains it this way: "Sin entered the world through one man, and death through sin, and in this way death came to all people, because all sinned" (Romans 5:12).

In short, death is the result of Adam's rebellion—and ours—against God. Defying the King of the universe is the highest form of treason. Sin is a capital crime—meaning our whole world sits on a kind of death row.

Yet God, in perfect justice and love, sent Christ to die for sins, to die in the place of sinners. And when Jesus rose from the dead, he served notice to every undertaker and every gravestone maker: "Your days are numbered!"

In Christ death has been defeated. The grave can't keep those whose trust is in Jesus. And at Christ's second coming death won't simply be defeated, it will be eradicated. He will swallow up death forever.

That's a great promise to keep in mind the next time you come face-to-face with death. ✤

GOD'S PROMISE TO ME

- By his death and resurrection my Son paid for sin and defeated death.
- At his second coming my Son will abolish death forever!

MY PRAYER TO GOD

Jesus, I praise you because you are the resurrection and the life. Those who believe in you will never die—at least not in the ultimate sense. Thank you for the hope of the gospel. Because of you, death has lost its sting.

day273

GOD DOES NOT WANT YOU TO BURN OUT

[Jesus] said to them, "Come with me by yourselves to a quiet place and get some rest."
MARK 6:31

Jesus' admonition here prompted some wise guy to quip, "Jesus is saying here that if we don't come apart and rest, we'll eventually just come apart!"

That's the idea! There's a work-rest, work-rest rhythm built by God into the very fabric of life (see Genesis 2:1–3). When we violate this natural order of things by excessive work or ministry involvement, we soon burn out. No wonder Jesus deliberately scheduled retreats for himself and his disciples — intentional trips into quiet or remote places.

What about you? How long has it been since you really rested? God promises to give you rest, and if you're seriously empty inside, he may even want you to take some extended time off. ✣

GOD'S PROMISE TO ME

- If you will pull away from your busy schedule, I will give you the rest you need.

MY PRAYER TO GOD

Lord, I often feel drained physically, emotionally and spiritually. Give me the wisdom to recognize the warning signs of burnout. I can't be effective for you if I am running on empty. I want the rest that you offer.

day274

GOD WILL DESTROY THIS WORLD AND ALL ITS TROUBLES

He carried me away in the Spirit to a mountain great and high, and showed me the Holy City, Jerusalem, coming down out of heaven from God. It shone with the glory of God, and its brilliance was like that of a very precious jewel, like a jasper, clear as crystal.

REVELATION 21:10–11

In the first century, while exiled on the barren island of Patmos, the apostle John was given this vivid glimpse of eternity.

Some call passages like this one a myth or fantasy. But the children of God know this snapshot of the future is anything *but* wishful thinking. Our heavenly Father reigns. History, as the old saying goes, is "His story." The day is surely coming when the curtain will fall on this sin-scarred world. Finally and forever we will see an end to sorrows, death, crying and pain.

In the midst of our tough times, we need to remember what the future holds — not uncertainty and fear, but the reassuring promise of a brand-new existence void of bad things and filled with God. "Dear friends, now we are children of God, and what we will be has not yet been made known. But we know that when Christ appears, we shall be like him, for we shall see him as he is" (1 John 3:2). ❖

GOD'S PROMISE TO ME

- I will bring an end to this old world and its troubles.
- I am preparing a heavenly home where we will live together forever.

MY PRAYER TO GOD

I praise you, God, for your perfect ways, your perfect plan and for the glorious future that awaits.

GOD SATISFIES THE LONGING SOUL

You, God, are my God, earnestly I seek you; I thirst for you, my whole being longs for you, in a dry and parched land where there is no water. PSALM 63:1

Sometimes it hits like a lightning bolt. At other times it comes gradually—like waking up from a deep slumber.

"It" is the sense that our lives are out of balance. We see ourselves as we truly are—frantic people, rushing through our days, trying so feverishly to have it all and do it all. We realize that all we have to show for our busyness is frustration and exhaustion. We experience feelings of regret, because we see (once again!) that whenever we choose a life jammed with nonstop activity, we are also choosing to shut the door on life's greatest treasures—intimacy with God and deep relationships with the people in our lives.

David made seeking God a high priority, especially when he felt threatened by enemies. Time with God was just the restorative medicine he needed, and it enabled him to live life without regrets.

If we make time with God a priority, we can experience joy, rather than regret. He satisfies those who long for him. ❖

GOD'S PROMISE TO ME

• I will satisfy the longings of those who seek me.

MY PRAYER TO GOD

O God, sometimes I don't truly know what I long for. I scramble around, searching in vain. Help me to long for you like I long for water or air.

day276 october 3

GOD ADOPTS YOU

When the set time had fully come, God sent his Son, born of a woman, born under the law, to redeem those under the law, that we might receive adoption to sonship.

GALATIANS 4:4–5

Most people in the world would agree with the statement that "We are all God's children." It's a nice sentiment. It just isn't what the Bible teaches. According to God's Word, unrepentant sinners are actually God's enemies (see Romans 5:10 and Colossians 1:21). It's only when we put our trust in the Lord Jesus Christ that we experience forgiveness and adoption into God's forever family (see Ephesians 1:5).

For a Christian going through hard times this "adoption" truth is the best of all possible news. God is not just a powerful Creator or a righteous Lord, he is a loving Father. He sees your trials. He listens to your pleas. He cares and protects and supports. He is never harsh or impatient with you. He is never "too busy" for you.

Take all the best qualities of all the best earthly dads you've ever known, add them together and multiply by infinity. That's the kind of father God is. ✣

GOD'S PROMISE TO ME

- You are my child if you accept the salvation I offer.

MY PRAYER TO GOD

Jesus, I do believe in you. I have accepted you as my Savior and Lord. Thank you for revealing yourself to me. Thank you for saving me. Because of your grace and my faith I am a child of the living God.

day277

GOD RESTORES THE HUMBLE IN SPIRIT

If we confess our sins, he is faithful and just and will forgive us our sins and purify us from all unrighteousness.   1 JOHN 1:9

There is nothing like a tough time to reveal what we're made of. When trouble rears its ugly, scary head, either we trust the promises of God and respond with obedience, or we panic and react sinfully.

Too often we are guilty of the latter. Things fall apart, and we become sarcastic, possessive, moody, self-centered, bitter, envious or a hundred other unflattering things. Now the situation is really messy—not only are we facing trouble, but we've complicated the matter by pulling away from God. Our doubt and disobedience have alienated us from the One we need most.

The good news is that intimacy with God can be restored by simply acknowledging our wrong attitudes and actions. Confession means we agree with God about our wrong choices and about his perfect forgiveness.

If you've added to your troubles by responding wrongly, confession is the bridge back to God. ✤

GOD'S PROMISE TO ME

- I am faithful and righteous.
- I forgive and cleanse those who acknowledge their sins.

MY PRAYER TO GOD

God, I am often guilty of reacting wrongly in the midst of tough times. My faith is small. Help me to stay close to you so that I do not fall apart spiritually at the first sign of trouble.

day278

GOD HEARS YOUR PLEAS OF DISTRESS

Evening, morning and noon I cry out in distress, and he hears my voice.   PSALM 55:17

Distress refers to the mental and emotional strain and/or physical danger resulting from a troubling situation. It can be mild—"a motorist in distress"—prompting uncertainty about the immediate future. Or it can be serious—"a baby in distress"—suggesting great trouble, immediate danger and need.

In Psalm 55 we find David in deep distress. His misfortune is a former ally and friend who has suddenly betrayed him and is now threatening his life. But David's unique circumstances are not as important as his response.

Notice his raw honesty as he continually cries out to God. Next, compare his initial desperation (see verses 1–15) with the confidence expressed in verses 16–23. What prompts such a mood swing? David knew that God always listened to him. ♣

GOD'S PROMISE TO ME

• I hear your prayers when you cry out in distress.

MY PRAYER TO GOD

Lord, like David, I need to bring my distress to you. Forgive me for the times I pout or complain to others, but do not bring my troubles to you—the one who can actually do something about them. You hear my desperate cries and come to my aid.

day279

GOD DRIVES AWAY YOUR FEARS

We will not fear, though the earth give way and the mountains fall into the heart of the sea.   PSALM 46:2

The next time you're at church, in a mall or at a sporting event, look at the people all around you. Then consider this: Each person is deeply afraid of something. Losing a child, health issues, problems on the job. Can you relate? What has the power to make you sweat bullets? Disease? Disaster? Death?

Psalm 46 is a hymn of trust sung by the ancient Israelites. It gives us insight into overcoming our unique fears. There are no "simple steps to follow"; the psalm simply reminds us of God. If God really is who he says he is, we need never be cowering souls who live in dread.

When a crisis looms in our path, our natural instinct is to panic. Precisely the opposite response is called for in Psalm 46. We need to be silent (or "still"—see verse 10) and focus on the fact that God is God. ❖

GOD'S PROMISE TO ME

- You don't have to fear because I am ready to help you in times of trouble.

MY PRAYER TO GOD

O God, you are my strong help in times of trouble. Forgive me for the times when I act as though you don't exist. I do not have to fear, no matter what I face. Teach me to pull back from troubles and focus on you.

GOD LOVES YOU IN TIMES OF DISTRESS

I will sing of your strength, in the morning I will sing of your love; for you are my fortress, my refuge in times of trouble. You are my strength, I sing praise to you; you, God, are my fortress, my God on whom I can rely. PSALM 59:16–17

It is the stuff of a first rate thriller motion picture. A delusional, paranoid king. A shadowy team of cold-blooded assassins. A young, innocent man running for his life.

Only it's not a fictional story; it's a slice of history from the life of David. He is "exhibit A" of the Biblical truth that godly people incur the wrath of the ungodly (see 2 Timothy 3:12).

In moments of great distress and crisis — and there are many recorded in the psalms — David demonstrates two refreshing qualities. First, he's always honest. He doesn't hide his feelings or mince words. He tells God all that is in his heart — good and bad. Second, he clings desperately to what he knows about the character of God.

Reread the passage above. What truths about God can help in your tough time? ✤

GOD'S PROMISE TO ME

- I am powerful.
- My love for you never fails.
- I am your refuge, your place of safety in distress.

MY PRAYER TO GOD

O God, you are powerful! Thank you for demonstrating your unfailing love to me day after day. When situations are bleak and hope seems gone, give me the faith to cling to you and look to you for salvation.

GOD DIRECTS YOUR WAYS

Direct my footsteps according to your word; let no sin rule over me.   PSALM 119:133

Going through difficulty is hard enough. Being in a mess and not having a clue what to do is even worse.

It gets complicated because sometimes our choices seem limited and at other times we have numerous options. What do we do? How do we know what's best?

We trust God's promise to provide guidance through his Word.

Imagine God as a wise and loving Father accompanying an insecure child on a long, hard journey. The Father is forever watching and directing, helping the child to make wise choices.

Don't face your troubles—and certainly don't make big decisions in the midst of trouble—alone. God wants to direct you. ✤

GOD'S PROMISE TO ME

- I will guide you in the ways that are best.
- I will help you make wise choices.

MY PRAYER TO GOD

You promise to guide me in the way that's best, Lord. Give me the sense and sensitivity to seek, to listen, to trust. I am so prone to wander off into dangerous places. Guard me and keep me from a stubborn, independent spirit. Speak loudly enough so that I can hear.

day282

GOD KNOWS ALL ABOUT YOU

From heaven the LORD looks down and sees all mankind; from his dwelling place he watches all who live on earth—he who forms the hearts of all, who considers everything they do. PSALM 33:13–15

When we are going through difficulties, we often feel somewhat invisible and greatly misunderstood. "No one really sees my struggle," we think. "And even if they do happen to notice, they don't really know what it's like to be in this situation."

That may be true of our fellow humans, but God knows.

According to today's promise, God sees. And he understands. Theologians refer to this all-seeing, all-knowing attribute of God as his *omniscience*. Nothing about us or our situation is hidden from him. God has total insight into how we got to this place, what we're thinking, what our motives and desires are, why we do what we do and what the future holds.

The verbs in the passage above speak volumes. Notice that God "looks down." He "sees." He "considers."

Believing in God's omniscience won't make your troubles go away, but it will diminish your feelings of aloneness. ✤

GOD'S PROMISE TO ME

- I see you and your situation.
- I made your heart, and I understand you.

MY PRAYER TO GOD

God, you see me and you know me. I feel alone and small and helpless. Thank you for the promise that you are always watching over me. You understand me and what I need to do. O, Maker of my heart, give me insight into what I am doing—and why—and what I need to do.

day283

GOD HELPS THOSE IN NEED

As for me, I am poor and needy; come quickly to me, O God. You are my help and my deliverer; LORD, do not delay.
PSALM 70:5

People talk at length about the trials of Job, but how about the travails of David? Of the approximate 75 psalms attributed to David, a shockingly high number reveal a man in great turmoil.

Psalm 70 is a classic example. The specific setting in which David wrote it is not known. But clearly he was—once again—in desperate need of rescue from some powerful adversary. And so he cried out urgently, acknowledging God as "my help."

David's honest lament forces us to ask ourselves, "To what or to whom do we turn when times get tough?" Is prayer our first response, or is God our last resort?

As one who spent a lifetime being delivered by God, David would likely urge us, "It's only when you depend fully on the Lord that you truly experience his help." ✤

GOD'S PROMISE TO ME

- I am your helper.
- I am your Savior.

MY PRAYER TO GOD

I am in need of your aid, God. Please help me before my troubles swallow me up. You are my helper and deliverer. I depend on you and not on my own wisdom or strength.

GOD HELPS YOU REACH YOUR GOALS

Commit to the LORD whatever you do, and he will establish your plans. PROVERBS 16:3

Ever set goals for your family? Perhaps you sat down as a family and decided on what you wanted to do or how you wanted to help each other grow. Setting goals together is a way of working as a team, as well as showing your love for each other.

As a member of God's family God wants to do the same thing with you: sit down together and work through your goals. Because he loves you and wants the best for you, he wants to hear your plans, hopes and dreams.

Sometimes we make plans without consulting God because we simply want our own way. Some of these plans may succeed; others fail. God wants us to submit our plans to him for his approval before we act. In this way, we show our love for and submission to him. ♣

GOD'S PROMISE TO ME

- If you commit your plans to me, I will help you reach godly goals.

MY PRAYER TO GOD

Heavenly Father, I'm glad you're so interested in my life that I can come and talk to you whenever I want. Thank you for helping me set good goals.

GOD IS CLOSE TO THE BROKENHEARTED

The LORD is close to the brokenhearted and saves those who are crushed in spirit.

PSALM 34:18

If we humans could write the script for life's tough times, first of all, there wouldn't be so many. We would then opt for more happy, "feel-good" endings — more diseases cured, more marriages saved, more kids saying "no" to drugs. In our version of things, God would be front and center — rending the heavens and making dramatic, "just in the nick of time" appearances. We'd have him speaking audibly — perhaps even holding daily briefings with lots of Q & A. He would tour disaster areas, giving out lots of hugs.

As it is, in times of trial God often remains invisible. He speaks in whispers through the pages of an ancient book. He designates proxies to do all his hugging.

His ways frustrate us, but they do not change the truth that he sticks by us when we feel brokenhearted or crushed. Do you have the faith to take him at his word? ❖

GOD'S PROMISE TO ME

• I draw near to those who are brokenhearted.

MY PRAYER TO GOD

Lord, you promised your followers you'd be with us, even in our darkest hours. I wish I could see you or touch you or hear you. But even if I can't, I trust you.

day**286**

GOD HAS SAVED YOU FROM ETERNAL DEATH

He who did not spare his own Son, but gave him up for us all—how will he not also, along with him, graciously give us all things? ROMANS 8:32

Whatever storm clouds are in your life right now, there was a time when you were facing an even greater crisis.

You were an enemy of God. Spiritually speaking you were on death row, having been rightly convicted of high crimes against the King of the universe (see Romans 6:23). But God did a shocking thing. He put his one and only Son to death in your place. Jesus took your punishment, and then, perfect justice satisfied, offered you a full, eternal pardon. More than that, God even offered to adopt you into his family so that you could share all his riches.

The point is this: If God willingly helped us out of our nightmarish predicament, does it make sense that he would allow lesser troubles to destroy us? ✣

GOD'S PROMISE TO ME

- I chose you.
- I gave you right standing with myself.
- I will give you my glory.

MY PRAYER TO GOD

Lord, you have chosen me and called me to yourself. I do not understand such love, such grace. But I praise you. Thank you for saving me from sin. You declare me righteous solely because of what Christ has done on my behalf. If you cared enough to rescue me from eternal dangers, surely you care enough to see me through temporary trials.

day287

GOD INVITES YOU TO COME TO HIM FOR HELP

He knows how we are formed, he remembers that we are dust.   PSALM 103:14

When we are scrambling around during tough times, trying to figure out what to do, our minds have a tendency to dream up all sorts of unlikely scenarios. Money woes, for instance, might prompt us to imagine an out-of-the-blue phone call from a billionaire like Bill Gates, offering to bail us out. Medical problems can get us daydreaming about an invitation to come consult—for free, of course—with the world's foremost specialists at a place like the Mayo Clinic.

Bottom line—what we want most in times of trouble is understanding and help from someone with the power to deal effectively with our situation.

God offers precisely what we want and need. He knows our every weakness and cares about them. We can trust that when we seek him for help in a situation, he'll care enough to do something about it. ❖

GOD'S PROMISE TO ME

- I understand your weaknesses.
- I want you to come boldly into my presence.
- I will give you mercy and grace in your time of need.

MY PRAYER TO GOD

Lord, you know my weaknesses and the temptations I face. You are never too busy for me. Thank you for the total, unhindered access I have to you.

GOD REVEALS TRUTH TO THOSE WITH CHILDLIKE HEARTS

Jesus said, "I praise you, Father, Lord of heaven and earth, because you have hidden these things from the wise and learned, and revealed them to little children. Yes, Father, for this is what you were pleased to do."　　　　　　　　　MATTHEW 11:25–26

Quick! You've just been given one of the greatest secrets of the universe. To whom will you tell it? Would you even think about sharing that secret with a child? More than likely you would head to the nearest phone and try to dial the president or some other world leader.

Jesus was known for his countercultural actions and sayings. After acknowledging the rejection he experienced in some of the leading cities around the Sea of Galilee, he made a declaration that probably shocked his listeners: God had revealed his truth to children. He explained his meaning a little further in the Gospel of Matthew: "Truly I tell you, unless you change and become like little children, you will never enter the kingdom of heaven" (18:3).

Children accept truth at face value. They don't "quantify" it or "shade" it fit their own beliefs. They simply believe. They also trust without reservation. Is that the kind of believer you are? ✤

GOD'S PROMISE TO ME

• I reveal my kingdom to those who are willing to trust me.

MY PRAYER TO GOD

God, your assurance to your people is that you will keep them from all evil. Thank you that though evil may come, it has no ultimate power over me. I want to trust, not worry.

day289

GOD IS CONCERNED ABOUT YOU

A friend loves at all times, and a brother is born for a time of adversity. PROVERBS 17:17

The Old Testament book known as Proverbs is essentially a divinely inspired king's best and most practical wisdom for everyday life. Not only did the king incorporate the above verse about friendship, he included another: "One who has unreliable friends soon comes to ruin, but there is a friend who sticks closer than a brother" (Proverbs 18:24).

In other words, a true friend is faithful. He or she will be there through thick and thin, to the very end. "Faithful friend" is a perfect description of God.

Now, think about the implications of that ancient wisdom. As your friend, God loves "at all times." How does that alter your attitude in your current trouble? ♣

GOD'S PROMISE TO ME

• I am your friend.

MY PRAYER TO GOD

O Lord, you are everything the Bible says you are — Creator, Sustainer, Provider, Father, Judge, Savior and King. I praise you for being the righteous ruler of the universe — and for making and saving me. But you are also my friend. I can count on you to stand by me in tough times.

day**290**

GOD'S PLANS SOMETIMES DIFFER FROM YOURS

God chose the foolish things of the world to shame the wise; God chose the weak things of the world to shame the strong. God chose the lowly things of this world and the despised things — and the things that are not — to nullify the things that are, so that no one may boast before him. 1 CORINTHIANS 1:27–29

"That's the craziest plan I ever heard!" Scientists and famous inventors probably hear those words a thousand times. Some of these "crazy" plans have resulted in the development of many inventions we hold dear, as well as scientific theories — like gravity — we take for granted as true.

God's plan to work in our world often seems "crazy". He uses the "foolish things" and the "weak things" and the "lowly things" to accomplish his purposes.

This promise also shows us that God's ways are not our ways. "'For my thoughts are not your thoughts, neither are your ways my ways,' declares the LORD" (Isaiah 55:8). When things don't make sense to us, it's time ask God for wisdom to discern what he is doing. ❖

GOD'S PROMISE TO ME

- My ways are not your ways.
- My plans are contrary to worldly wisdom.

MY PRAYER TO GOD

Lord, I'm grateful that your "foolish" plans included me. I'd be a fool if I didn't take you at your Word and trust you.

GOD'S KINGDOM WILL LAST FOREVER

Your throne, O God, will last for ever and ever; a scepter of justice will be the scepter of your kingdom.   Psalm 45:6

You have only to read the news on a continual basis to see how nations and regimes rise and fall. That's because conquerors come and go. There will always be a new king, leader or politician on the horizon.

This transitory nature of our world can be dismaying for those of us who crave permanence. For true permanence we have only to turn to God.

In this psalm the psalmist declares the eternal nature of God's kingdom. Unlike earthly kings who come and go, God's kingdom will last for all eternity. The word *temporary* is not in God's nature. Instead, we can count on him to always be King, always be just, and—best of all—always welcome new citizens to his kingdom. ❖

GOD'S PROMISE TO ME

- I will be King forever.
- I will be fair forever.

MY PRAYER TO GOD

Almighty God, I can only echo the traditional coronation phrase, "Long live the King." Your throne will last forever. In this world of passing regimes, the concept of forever is hard to fathom. But it gives me comfort nevertheless.

GOD ACTS FOR THE GOOD OF THOSE WHO WAIT ON HIM

Since ancient times no one has heard, no ear has perceived, no eye has seen any God besides you, who acts on behalf of those who wait for him. Isaiah 64:4

"Good things come to those who wait." We hear this old saying, but do we really believe it in our instant society, where waiting is viewed as positively as a root canal?

According to the Old Testament prophet Isaiah, God's plans are always worth the wait. This was good news coming after the prediction of Judah's exile and God's judgment of the nations. Though God's people would suffer for a time, eventually, God would restore them.

Waiting implies hope—hope that God will act in his perfect time frame. This is waiting with anticipation. Consider the anticipation a child exhibits, beginning in December, as thoughts turn toward Christmas. He or she waits with excited anticipation, knowing that something good will happen.

Good things do indeed come to those who wait ... on the Lord. ❧

GOD'S PROMISE TO ME

- I have good plans for you.
- If you wait for me, I will act on your behalf.

MY PRAYER TO GOD

Hear my cry, O Lord. I am waiting on you to act. Help me not to put a time limit on when I think you should act. I want to trust that you will act in just the right time.

day293

GOD IS BIGGER THAN YOUR PROBLEMS

Great is the LORD and most worthy of praise; his greatness no one can fathom. One generation commends your works to another; they tell of your mighty acts. They speak of the glorious splendor of your majesty—and I will meditate on your wonderful works.

PSALM 145:3–5

Have you ever heard the old saying: "Big God, little problems; little God, big problems"?

It's a simple reminder of the truth that our response during times of trouble is a direct reflection of our view of God.

If we see God as he truly is—majestic, infinite, all-seeing, immanent, awesome, strong and compassionate—we will be more inclined to rest and trust. If, on the other hand, we imagine God to be absent, distant, impotent, unaware or indifferent, we will surely panic.

What is your common response when things fall apart? Do you focus on the magnitude of your problems or the magnificence of our God? ❖

GOD'S PROMISE TO ME

- I am great and worthy of praise.
- I am majestic, glorious and able to do miraculous things.

MY PRAYER TO GOD

O, Lord, you are worthy of praise, far greater than I can even imagine. Forgive the times I take my eyes off you. You are worthy of my full attention and total trust. There is none like you. Teach me to better focus on your greatness and majesty so that I might have perspective in times of trial.

day294

october 21

GOD IS ABLE TO DO ANYTHING

You are the God who performs miracles; you display your power among the peoples.

PSALM 77:14

Almighty. Invincible. Unstoppable. Supreme. All great words to describe the infinite power of the living God.

Theologians like to refer to God's limitless strength as his *omnipotence*—from the Latin words *omni*, meaning "all" and *potens* meaning "power." In short, God has all power. There is nothing too difficult for him (see Genesis 18:14).

People in trouble have every right to call upon God's awesome power. It honors the Lord when we ask him for "God-sized" things. But a word of caution is in order: Don't think of God's might as being displayed only when your problems are dramatically taken away. Sometimes the greater miracle occurs when you are able, because of God's sustaining strength, to endure crushing troubles. ✤

GOD'S PROMISE TO ME

- I am the God of miracles and wonders.
- I possess awesome power.

MY PRAYER TO GOD

O, Lord, you are able to do miracles and work wonders. Remind me daily of your limitless power. I serve a God who can do anything and everything. You demonstrate your infinite strength among the nations. Display that same might in my life today. If you choose not to deliver me from my trials, then give me the ability to hang on and keep trusting you.

day295

GOD HOLDS YOU CLOSE

He tends his flock like a shepherd: He gathers the lambs in his arms and carries them close to his heart; he gently leads those that have young.   ISAIAH 40:11

Some years ago an elderly college librarian put a sign on her desk offering "free hugs" to students. Initially the sign provoked only raised eyebrows. But before long a few disheartened and lonely students began to take the librarian up on her offer. Soon the trickle became a stream, and during final exam weeks it is said that there would often be a line of stressed-out students waiting for a brief bit of tender loving care.

Sometimes when everything in our lives is going south, a little TLC is all we need to make it through the day. A shoulder to cry on, the touch of a caring human being, a pat on the back, a hug. God knows that we need those things and provides people to act as his hands in this world. But in addition to that, God himself promises to gather us in his arms.

Will you let the Sovereign Lord hold you close to his heart right now? ❖

GOD'S PROMISE TO ME

- I will lead you.
- I will carry you in my arms.
- I will hold you close to my heart.

MY PRAYER TO GOD

Shepherd, you faithfully feed and guide your flock. Thank you for your protection and provision. You are gentle, and you hold me in your arms. What an amazing promise! When I am afraid or worried or tired, remind me that you desire to carry me with all tenderness.

GOD TAKES CARE OF YOU

The LORD is gracious and righteous; our God is full of compassion.   PSALM 116:5

It would be odd to write a book on God's promises for people in tough times and not mention Psalm 116. The lyrics of this ancient song describe a distressing, near-death episode using dark words such as "cords of death," "anguish of the grave," and "distress and sorrow" (116:3).

Whatever the specific situation, clearly this was not a carefree time in the psalmist's life. Nevertheless, his troubled soul found encouragement and help in remembering God's compassion. God was gracious to him. He showed favor and kindness.

If you want a stunning picture of God's compassion to the scared and hurting, read all 19 verses of this remarkable psalm. God is pictured as being absolutely attentive to the prayers of his helpless children—he "turned his ear to me" (verse 2). He is protective and gentle to us because we are precious to him.

It's when we experience God's compassion that we're able to move from problems to praise. ✤

GOD'S PROMISE TO ME

- I am compassionate.
- I want to show you mercy.

MY PRAYER TO GOD

O, Lord, you are compassionate and full of mercy. Thank you for not treating me as I deserve. You are good to your children, taking care of their every need. I praise you for being so gentle and loving. In dark times enable me to fix my mind on your proven track record of kindness.

GOD IS UTTERLY DEPENDABLE

Yet the LORD longs to be gracious to you; therefore he will rise up to show you compassion. For the LORD is a God of justice. Blessed are all who wait for him!   ISAIAH 30:18

The word *faithful* means reliable or trustworthy. A faithful person is dependable; you can count on them. A faithful husband is true to his wife. What the faithful employee promises, she will do. A faithful friend will stand by you "until the cows come home," as they say in some parts.

Of course, no flawed, fallible human is one hundred percent faithful. Only God measures up to that perfect standard. He is our faithful God who always keeps his promises (see Numbers 23:19). The Lord is devoted to us. One psalm repeats the phrase, "His love endures forever," 26 times in 26 verses (see Psalm 136).

Whatever your trouble, God is there. He will not abandon you. Turn to him and let him show you how reliable he is. ✤

GOD'S PROMISE TO ME

- I want to show you my love and compassion.
- I am a faithful God.
- You are blessed if you wait for my help.

MY PRAYER TO GOD

God, you are waiting to show me love and compassion. Why do I look elsewhere for help? You are the one, true, faithful God. Give me the courage to wait on you. Strengthen my faith as I see your faithfulness in my life.

GOD IS PERFECTLY FAIR

The leaders of Israel and the king humbled themselves and said, "The LORD is just."

2 CHRONICLES 12:6

Life sure doesn't seem very fair, does it? We all see people who passively ignore or actively despise God and enjoy abundant health, wealth, advantage and ease. And we know those who love and serve God with great passion and live under a barrage of problems. How can this be? How do we reconcile the great injustices of the world with the claim that our Maker and Ruler is always just?

This is, of course, a theological can of worms. The short answer is that just because we don't seem to see universal, perfect justice *right now* doesn't mean we never will.

One day heaven's court will convene with almighty God presiding. All the evidence for everything will be presented. Every single motive will be considered and judged. Wrong thoughts and actions will be addressed. Every honorable response will be commended. ✤

GOD'S PROMISE TO ME

- I am just and fair.
- I am the upright, faithful God who can do no wrong.

MY PRAYER TO GOD

Sometimes, Lord, when I look around, I wonder why the wicked prosper and the righteous suffer. Help me to keep me eyes on you and on the truth of your Word. You are just and fair in all you do. When I am suffering, keep me from complaining and doubting. Teach me to rely fully on your upright character.

day299

GOD'S WORD SPEAKS TO THE TROUBLED

All Scripture is God-breathed and is useful for teaching, rebuking, correcting and training in righteousness, so that the servant of God may be thoroughly equipped for every good work.   2 TIMOTHY 3:16–17

A lot of people view the Bible as nothing more than an anthology of strange, dusty, old stories compiled by the superstitious residents of another time.

But notice what the Bible claims for itself in the passage above. It says it is "God-breathed" from beginning to end. It claims also the ability to "thoroughly equip" us for life (the term was used to describe the outfitting of a boat or wagon for a long journey).

When we factor in other verses about the Bible being "alive and active" (Hebrews 4:12), we begin to realize the tremendous resource the Bible can be to those in trouble.

Are you letting God speak to you through his Word? ✤

GOD'S PROMISE TO ME

- My Word can teach you and help you.
- My Word can prepare you for good works.

MY PRAYER TO GOD

O Lord, thank you for revealing yourself to the world through the Bible. Your Word is a trustworthy and useful guide for life. Teach and correct me. Prepare me spiritually for whatever the future holds.

day300 october 27

GOD GIVES YOU SKILL FOR LIVING

For the LORD gives wisdom; from his mouth come knowledge and understanding.

PROVERBS 2:6

Supposedly mankind's knowledge is now doubling every three or four years. Unfortunately, despite living in the information age, despite computers, the Internet and an ever-increasing emphasis on education, large numbers of people continue to do really foolish things. Why?

The ancient Hebrews defined wisdom as "skill in living." To their way of thinking, wisdom was much more than just knowing facts about a subject. It was the ability to apply truth to real-life situations in a fashion that honored God.

We all need such "skill in living" every day. But we especially need wisdom when we're going through tough times. A wrong decision or foolish reaction when we're in a mess can make our troubles even worse.

Ask your wise heavenly Father to show you what's right and best. He will do it. ✤

GOD'S PROMISE TO ME

- I give you my wisdom.
- I am the source of knowledge and understanding.

MY PRAYER TO GOD

You are wise, Lord. Remind me of the truth that much of what the world calls "wisdom" runs counter to your character. You give wisdom and insight to those who seek you. How often I lack deep understanding! Heavenly Father, keep me from making bad decisions. Let me see my situation from your perspective.

GOD SUPPLIES ALL THAT YOU NEED

Grace and peace be yours in abundance through the knowledge of God and of Jesus our Lord. His divine power has given us everything we need for a godly life through our knowledge of him who called us by his own glory and goodness.　　2 PETER 1:2–3

You're going through a hard time. You feel abandoned and anxious. You feel helpless, powerless and clueless.

Most people in such straits react in one of four ways. Some embrace the philosophy of *hedonism*. They try to escape their problems using the pleasures of food, entertainment, shopping, chemicals and so on. Others give in to *pessimism* or *cynicism*. Still others pin their hopes on *humanism*, which is based on human strategies and the counsel of others. A final group resorts to *supernaturalism*—mind readers, astrology and so on.

The apostle Peter offers us a better response—pursuing an ever-deeper relationship with Jesus. In Christ we find grace and peace. As we come to know him more and more, we'll experience his goodness, and we'll better understand that Jesus provides all we need to live as we should. ❖

GOD'S PROMISE TO ME

- I will bless you with favor and peace.
- I give you everything you need for living a godly life.
- You will receive my glory and goodness.

MY PRAYER TO GOD

God, you bless me with grace and peace as I come to know Jesus more and more. Open my eyes, Lord. I want to see Jesus. Teach me how to develop a more intimate relationship with you.

GOD SAVES THOSE WHO CALL ON HIM

Everyone who calls on the name of the LORD will be saved. JOEL 2:32

It's not a flawless system by any means—what human invention *is* perfect in an imperfect world? Still, the 9–1–1 emergency telephone number is pretty amazing.

As most people know, 9–1–1 is the digit sequence North Americans dial when they find themselves in emergency situations. In most cases, depending on where we are, we can press those three numbers on any type of phone to request—and receive—help from the police, fire department or EMT personnel within a matter of minutes.

Long before the days of 9–1–1, the prophet Joel foresaw a terrible day of trouble and judgment. He urged, not a phone call to a fellow human being, but calling out, crying out directly to God. And he promised that the desperate pleas of humble people would never fall on deaf ears. The Lord, indeed, rescues all those who look to him.

Jesus later said the same thing in different words: "Whoever comes to me I will never drive away" (John 6:37).

Are you facing a hard or terrifying situation? Call on the name of the Lord. He stands ready to help. And he is able to save. ✤

GOD'S PROMISE TO ME

- If you call on my name, I will be faithful to save.

MY PRAYER TO GOD

Lord, thank you for the promise to hear and answer my cries for help. Your rescue of me may not end up looking like what I imagined, but you do promise to deliver. Grant me the faith to believe this promise with all my heart.

day**303**

GOD IS ON THE THRONE

The LORD reigns, let the nations tremble; he sits enthroned between the cherubim, let the earth shake.   PSALM 99:1

In the darkest moments of our worst times it is difficult not to give in to despair. Every direction we turn we see trouble brewing. Meanwhile, where is God? Does he see? Does he hear our cries? Does he care? Has he lost control? Why doesn't he do something?

If that is where you find yourself today, a truth that can make a real difference is the promise above. God is on his throne. He reigns over the universe and rules over your life. No matter how bleak things seem, the fact remains that God is in charge.

It's interesting to read what happened when the curtains of heaven rolled back, so to speak, and allowed the prophet Isaiah (see Isaiah 6) and the apostle John (see Revelation) a glimpse of the Lord on his throne. The experience didn't deliver either man from a life packed with trouble. But the reminder that God reigns changed each of them forever. ❖

GOD'S PROMISE TO ME

- I am the King of the universe.
- I am on my throne.

MY PRAYER TO GOD

I praise you, Lord. By faith I proclaim that you reign over all. You are on your throne, and everyone and everything is subject to you. When my faith is weak and I am tempted to despair, remind me that you are still in charge. Give me a fresh vision of your kingship over the whole world—and over my world.

day304

GOD TREATS YOU WITH TENDER MERCY

As a father has compassion on his children, so the LORD has compassion on those who fear him.   PSALM 103:13

Compassion is *awareness*. It's a big-hearted, other-centeredness that opens one's eyes to the hurting and enables one to feel their pain.

Compassion is *attitude*. It's a strong desire to reach out and alleviate the misery of others.

Compassion is *action*. It's a generous lifestyle of demonstrating tender concern to those who suffer.

We all know compassionate people. What would we do without them? But in moments of crisis, what we need most is a touch point with the source of all compassion—our loving heavenly Father. Perfect compassion is what the Lord offers us when we hurt. He will move heaven and earth to help us in our time of need. ✤

GOD'S PROMISE TO ME

- I am a father to you.
- I am tender and compassionate to those who revere me.

MY PRAYER TO GOD

You are a father to your children—a perfect Father. Thank you, Lord, for being strong and gentle, holy and approachable. When your children hurt, you hurt. Your desire is to protect me and give joy. O Father, let me know your gentle concern as I draw near to you today.

day305

GOD ABOUNDS IN LOVE

Rend your heart and not your garments. Return to the LORD your God, for he is gracious and compassionate, slow to anger and abounding in love. JOEL 2:13

Ever sinned in spectacular fashion? Stubbornly? Blatantly? Willfully? Repeatedly? If so, you've no doubt experienced the heaviness of guilt. Here's betting you also got well acquainted with shame and disgrace and condemnation.

Maybe you're even in that place today. And maybe you're keeping God at a safe distance, fearing you just might be a candidate for divine smiting.

Here's good news from Joel. God says, "Come home." God says, "Return to me." The word *return* can also be translated "repent." Repent simply means to turn around. It means to get off the wrong path and get back on the right one.

Notice God doesn't want you to merely *act* sorry. He wants you to *be* sorry—by letting your whole heart be broken by the ugliness of your sin.

And if you do return? You'll find God is gracious. He forgives. He abounds in love for you. *Abounds* means abundance. It means large amounts, lots, excess.

How about that? No matter how excessive your sin, it's never as much as God's love! ❖

GOD'S PROMISE TO ME

- No matter what you've done, you can return to me.
- I am gracious and compassionate.
- I am slow to anger and abounding in love.

MY PRAYER TO GOD

Heavenly Father, thank you for this hard-to-believe promise: You abound in love. When I blow it, I can return to you and find compassion, not anger. Cause that truth to sink deeply into my heart.

day306

november 2

GOD GIVES YOU HIS SPIRIT

When he, the Spirit of truth, comes, he will guide you into all the truth. He will not speak on his own; he will speak only what he hears, and he will tell you what is yet to come.

JOHN 16:13

Salvation would have been fantastic even if God had only canceled out our sins. We would have had ample reason for praise if God had merely guaranteed to get us to heaven one day. But God did so much more.

He not only granted full forgiveness and the staggering promise of eternity with him, he also comes to live within us, guiding us into "all the truth."

Do you see the implications? We are not alone. We are not weak. We have not been left without guidance. And it gets even better. The Spirit's presence assures us of infinite future blessings.

When life goes haywire, you don't have to scramble around looking for God. He's with you. He's in you. He's also for you. ✤

GOD'S PROMISE TO ME

- I own you.
- I have placed my Spirit in your heart.

MY PRAYER TO GOD

Your Spirit, God, lives within me. Thank you for your powerful presence. I want to live a holy life so you will feel at home in my heart. I want to yield to you. I want to follow your lead. Cause your power to flow through me today.

day**307**

GOD HAS GIVEN YOU NEW LONGINGS

So I say, walk by the Spirit, and you will not gratify the desires of the flesh. For the flesh desires what is contrary to the Spirit, and the Spirit what is contrary to the flesh. They are in conflict with each other, so that you are not to do whatever you want.

GALATIANS 5:16–17

Here's a statement no Christian can rightfully make: "I don't want to do what God says." Such a declaration simply doesn't fit with what God's Word tells us.

When we put our faith in Christ and the Holy Spirit took up residence inside us, we were fundamentally changed. We were given new life, new standing with God, a new nature and new desires—new longings to please God, to obey him, to do and be what he asks.

Do we want to worship God in the midst of difficulty? Yes! Whether we sense such a holy desire or not, the fact is, it is part of us. Do we feel like worshiping? Maybe not on the surface, but worship is the deep longing of our redeemed hearts. Such a desire must be in us—because God is in us.

The goal of the walk of faith is to live out the new longings that God has already planted within us. At no time is this more crucial than when we are going through difficulty. ✤

GOD'S PROMISE TO ME

- I have given you my Spirit.
- As you listen to the Spirit's counsel, you will live as you should.

MY PRAYER TO GOD

Thank you, God, for coming to live inside me. Teach me to make decisions based, not on feelings, but on the facts of your Word. Show me how to follow the leading of the Spirit. Continue to help me understand the truth that you have filled me with longings that honor you.

day308

november 4

GOD HAS GIVEN YOU A NEW IDENTITY

Our citizenship is in heaven. And we eagerly await a Savior from there, the Lord Jesus Christ.   PHILIPPIANS 3:20

What do Christians mean when they say, "this world is not my home"? What is the Bible saying when it calls us "citizens of heaven"?

In 42 BC the Macedonian city of Philippi became a Roman colony. A few years later the Emperor Octavian ordered thousands of Italian people to relocate there. Though far from their homeland these expatriates enjoyed all the privileges of full Roman citizenship.

The apostle Paul used this situation to help the Philippian Christians understand that followers of Christ are "foreigners and exiles" (1 Peter 2:11) in this world. We're here only temporarily, and only by our "Emperor's" orders. Our true citizenship is in heaven (see John 14:2–3). Our current troubles and trials will not last forever. One day our service will be complete, and we will be summoned home. ✣

GOD'S PROMISE TO ME

• I have made you a citizen of heaven — this world is not your home.

MY PRAYER TO GOD

What joy to know that I'm listed among the residents of eternity. I praise you, God! Thank you for giving me eternal life. Though this life is filled with trouble, I know I'm only passing through. Grant me an eternal mindset so I can endure the temporal difficulties that come my way.

GOD VALUES YOUR OBEDIENCE

Does the LORD delight in burnt offerings and sacrifices as much as in obeying the LORD? To obey is better than sacrifice, and to heed is better than the fat of rams. 1 SAMUEL 15:22

Through the prophet Samuel, God gave Saul, the new king of Israel, crystal clear instructions: (1) Attack and defeat the godless city Amalek, and (2) completely destroy everything in it.

Saul promptly obeyed God's first directive. But then he decided to "improve on" the second. He spared Amalek's king, and he kept alive the nation's choicest livestock, intending to offer those sheep and cattle to God in sacrifices.

God was not impressed by Saul's plan. He was not pleased with Saul's independent thinking. Through Samuel God reminded Saul—and all believers everywhere—of a great truth. More than anything else God wants our obedience.

Why? Because when we faithfully carry out the commands of God, it demonstrates that we trust God. And remember, without faith, it is impossible to please him (see Hebrews 11:6). Jesus said that complete obedience to the Lord is the one sure proof of our love for him (see John 14:21). If we say we love God, if we claim to trust him, we must obey him. ✤

GOD'S PROMISE TO ME

• Obedience to me brings blessing.

MY PRAYER TO GOD

God, forgive the times when I try to rationalize your clear words or justify my disobedient actions. Give me an obedient heart that loves and trusts you above all else.

GOD WANTS YOU TO EXPERIENCE ABUNDANT LIFE

I have come that they may have life, and have it to the full.   JOHN 10:10

Far too many believers in Christ are living what writer Dallas Willard has called "vampire Christianity." By that phrase he means they are preoccupied with the blood of Christ, but not so much the life of Christ.

Jesus did not come only to forgive our past misdeeds. And he didn't come just to offer us the future hope of heavenly glory. He came, as the promise above states, to give us life now—life in all its fullness—a richer, deeper, more satisfying existence.

If Christianity is only about a pardon for sins and a ticket to heaven one day, that's wonderful news—but not much help when your life is unraveling. On the other hand, if knowing Christ brings meaning, clarity and perspective then even hard times can be profitable. Such times are not fun, certainly, but through difficulties, we experience and encounter the one who is life itself (see John 14:7). ❖

GOD'S PROMISE TO ME

• I offer you a rich, satisfying life.

MY PRAYER TO GOD

Jesus, your purpose in coming was to give me a full and meaningful life. Forgive me for the times I settle for a drab, ho-hum life or am so preoccupied with the stuff of earth that I fail to seek you or even hear you.

day311

YOUR RIGHTEOUSNESS IS LIKE THE SUN

The path of the righteous is like the morning sun, shining ever brighter till the full light of day. But the way of the wicked is like deep darkness; they do not know what makes them stumble. PROVERBS 4:18 – 19

The book of Proverbs is a mother lode of practical wisdom. It offers us priceless counsel by repeatedly contrasting one kind of person with another: the wise man with the fool; the sluggard with the hard worker; the prudent and the simple.

In the broadest sense, however, Proverbs really contrasts two radically different lifestyles: the way of the righteous person — who lives according to God's law — versus the way of the wicked person — who rejects God's rule over his or her life.

The differences are nowhere more startling than in today's promise. There the path ("the way of wisdom," verse 11) of the righteous person is described as well-lit — with that illumination intensifying over time. The "way of the wicked" (verse 19), meanwhile, is said to be the way of "darkness." It's worth noting here that the writer uses a word that means "a thick, deep, almost tangible darkness" (see Exodus 10:22).

In other words, when we live as God intends, we see clearly and live with security. When we take a different path, we stumble (verse 19) and fall. The promise? Follow God's path, and you will walk in the light. ✤

GOD'S PROMISE TO ME

• When you walk with me, I will illumine your path.

MY PRAYER TO GOD

God, I want to be wise, not foolish. I want to walk on the righteous path, in the light of your truth. When I start to stray, discipline me in your love.

day**312**

GOD PRODUCES CHANGE IN AND THROUGH YOU

I am the vine; you are the branches. If you remain in me and I in you, you will bear much fruit; apart from me you can do nothing.　　　　　　　　　　JOHN 15:5

One of its most appealing features of the gospel has to be the prospect of change. Old, wrong attitudes and habits are replaced. New abilities and opportunities for impact are given. In short, God wants to work in us and through us.

In describing this process of spiritual growth, the Bible often uses agricultural imagery. For example, in the words of Christ above, as we mature in our faith, we bear "fruit." But notice what Jesus says: We must "remain" in him. Separate a branch from its life-giving vine, and the branch not only ceases to bear fruit, it withers and dies.

In this same chapter of John, Christ reveals that branches must be pruned to increase their production of fruit (see verse 2). This is an unsettling image and a painful thought, but the idea seems to be twofold. There can be no growth or fruitfulness without pain. The Lord uses our troubles for his glory and our good. ❖

GOD'S PROMISE TO ME

- You will bear fruit when you remain in me.

MY PRAYER TO GOD

Please, change me, Lord. Use me. Apart from you, I can do nothing. Help me to cling to you when times are tough, knowing that faithfulness always leads to fruitfulness.

GOD GIVES YOU THE ABILITY TO LOVE

The fruit of the Spirit is love.   GALATIANS 5:22

In 1 John 4:16, we read that God is love. His entire nature is wrapped up in love. Yet we must not picture a grandfatherly character who dispenses good feelings with lollipops. God is all-powerful, all-knowing, holy and just. Yet because God is perfect, all of his characteristics are perfect. God is completely holy and perfectly just while also being totally loving.

As human beings, we cannot be perfectly anything. The Bible promises, however, that the Holy Spirit will produce love in our lives because God himself has come to take up residence in us.

What will that look like? A funny thing about love is that it can't stay put. It needs to be given and given and given. Because of God's love within us, we have an unlimited source of love from which to draw. As the apostle John explains, "We love because he first loved us" (1 John 4:19). This is a love that thinks of others first, a love that cares, a love that sacrifices. This kind of love characterizes God's people. ❖

GOD'S PROMISE TO ME

- My nature is to love.
- When my Spirit lives in you, you will live in my love.
- My Spirit produces the fruit of love in you.

MY PRAYER TO GOD

God, you are love. Nothing will happen to me that is not permitted within the scope of your love. I want to overflow with the constant refreshing fountain of your love so that it will spill out in my actions and words. Even in difficult circumstances with difficult people, help me find the path of love.

GOD GIVES YOU SUPERNATURAL JOY

The fruit of the Spirit is ... joy.   GALATIANS 5:22

If it's short-term pleasure or laughter you want, well then, you can almost certainly find it, and God need not be involved. Entertainment, comfort, luxury—these experiences are readily available in our culture. Happiness is a bit more tricky. Circumstances have to fall into place just so—but happiness can be found for brief periods.

Then there's the rare jewel of joy. Joy is the quiet delight that comes from knowing we are right with God. It is a deep pleasure of soul that comes from living consciously in God's presence (see Psalm 16:11). Joy isn't giddiness or feeling tingly; it is an abiding radiance and elation that fills us when we give the Spirit of God total freedom to work in us however he wants.

For many Christians—especially those in crisis—joy is the most elusive of fruits. But it need not be. The Spirit of God specializes in producing this quality in the people of God. Will you let him have his way in you today? ❖

GOD'S PROMISE TO ME

• When you allow my Spirit to reign in your life, I will fill you with joy.

MY PRAYER TO GOD

Holy Spirit, I need the joy that only you can give. Forgive me for the times I let circumstances control my moods. Let me experience your presence today and the quiet thrill that comes from walking with you.

day315

GOD GIVES YOU WONDERFUL PEACE

The fruit of the Spirit is ... peace.   GALATIANS 5:22

The world is not terribly impressed with Christian t-shirts, billboards and bumper stickers. And, truth be told, many unbelievers are actually turned off by these impersonal attempts at witnessing. However, the world is stunned when they see a Christian overflowing with peace despite personal crisis. "Her life is falling apart, but she isn't. How come?" "If I were in his shoes, I'd be a nervous wreck, but he is so calm. Why?"

The peace that the Holy Spirit produces within us is supernatural tranquility of soul. Storms can be raging all about us, but within us is the calm assurance that God has already saved us from our worst predicament—sin and death. Would he rescue us for the world to come only to turn around and abandon us in this world? Of course not!

The Spirit-filled Christian is peaceful because he or she knows the perfect love that drives away fear (see 1 John 4:18). Ask God to give you this soothing and eye-catching quality. ✤

GOD'S PROMISE TO ME

- When you give my Spirit free reign in your life, you will know my perfect peace.

MY PRAYER TO GOD

I want to be marked by your peace, Lord. I need it so that I don't worry and fret. More than that, I need it for your glory—so that others might see the wonderful comfort and assurance available only in you. Teach me how to rest in the knowledge that you are in control.

day316

GOD GIVES YOU UNEARTHLY PATIENCE

The fruit of the Spirit is . . . forbearance.   GALATIANS 5:22

Why does it seem that trouble always rears its head just when we start to make real progress? And why do so many difficulties linger for what seems an eternity?

Why are some people so annoying? And what recourse do we have when we can't swap the irritating folks in our lives—family members, co-workers, neighbors—for a more congenial bunch?

When we're in these kinds of situations, when we're feeling stuck, restless and unable to change anything, we need the miracle of God's patience.

The word the apostle Paul uses here—*forbearance*—is a word that means endurance, patience or perseverance. This is the quality of being long-suffering.

The next time circumstances put you in an unpleasant "holding pattern," the next time an annoying person pushes your buttons, relinquish control of the situation and your own emotions and offer it to the One who has an endless supply of patience. The results really are miraculous. ✤

GOD'S PROMISE TO ME

• Those controlled by my Spirit can experience unearthly patience.

MY PRAYER TO GOD

I want to know your patience, Lord. Forgive me for getting irritated with situations and people. I want to be even-keeled. I want to be willing to wait for you no matter how long it takes.

day317

GOD SUPPLIES YOU WITH HIS KINDNESS AND GOODNESS

The fruit of the Spirit is ... kindness, goodness. GALATIANS 5:22

On that ghastly Friday morning, which ironically has become known as "Good Friday," Jesus is a swollen, bloody mess. Most of his friends hightailed it hours ago, leaving him alone to face the physical agony of crucifixion, the emotional anguish of a jeering crowd and the spiritual horror of separation from God the Father.

Yet during this entire nightmare, Jesus has responded, well, *strangely*. On the way to his execution he has paused to console a group of grief-stricken women. He has used what little breath he is able to catch to pray for those who have been so merciless to him. He has demonstrated compassion and forgiveness to a criminal dying at his side. And he has taken pains to see that his grief-stricken mother is cared for by a friend.

In the ultimate tough time, Jesus models kindness and goodness. And because his Spirit lives in us, we also have the capacity to use personal tragedy as an opportunity to care for others. ✤

GOD'S PROMISE TO ME

- Those controlled by my Spirit will be marked by pure kindness and goodness.

MY PRAYER TO GOD

Cause your kindness and goodness to flow through me, Lord. It is not natural for me to think of others or to think of glorifying you when my life is filled with pain. Teach me to live supernaturally. I want to be selfless like you, Jesus—always seeking to bless others.

day318

november 14

GOD PROMISES THE FRUIT OF FAITHFULNESS

The fruit of the Spirit is ... faithfulness. GALATIANS 5:22

Throughout the Bible we read of God's great faithfulness to his people. Moses told the Israelites, "Know therefore that the LORD your God is God; he is the faithful God, keeping his covenant of love to a thousand generations of those who love him and keep his commandments" (Deuteronomy 7:9). In this verse we get a clue about what faithfulness means—it has to do with trustworthiness, keeping promises, dependability, reliability.

In Jesus' parable of the shrewd manager, he pointed out that those who are faithful in small matters will be entrusted with greater responsibilities (see Luke 16:10). Faithfulness begins with the little things. The Bible promises that as we remain faithful, we will one day share in Christ's kingdom: "We have come to share in Christ, if indeed we hold our original conviction firmly to the very end" (Hebrews 3:14).

As we pray for the fruit of faithfulness in our lives and those of others, we are praying that we—and they—will be trustworthy, responsible and reliable. We also pray that as others notice this faithfulness, God will continue to entrust us with greater responsibility for building his kingdom. ✤

GOD'S PROMISE TO ME

- My Spirit grows the fruit of faithfulness in your life.
- The fruit of faithfulness will keep you until the end.

MY PRAYER TO GOD

Lord, I pray that I will be known as a faithful person, one who is trustworthy, dependable, reliable and who keeps my word. May I continue to trust you unwaveringly and so receive what you have promised.

day**319**

GOD GIVES YOU THE CAPACITY TO BE GENTLE

The fruit of the Spirit is ... gentleness.   GALATIANS 5:22–23

In Jesus' Sermon on the Mount he told his followers, "Blessed are the meek, for they will inherit the earth" (Matthew 5:5). And later in his ministry he characterized himself as "gentle and humble in heart" (Matthew 11:29). Many Bible versions use the word *meek* for the word translated as "gentle" in Matthew 5:5. Our culture often thinks of *meek* as weak and spineless. Gentle, however, gives a sense of tempered strength. When Jesus angrily cleared the temple, he stayed focused on his goal, and his anger was directed appropriately. Gentleness can be strong when it needs to be.

God promises to bless those who are gentle and humble. That's just the opposite of what we see in the world. Often those who succeed are wealthy, harsh and willing to step on anyone to get ahead. But in God's economy those who are gentle will receive everything—the "earth" refers to the future inheritance of God's kingdom.

When we ask for the fruit of gentleness in our lives, we are praying for an attitude of humility that, while strong, is considerate toward others. As we see in the example of Jesus, gentleness can be tough, disciplined and powerful. ✤

GOD'S PROMISE TO ME

- My Spirit grows the fruit of gentleness in your life.
- Great blessings are in store for those who are strong in their faith and gentle in their relationships with others.

MY PRAYER TO GOD

Lord, thank you for dealing with your people gently, even though you are at the same time sovereign, supreme, holy and just. I want to be a person of principle, a person of strong faith, who stands firm for you, and yet a person with powerful gentleness.

day320 november 16

GOD GIVES YOU SELF-CONTROL

The fruit of the Spirit is ... self-control.   GALATIANS 5:22–23

In a very real sense, without self-control it is difficult to have the other eight fruit of the Spirit growing in our lives. The Holy Spirit works to grow the fruit of self-control so that we can restrain our natural instincts—lashing out in anger or yielding to temptation. Self-control helps us, human as we are and provoked as we can be, to act in a Christlike manner.

When we lack self-control Satan declares open season on our lives. He sends in temptations and frustrations by the truckload and then stands back happily to watch our not-so-godly reactions. On the other hand, Peter wrote that we should add "to knowledge, self-control" (2 Peter 1:6). That's our defense against temptation.

As we ask for self-control in our lives, we need to trust that God will equip us to act and react correctly to the temptations and frustrations we face. ❖

GOD'S PROMISE TO ME

- My Spirit grows the fruit of self-control in your life.
- Godly self-control will lead to patient endurance and godliness.

MY PRAYER TO GOD

Lord, thank you for the fruit of self-control that the Holy Spirit grows in us. Help me to respond to life with the self-control that you give me.

YOU WERE BOUGHT BY THE BLOOD OF CHRIST

Now in Christ Jesus you who once were far away have been brought near by the blood of Christ. EPHESIANS 2:13

What is the most expensive item you've ever purchased? A house? A car? Perhaps you quipped that you paid for the item with your blood, sweat and tears. Because it was so costly, this item undoubtedly has great value to you.

Each person who acknowledges their sin becomes the most expensive "item" God has ever purchased. The precious blood of his Son was the payment demanded to free us from our sin debt—one we couldn't pay ourselves. This means we have great value to God. Once we were estranged, now—through the blood of Jesus—we "have been brought near."

The next time you're feeling as if you're not valued, consider the price God paid for your life. It cost him his Son to show just how much you're worth. ❧

GOD'S PROMISE TO ME

- I bought you. You are mine.
- You have great worth.

MY PRAYER TO GOD

Lord, it's difficult for me sometimes to comprehend such an amazing act of love. Since you paid the price for my sin, I choose to live for you.

day322

november 18

YOU WERE CREATED FOR GOD

For in him all things were created: things in heaven and on earth, visible and invisible, whether thrones or powers or rulers or authorities; all things have been created through him and for him. COLOSSIANS 1:16

Many times in the news you read or hear of people who are described as "self-made" people. These include successful businesspeople and prominent actors or artists who worked their way up from the bottom and established great careers. "I did it my way" is the motto of many.

If we're honest, we sometimes like to think of ourselves as "self-made" people whenever someone compliments our skill or accomplishments. But according to the apostle Paul there is one inescapable fact we can't overlook: We were created by God for God's own purposes.

So what does this mean? It means our lives are not our own. God has a unique purpose for each one of us. He desires that we live out the truth of this by first acknowledging his sovereignty—his right to rule over us and overrule our plans.

Is he Lord over *your* life? ❖

GOD'S PROMISE TO ME

- I created you for a purpose.

MY PRAYER TO GOD

Lord, you created me for a reason. Help me be all that you created me to be.

326

GOD ENCOURAGES THOSE WHO WAIT ON HIM

I wait for the LORD, my whole being waits, and in his word I put my hope.
PSALM 130:5

After a while tough times can make you feel like a boxer in a brutal championship bout. For a short time you were holding your own — even getting in a good counterpunch now and then. But for the last few rounds your opponent has trapped you up against the ropes and come close to knocking you out. Now you're slumped in your corner, so weary you don't know who or where you are. The fight's not even close to being over. People are shouting instructions and trying to give you encouragement, but if you are going to make it to the next round, much less the end of the fight, you'll need much more than verbal motivation.

When you endure a long-term difficulty, you'll understand and relate to this analogy. Thankfully, God sees and knows the difficulty you face. That's why he encourages you to wait for the strength and help that can only come through him.

If you're worn-out and ready to quit, ask God to help you keep waiting. ✤

GOD'S PROMISE TO ME

- I encourage those who wait on me.
- You will never wait for me in vain.

MY PRAYER TO GOD

O Lord, I need your limitless strength so that I can keep going even in the midst of hard times. The only way to experience your strength is to wait on you.

day324 november 20

GOD'S WORD KEEPS YOU FROM SIN

I have hidden your word in my heart that I might not sin against you. PSALM 119:11

In the game of football it's called "piling on"—you're already down when suddenly you get pummeled again by your opponents. In real life, it's called "spiritual warfare," and it's often much more subtle. You're suffering through a hard time when suddenly the enemy comes at you with what actually looks like *relief.*

Ah, how vulnerable we are in such moments! "After all I've had to endure lately, I think I deserve a little break." How easy it is to rationalize. "Would it really be so wrong for me to _____? Why not?"

Of course this is the nature of temptation. On the front end sin looks "heavenly." On the back side it is always makes bad situations worse.

Our only hope is living out the promise above. By filling our hearts and minds with the truth of God's Word, we are able to recognize the enemy's lies. This is how we stay pure in hard or tempting times (see Matthew 4:1–11). This is how we avoid Satan's deceptive attempts to hit us when we're down. ✤

GOD'S PROMISE TO ME

- I have given you my Word.
- Hiding my Word in your heart will keep you from wrong attitudes and actions.

MY PRAYER TO GOD

God, when I hide your Word in my heart, I can keep from sin. Grant me the wisdom to seek you and to hide your Word in my heart. I need discernment to apply your truth to everyday situations, especially when I am going through difficult times.

GOD HAS SET YOU FREE IN CHRIST

To the Jews who had believed him, Jesus said, "If you hold to my teaching, you are really my disciples. Then you will know the truth, and the truth will set you free." ... So if the Son sets you free, you will be free indeed. JOHN 8:31–32,36

The United States Penitentiary near Marion, Illinois, is a somber sight. Its windowless buildings, imposing guard towers and series of barbed-wire fences remind us that the human heart is capable of great evil and that wrong choices have devastating consequences.

But Christ's words above remind us of another, greater truth. People trapped in destructive lifestyles, and those enslaved by guilt and shame, can experience ultimate freedom.

Hardened sinners can be released from sin's terrible penalty and power. Weary religious folks can be unshackled from their exhausting, futile efforts to live by a million "do's and don'ts."

Christ came to set us free. Free from condemnation and shame. Free from the impossibility of trying to earn God's approval or please fickle people. Free to marvel at the wonder of forgiven sin. Free to enjoy the rich banquet of his endless grace.

Are you living in freedom today? ✤

GOD'S PROMISE TO ME

- My truth will set you free.
- The freedom I give is true freedom.

MY PRAYER TO GOD

O Lord, this is an amazing truth! You have set me free to obey you. Teach me to believe the paradox that I am most free when I am living as your servant. Help me to better understand your grace.

GOD CAN CLEANSE YOU COMPLETELY

"Come now, let us settle the matter," says the LORD. "Though your sins are like scarlet, they shall be as white as snow; though they are red as crimson, they shall be like wool."

ISAIAH 1:18

You've *seen* them ... those commercials featuring miracle stain removers. According to the pitch it doesn't matter what substance you're trying to clean up—wolf blood, cat vomit, jet fuel, road tar, etc. "If you'll just use Mess-B-Gone (only $19.95 if you call in the next 10 minutes!), your carpet or sofa or flat panel TV will be clean in a flash!"

Perhaps you've tried such products, only to realize that Mess-Be-Gone is better at removing money from your wallet than it is at removing maple syrup from your college diploma.

We all have legitimate reasons to be skeptical when an offer sounds too good to be true. But here's a pledge you can take to the bank: God is willing to cleanse any and every sin. No act is too awful, too big, too outrageous.

It's true. Even *that* sin, *that* unspeakable act, is forgivable. Except for the sin of refusing to trust in Christ, you can't imagine a sin that God can't pardon. "God's grace," as the old hymn says, "is greater than all our sin."

What terrible mess would you like to bring to God for a miracle clean-up today? ♣

GOD'S PROMISE TO ME

• I will blot out and take away the stain of sin.

MY PRAYER TO GOD

God, what an amazing promise! What an incredible Savior! Thank you for dealing fully and finally with my sin. Thank you for forgiveness in Christ.

GOD HELPS YOU RESIST TEMPTATION

With flattery he will corrupt those who have violated the covenant, but the people who know their God will firmly resist him. DANIEL 11:32

Because of some long-term unwise choices, the Walkers are now facing serious financial troubles. Their economic woes have been the source of constant tension and stress at home. Interestingly, in the midst of this major money crunch, Denise has gained thirty pounds and is thinking about reneging on a financial commitment to her church's building campaign. Meanwhile, Donald has been escaping regularly into the world of Internet pornography while he considers partnering with an old college buddy in a "can't lose" (highly questionable) business deal.

The Walkers' situation reminds us that when we feel weakened and worried by the pressures and problems of life, certain temptations can seem irresistible. We're tempted to compromise our principles. But the Old Testament prophet Daniel reminds us that people who know God can resist temptation because they recognize the enemy's hand in it.

How would you counsel the Walkers using the promise above? ❖

GOD'S PROMISE TO ME

- Temptations are a fact of life.
- I will enable you to resist temptation.

MY PRAYER TO GOD

My temptations are not unique; everyone struggles, Lord. I want to know you so well that I will be able to say a firm "no" to temptation.

day**328**

GOD HAS PROVIDED ALL YOU NEED

Praise be to the God and Father of our Lord Jesus Christ, who has blessed us in the heavenly realms with every spiritual blessing in Christ. EPHESIANS 1:3

Maybe you've seen on TV the cycling enthusiasts who race annually from California to New York. Averaging some 20 hours of furious pedaling daily, these amazing athletes zip through deserts, mountains and cities—almost three thousand miles total—in less than one week.

How in the world do they do it? Here's the secret: Each rider is followed by a three- to four-person support team in a fully-equipped RV. Everyone and everything the cyclist might need—a coach, mechanic, massage therapist, trainer/nurse, dietician, chef, cheerleader, plus food, water, and spare bikes and parts—can be found in that chase vehicle.

In a similar but much more glorious way, God has provided us with all the spiritual blessings needed to make it through the most difficult parts of the race of life. ✤

GOD'S PROMISE TO ME

- I am the God who blesses.
- I have already given you every spiritual blessing you need to live in a fallen world.

MY PRAYER TO GOD

O God, thank you for your abundant blessings. How easy it is to forget that you are the source of every good thing. Because of Christ, I have been given every spiritual blessing I need. When I feel empty and dry, remind me that you stand ready to give me whatever I need.

GOD WANTS TO SHOW YOU THE GOOD PATH

This is what the LORD says: "Stand at the crossroads and look; ask for the ancient paths, ask where the good way is, and walk in it, and you will find rest for your souls."

JEREMIAH 6:16

The speed limit is 65, but you set the cruise on 80 because you want to get home. After five minutes you see flashing red lights behind you.

On the way to work you realize you left your laptop at home with the browser open. Just then you get a text from your spouse that reads: "Would you care to explain these emails I'm reading on your computer?"

Writing to the people of Israel who were facing major trouble because of their refusal to live as God commanded, Jeremiah stated a simple truth: It's only when we walk in God's ways that we find real rest for our souls.

When we ignore the rules, we eventually pay the consequences. That's true on the road, in marriage—anywhere in life. We will reap what we sow.

Are you anxious right now? Are you fearful of being found out and paying a huge price? Here's an easy cure, a sure path to peace. You are at a crossroads. Stop. Ask God to show you his ancient, proven, good way. Then determine, by his grace and with his help, to walk that path and no other. ✤

GOD'S PROMISE TO ME

- I will show you the way in which to live.
- If you live my way, you will find rest for your soul.

MY PRAYER TO GOD

Father, forgive me for foolishly thinking I can ignore your truth and find blessing and peace. There is no true rest for my soul unless and until I submit to your will and your plan for my life. Grant me the grace and courage to do that.

day330

GOD HELPS WHEN YOU'RE OVERWHELMED

Our God, will you not judge them? For we have no power to face this vast army that is attacking us. We do not know what to do, but our eyes are on you. 2 CHRONICLES 20:12

In one of the darkest moments of his life, with a vast enemy army advancing against his nation, King Jehoshaphat prayed the above prayer. He looked toward heaven instead of just at the seemingly invincible enemy.

Ever feel like that—alarmed and confused by looming troubles? Or perhaps you're feeling overwhelmed and defeated after a series of painful circumstances. If that describes you today, follow in Jehoshaphat's footsteps. Turn your eyes to the One who truly is invincible. God knows how you feel: depleted and sorely in need of assistance. As Jehoshaphat said, "We do not know what to do, but our eyes are on you."

Feeling at the end of your resources? Instead of focusing on fear, focus on the Father. Ask him to provide help in your time of need. ✣

GOD'S PROMISE TO ME

- When trouble comes, keep your eyes on me.
- I will help you.

MY PRAYER TO GOD

Lord, sometimes I feel so overwhelmed, all I can say is, "help!" When I don't know what to do, help me trust you.

day331

GOD GIVES CONFIRMATION THAT YOU ARE HIS CHILD

So you are no longer a slave, but God's child; and since you are his child, God has made you also an heir. GALATIANS 4:7

Nothing can send a believer into a tailspin of doubt like long-term trials or short-term crises.

Why is all this happening to me? I can't believe a loving God would let his own children go through such trauma—so, maybe that means I'm not really his child?

In the midst of such turmoil we need the comfort of the promise above. It is found in the midst of the apostle Paul's explanation of our spiritual adoption into God's family at salvation. For an adoption to be legal in ancient Roman culture, seven witnesses were required to attest to the validity of the proceedings.

In essence, Paul is saying that we are truly God's children. God has made us heirs with his Son Jesus. That means we have all of the legal rights that Jesus has.

If you are struggling in this area, ask a friend today, "How and where do you see God at work in my life?" ♣

GOD'S PROMISE TO ME

• My Spirit provides assurance that you are my child.

MY PRAYER TO GOD

O Father, in times of trial, I am bombarded by doubts. Tough times often make me wonder if I really am your child. Thank you for the presence of your Spirit, who provides assurance that I belong to you.

day332 november 28

GOD'S SPIRIT GIVES YOU INSIGHT

This is what we speak, not in words taught us by human wisdom but in words taught by the Spirit, explaining spiritual realities with Spirit-taught words. 1 CORINTHIANS 2:13

Question: What do people of the world do when facing trouble? Answer: Typically, they seek worldly counsel.

They watch talk shows, read advice columns, call psychics, consult horoscopes, question friends, buy self-help books, and/or attend assorted seminars.

This is not to say that all of these sources of counsel are always wrong; the point is there is a much more reliable and excellent source of ultimate knowledge. He's called the Holy Spirit, and he lives inside everyone who trusts Jesus as Savior.

The question then is why would any Christian settle for fallible counsel and insight when they already have internal access to infallible truth and knowledge?

If you've got questions, the Spirit has answers. ♣

GOD'S PROMISE TO ME

- I have given you my Spirit.
- My Spirit will show you the depths of my blessings.

MY PRAYER TO GOD

God, you have given me your Holy Spirit. Thank you! What would I do without your presence in my life? Only your Spirit can help me understand all the spiritual blessings I've been given.

GOD QUENCHES YOUR THIRSTY SOUL

Whoever drinks the water I give them will never thirst. Indeed, the water I give them will become in them a spring of water welling up to eternal life.   JOHN 4:14

The renowned British author C. S. Lewis once observed that if we find within ourselves longings that nothing in this world can satisfy, the only logical conclusion is that we were created for another world.

Of course all of us have longings. Look around at all the fidgety, searching people. Look also at the countless ways people try to fill the gnawing emptiness inside them.

Now observe Jesus of Nazareth, standing at Jacob's well conversing with a woman with a dried-up spirit. Listen as he proclaims himself the solution for her soul's deepest longings.

Tough times provide the unexpected blessing of putting restless people in touch with their soul's desperate condition. If you can relate to such spiritual thirst you would do well to accept Jesus' offer of living water. Your problems likely will not change, but you will. ❖

GOD'S PROMISE TO ME

- I alone can quench your spiritual thirst.
- I give eternal life.

MY PRAYER TO GOD

Jesus, you are the only one who can satisfy a thirsty soul. The life that you give supplies continual refreshment. Teach me the holy habit of looking to you alone for whatever my soul is thirsty for. Make me a source of encouragement and help to those who are spiritually dry.

GOD IS SHAPING YOUR CHARACTER

We all, who with unveiled faces contemplate the Lord's glory, are being transformed into his image with ever-increasing glory, which comes from the Lord, who is the Spirit.

2 CORINTHIANS 3:18

It begins as a big, shapeless block of marble. Over an extended period of time, the sculptor chips and smoothes the stone. At last the day comes for the great unveiling. The giant covering is yanked away, and there stands a breathtaking, lifelike masterpiece—a reflection of the artist's genius.

In effect this is what God is doing in and with us. He is the great craftsman, dedicated to taking our ordinary, unimpressive lives and transforming them into unique and eternal works of art. More precisely he is about the business of making us just like his Son.

The process itself is painstaking and at times painful. But the point—the glory of God—and the product—a fully redeemed and re-created life—make it worth whatever price we must pay.

Are you willing to pay the price? ❖

GOD'S PROMISE TO ME

- My Spirit is working in you.
- I am conforming you to my image, so that you will reflect my glory.

MY PRAYER TO GOD

O Father, thank you for loving me enough to work in me. Make me aware of your presence. Make me cooperative with your indwelling Spirit. I can't always see signs of change, but I pray that others can.

day335

GOD'S CHILDREN WILL FACE TROUBLE IN THIS LIFE

Very truly I tell you, it is for your good that I am going away. Unless I go away, the Advocate will not come to you; but if I go, I will send him to you. JOHN 16:7

A lot of Christians are disappointed or even disillusioned in their faith because somewhere along the line they bought into the popular fallacy that being a child of God guarantees a life of unending blessing: health, wealth, comfort and ease.

Nothing could be further from the truth. In the book of Job we read, "Yet man is born to trouble as surely as sparks fly upward" (Job 5:7). Indeed, suffering is a fact of life in a fallen world.

Consider the names and descriptions given the Holy Spirit. Jesus described him as our Advocate (see John 14:16,26). Other passages and/or Bible translations call him our Helper, our Comforter and Counselor. Such terms and phrases clearly imply we will routinely find ourselves in desperate situations.

We need to adjust our expectations accordingly. We will face trouble, but we will never be alone. ♣

GOD'S PROMISE TO ME

• My Spirit will be with you in all your times of trouble.

MY PRAYER TO GOD

I should never be surprised by trouble, Lord. The Bible and human experience indicate that hard times are to be expected in this life. Thank you for sending your Spirit. I do not go through difficulty alone. You are with me always—to counsel, help and pray for me.

day336

GOD WILL GIVE YOU PERFECT COUNSEL

Blessed are those who find wisdom, those who gain understanding.   Proverbs 3:13

For many decades, millions of desperate and confused people sought guidance from two syndicated columns: "Ask Ann Landers" and "Dear Abby." Some people have actually built their lives upon the guidance they received from various advice columnists. Are advice columnists the best we can do for gaining wise counsel?

If we want surefire counsel based in truth, if we want guidance that works, we need the wisdom that comes straight from God. This wisdom is the only advice that will satisfy us. As the above proverb promises, "blessed are those who find wisdom."

If you're scratching your head as you ponder your next move, take your questions to God himself. As you listen to the Word and the Spirit, you'll eventually know the best course of action. ✤

GOD'S PROMISE TO ME

- I will give you wisdom.
- I will gladly show you what to do.

MY PRAYER TO GOD

O Lord, when times get tough, it is hard to know what to do. I need wisdom from above. I praise you for being the source of all wisdom. Help me to remember your willingness to help in my times of trial.

GOD HAS A PLAN FOR YOU

I cry out to God Most High, to God, who vindicates me.   PSALM 57:2

The most famous and most distributed gospel tract in the world is Campus Crusade's *The Four Spiritual Laws*, which begins with these words: "God loves you and offers a wonderful plan for your life."

What a great reminder of the truth that God has a unique purpose for each of us. Yes, he has plans for you—a special place for you to fit, a key role for you to play in his divine drama.

This is true no matter what trials you're facing right now. In fact, because of God's sovereignty even your messes are somehow a part of God's cosmic plotline.

David grasped this truth. As a result, he was able to look heavenward and express trust in a time of great personal trouble.

God *will* fulfill his purpose for you. He really does have a wonderful plan for your life. Latch on to this extraordinary promise today. ♣

GOD'S PROMISE TO ME

- I will fulfill my purpose in your life.

MY PRAYER TO GOD

O God, in the midst of tough times, it's hard to remember that you're in control. You sit enthroned above the heavens and will fulfill your purpose in my life. Instead of complaining and doubting, I will wait patiently for your goodness and trust confidently in your infinite power.

GOD WILL HONOR YOUR INTEGRITY

The blameless spend their days under the LORD's care, and their inheritance will endure forever.   PSALM 37:18

Maybe last month it was a relational disaster. This week it might be trouble at work. Next week could bring a health crisis. After awhile the unrelenting stream of tough times takes its toll.

"What's the use?" we cry. "I try to do right, and for what? Life keeps beating me up. I can't get ahead. I'm not sure it pays to try to live a godly life. I struggle as much or more than my neighbors who could care less about God!"

Troubles certainly have a way of wearing us down. And, if we're not careful, they can erode even our bedrock convictions. The promise above is a good reminder of why we must be vigilant not to take ethical shortcuts.

Those who maintain their integrity, those who continue doing right—even when everything and everyone else is wrong—will one day receive the ultimate reward. ❖

GOD'S PROMISE TO ME

- I will take care of my innocent children.
- You will receive an eternal reward.

MY PRAYER TO GOD

Life doesn't seem fair at times, Lord. And integrity often seems like it doesn't matter. But it does matter, God. You see everything. Nothing escapes your gaze. You promise to care for the pure and reward the faithful. Give me the spiritual tenacity to hang in there until the day when you exalt those who steadfastly trust in you.

day**339**

GOD HAS DETERMINED THE LENGTH OF YOUR LIFE

Show me, LORD, my life's end and the number of my days; let me know how fleeting my life is. You have made my days a mere handbreadth; the span of my years is as nothing before you. Everyone is but a breath, even those who seem secure. PSALM 39:4–5

At some deep level we realize we're mortal creatures. However, most of us on most days avoid such thoughts. We might mention getting older, or comment on how time flies, but then we quickly change the subject. The brevity of life is a sobering and unnerving topic.

And yet, the promise that God has allotted each of us a specific number of days—no more and no less—is a life-changing, even freeing truth. We need not be afraid to walk into any situation, for we can know that God will not take us a moment before he already has planned to.

Live wisely and make wise choices and be set free by knowing that God has your life in the palm of his hands. He will bring you to be with him when he has determined to do so. ❖

GOD'S PROMISE TO ME

- I have given you a set number of days.

MY PRAYER TO GOD

This promise motivates me, Lord, to live wisely and well. I want to make each day count, for I only have a set amount. Thank you that I can trust every moment of every day of my entire life to you.

GOD TURNS TROUBLE INTO TRIUMPH

Our light and momentary troubles are achieving for us an eternal glory that far outweighs them all. So we fix our eyes not on what is seen, but on what is unseen, since what is seen is temporary, but what is unseen is eternal. 2 CORINTHIANS 4:17–18

A few envied women have "effortless" pregnancies—no morning sickness, plenty of energy, minimal weight gain—culminating in quick deliveries and recoveries. The average woman, however, struggles with some combination of nausea, weariness, back pain, mood swings, a long, tortuous labor—and perhaps even a medical complication or two along the way. For this majority, nine months can seem like nine years.

Yet the old clichés are true. The teary-eyed mom holding her newborn is quick to admit, "It was worth every bit of the trouble." All the discomfort and stress is swallowed up by the joy of new life.

This is the idea in the apostle Paul's words about our temporal struggles. From our vantage point tough times seem gigantic, endless and pointless. But by the light of eternity we will one day see them as "temporary" and responsible for immeasurable good.

It is this kind of thinking that will get us through—looking ahead, anticipating the lasting joy that God will bring forth from our temporal troubles. ❖

GOD'S PROMISE TO ME

- In light of eternity your troubles are temporary.
- I will give you a joy that lasts forever.

MY PRAYER TO GOD

It takes great faith to read the passage above with real conviction. My troubles seem huge, Lord. Give me eyes to see how temporary my trials are and how eternal your blessings are.

day**341**

GOD PROVIDES SATISFACTION AS YOU LIVE BY HIS WORD

Direct me in the path of your commands, for there I find delight.   PSALM 119:35

The Bible frequently pictures our earthly existence as a foot journey. In other words, we "walk" through this life. And as we do we must choose. We can join the throng of travelers on the popular, broad roads that ignore the Creator and lead ultimately to destruction (see Matthew 7:13–14). Or we can choose, with the dwindling minority, to walk with the Lord.

Choosing Christ means a tough, often lonely, trip along a narrow path. This way—Jesus' way—will take us straight into dangerous territory. We will have frightening moments. We will be tempted repeatedly by appealing yet misleading shortcuts. We will, on occasion, feel lost—or feel all is lost.

But in truth we are safest and most satisfied when we stay on Christ's path, walking along the way outlined in the Word of God. This plodding life seldom brings the thrills that we might find at an amusement park. But it results in a lasting joy that most travelers will never know. ❖

GOD'S PROMISE TO ME

- You will find satisfaction to the degree that you obey my Word.

MY PRAYER TO GOD

This world offers an endless variety of paths, Lord. Help me see that true joy and satisfaction can be found through walking with you. I want to walk the narrow way with Christ, not the broad path that leads to destruction.

GOD COMFORTS YOU SO YOU CAN COMFORT OTHERS

Praise be to the God and Father of our Lord Jesus Christ, the Father of compassion and the God of all comfort, who comforts us in all our troubles, so that we can comfort those in any trouble with the comfort we ourselves receive from God. 2 Corinthians 1:3–4

If we're honest, what we'd really like is deliverance *from* our troubles. We want all our problems to go away—and never come back. One day we'll get that wish in a place called heaven. But for now the best we can hope for is comfort *in the midst* of all our pain.

The verb "comforts" that Paul uses to describe God's response in our times of calamity conveys the idea of being "called alongside." In other words, when we're at our lowest point, God shows up, often in a quiet, almost imperceptible way. He provides consolation, encouragement and strength through that genuine hug from a Christian friend, that song lyric, the Bible verse that jumps off the page, the encouraging letter or email. All these are the work of God, his tools of consolation to enable us to keep going.

And out of that renewed strength, guess what? God wants us to come alongside someone else in pain and pass along the encouragement we've received. ✤

GOD'S PROMISE TO ME

- I will comfort you in all your troubles.
- I will use you to come alongside others who are hurting.

MY PRAYER TO GOD

You comfort me in all my troubles. Thank you for caring for me, Lord. I want to be a conduit of your encouragement and a strengthener of my brothers and sisters.

day**343**

GOD USES HARD TIMES TO GET YOUR ATTENTION

It was good for me to be afflicted so that I might learn your decrees.   PSALM 119:71

If difficulties in our lives merely strengthen a prideful reliance on our own human strength and will . . .

If personal pain becomes our obsession, and relieving it becomes our chief goal in life . . .

If our troubles serve only to drive us to bitterness and envy and despair . . .

Then we have squandered a wonderful opportunity to know God better.

C. S. Lewis once wrote, "God whispers to us in our pleasures, speaks to us in our conscience, but shouts in our pains: it is His megaphone to rouse a deaf world." In another place Lewis called suffering God's "severe mercy."

If you are hurting, stop looking around or looking within yourself for answers. Resist the temptation to become angry and sullen. Instead, consider the fact that God is trying to get your attention. He wants to reveal himself and his truth to you.

This is how suffering becomes a blessing in your life. ♣

GOD'S PROMISE TO ME

- I use suffering to get you focused on what's true.

MY PRAYER TO GOD

You use suffering in my life to get my attention, Lord. Forgive me for missing the point, for complaining, pouting, and accusing you of being cruel or indifferent. You are wise and good. Suffering is never enjoyable, but it can be profitable in my life if I don't fight it. Help me to learn the lessons you have for me.

GOD KEEPS HIS PROMISES

Therefore the Lord himself will give you a sign: The virgin will conceive and give birth to a son, and will call him Immanuel. ISAIAH 7:14

On a journey, as you navigate by reading the signs on a highway, you have the expectation that the signs are accurate and will help you get to your destination as promised.

God also provides "signs" to help his people understand that he keeps his promises. These "signs" are prophecies of events that would take place.

When God promised that a Savior would be born, he used the prophet Isaiah to tell the people what to look for: "The virgin will conceive and give birth to a son." By this amazing sign the people would know that the Messiah came from God.

We celebrate the Advent of the Savior because God faithfully kept his promise. You can trust him to keep all of his promises. ❖

GOD'S PROMISE TO ME

• I always keep my promises.

MY PRAYER TO GOD

Thank you, Lord, for keeping your promises. Your faithfulness astounds me and fills me with joy and peace.

JESUS IS COUNSELOR, GOD, FATHER, PRINCE OF PEACE

For to us a child is born, to us a son is given, and the government will be on his shoulders. And he will be called Wonderful Counselor, Mighty God, Everlasting Father, Prince of Peace.   ISAIAH 9:6

The Old Testament prophet Isaiah saw that through a child would come the fulfillment of God's promise to deal with sin forever. This child would grow to be a man who would die as a perfect sacrifice for sin and then would return to heaven. Jesus said of himself, "The Son of Man will be seated at the right hand of the mighty God" (Luke 22:69).

Jesus is the *Wonderful Counselor*. He knows all things, speaks what the Father says and can give us the perfect advice we need. Jesus is the *Mighty God*. Here we find the mystery of the Trinity. Jesus is himself God; God's attributes are his attributes. He is the Son, yet he is God. Don't try to understand it—just rejoice in it! Jesus is the *Everlasting Father*. He desires a relationship with us. He is not just an impersonal, all-powerful God; he is our Father—forever. Jesus is the *Prince of Peace*. In this world we will not have complete peace, but Jesus promises to give us inner peace and to one day bring peace to all his people. What a day that will be! ❖

GOD'S PROMISE TO ME

- I am the Wonderful Counselor, Mighty God, Everlasting Father and Prince of Peace.

MY PRAYER TO GOD

You are everything this verse says, Lord. Nothing stands in your way; nothing is outside of your authority. I pray for peace in the midst of my hard times. I understand that it is through times of trial and difficulty that people grow and mature.

day346

YOUR LIFE CAN HAVE A SURE FOUNDATION

As for everyone who comes to me and hears my words and puts them into practice, I will show you what they are like. They are like a man building a house, who dug down deep and laid the foundation on rock. When a flood came, the torrent struck that house but could not shake it, because it was well built.   Luke 6:47–48

Hurricanes. Tornados. Mudslides. Floods. Wildfires. Tsunamis. Volcanoes. It almost doesn't matter where we choose to live—everybody faces the threat of some kind of natural disaster.

And even if we do somehow manage to avoid life's *natural* disasters, we don't avoid emotional or marital or financial or occupational crises.

Jesus revealed where we can find ultimate security: through turning to him, listening to him, and obeying him.

It's important to pay close attention to the promise—to note what Jesus says and doesn't say. He doesn't say that if we build our lives on his truth we will avoid all the storms and troubles of life. He does say that if we make him our foundation, we will endure the worst storms.

Are you facing storms? Are you feeling shaky? Renew your resolve to draw near to Jesus, to listen to his words, and to be a doer of his Word (see James 1:22). Then watch what happens! ✣

GOD'S PROMISE TO ME

- If you come to me, listen to me and live as I command, your life will have stability and security.

MY PRAYER TO GOD

Lord Jesus, you call me to follow you. I want to walk with you and listen to you and live as you lived. In a shaky, uncertain world, I want to experience the security and stability that only you can bring.

GOD IS MAKING YOU HOLY

Now that you have been set free from sin and have become slaves of God, the benefit you reap leads to holiness, and the result is eternal life.   ROMANS 6:22

Sanctified is a religious word Christians don't use much anymore. It means, literally, "to be set apart" for God's special use. It reminds us that a holy God can only be served by that which has been made holy.

Holiness happens in one sense when we trust in Jesus Christ, recognizing his death on the cross as the only sufficient payment for our sins. At that moment we become "set apart" in the eyes of God. We are no longer regarded as common and corrupt. We are actually sanctified—made pure and holy in the fullest, most eternal sense of the terms.

Then comes the messy business of practical holiness: learning to live out our new, true nature. Pure attitudes, God-honoring decisions, holy habits—these marks of a sanctified life take a lifetime to develop.

Like it or not, trials are some of the most effective tools God has in his relentless quest to set us apart. If trouble is what it takes to transform us, trouble is what God will allow us to experience. ✤

GOD'S PROMISE TO ME

- I have freed you from the power of sin.
- You are my slave.
- I am making you holy.

MY PRAYER TO GOD

I praise you, God, for making me holy. Because of Christ I am clean and acceptable in your sight. I am called to live my life as a "sanctified" slave of God. As I encounter difficulties today, I want to respond in ways that "set me apart" from my old ways of thinking and living.

day348 december 14

JESUS CAME TO SEEK THE LOST

For the Son of Man came to seek and to save the lost. LUKE 19:10

It's popular in church circles these days to speak of "seekers." Typically this is the label used to describe people who seem curious to know more about Jesus. They may be intrigued by the gospel message or attracted by the life of a Christian they know. So they visit church. They ask questions. They are open to spiritual conversations.

The Bible speaks of "seekers" differently. Jesus said in John 6:44 that "No one can come to me unless the Father who sent me draws them."

Put simply the real "seeker" is the Lord. Jesus said this plainly in Luke 19:10. It happened in Jericho, after Jesus invited himself to the home of a notoriously dishonest tax collector named Zacchaeus, and after Jesus proclaimed him right with God. "I came" Jesus said, "to seek and to save the lost."

This shouldn't shock us. Builders build. Kickers kick. Teachers teach. Plumbers plumb. What else would a Savior do, but save?

Be encouraged as you pray for friends and family members who may or may not appear to be "seeking." What matters is that Jesus is seeking after them. Why? Because he wants to save them. ✤

GOD'S PROMISE TO ME

- I seek lost people.
- I want to save lost people.

MY PRAYER TO GOD

God, thank you for sending the Savior into the world; and for drawing people to yourself. I ask you today to work in the heart of _____. I ask you to save them.

GOD HAS MADE YOU PART OF HIS ROYAL PRIESTHOOD

To him who loves us and has freed us from our sins by his blood, and has made us to be a kingdom and priests to serve his God and Father—to him be glory and power for ever and ever!   REVELATION 1:5–6

Most of us wear a variety of hats: child, sibling, parent, homeowner, neighbor, employee, taxpayer, hobbyist, club member—and the list keeps on going.

If we're a believer in Christ, we can add to that list. When we respond to God's grace and put our trust in Christ, we become a "new creation" (2 Corinthians 5:17). And that's not all. Through our faith, God declares us his beloved "children" (John 1:12). The Bible further identifies us as God's "servants" (1 Corinthians 4:1), "ambassadors" (2 Corinthians 5:20) and "soldier[s]" (2 Timothy 2:3)—among other designations.

There's one more encouraging identity to ponder. The apostle John, in the opening chapter of Revelation describes believers as "priests." The idea here is that, just like the priests of the Old Testament, we have been set apart by God to serve God. We help others encounter God. That is our express purpose as a part of God's "royal priesthood"—to live our lives fully for him. ❖

GOD'S PROMISE TO ME

- I have made you to be a priest so that you might serve me.

MY PRAYER TO GOD

Jesus, thank you, not only for freeing me from sin, but also for granting me the high privilege of serving you forever. Let me begin by serving you this day.

day350

GOD CREATED EVERYTHING TO BRING HIM GLORY

You are worthy, our Lord and God, to receive glory and honor and power, for you created all things, and by your will they were created and have their being. REVELATION 4:11

Interspersed between Revelation's graphic descriptions of terrible judgment "as it will be" on earth are several incredible glimpses of heaven "as it is."

The unearthly colors. The strange and fantastic creatures. John has no words for such sights. Consequently he struggles to find comparisons, using the word "like" more than 60 times.

Yet when it comes to describing heaven's top priority, John has no difficulty. Everything and everyone is focused on God. The Lord God Almighty is the revered center. He is the adored One. The indescribable One on the throne is the recipient of thunderous praise and unceasing worship.

Interesting, isn't it? Those with the clearest view of ultimate, eternal reality understand that everything—everything!—was made by God and for God. All things and all people were created to point to God, to exalt him, to serve him, to make much of him.

Is that true of your life? God gave you breath so that you might give him praise. Have you given yourself back to God for that purpose? ✤

GOD'S PROMISE TO ME

- I made you for my purpose and my glory.

MY PRAYER TO GOD

Great God of heaven, grant that I might see you as you truly are, and that I might worship and glorify you as you truly deserve.

GOD SUPPLIES EVERYTHING YOU NEED

My God will meet all your needs according to the riches of his glory in Christ Jesus.
                                                                            PHILIPPIANS 4:19

The first-century Christians at Philippi were generous. On several occasions they collected and sent financial aid to the apostle Paul. Later, when they learned Paul was in a Roman prison, they promptly dispatched Epaphroditus to relay their concern and to present Paul with a large financial gift to make his incarceration more bearable (see Philippians 4:18).

Perhaps all this giving severely depleted their material resources. Or maybe the economy in Macedonia took a turn for the worse. Whatever the case, the implication of the last few paragraphs in Philippians is that these open-handed believers suddenly were facing financial needs of their own.

Paul's inspired words contain a wonderful promise: God will provide for his children. The verse also reminds us of the divine law of reciprocity stated elsewhere: "Honor the LORD with your wealth, with the firstfruits of all your crops; then your barns will be filled to overflowing, and your vats will brim over with new wine" (Proverbs 3:9 – 10). ❖

GOD'S PROMISE TO ME

- I will supply all your needs.

MY PRAYER TO GOD

Lord, you pledge to meet the needs of your children. Keep me from being stingy — with my time, treasure or talents. Deepen my conviction that I can give myself and my stuff — freely and fully — and that you will be faithful to provide all I need out of your glorious riches.

day352

GOD USES SORROW FOR HIS PURPOSES

Godly sorrow brings repentance that leads to salvation and leaves no regret, but worldly sorrow brings death.   2 CORINTHIANS 7:10

When most people think of tough times, they think of physical or fiscal trouble. But what about spiritual difficulty? What about those occasions in life when we become aware of the wrongness of certain attitudes or actions?

Second Corinthians 7 addresses this topic of godly sorrow. The apostle Paul had previously written a stern letter to the church at Corinth, rebuking the believers for certain wrong actions. They might have become hostile in the face of such confrontation. Or they might have reacted with worldly regret—a self-centered, superficial remorse about being caught.

Instead the Christians at Corinth reacted with true, godly sorrow. They saw their sin, in all its ugliness, as an affront to a holy God. From this place of genuine spiritual sorrow they humbly sought forgiveness and the power to change.

God can use sorrow for our good and his glory—but not if we are hard-hearted and hardheaded. ✣

GOD'S PROMISE TO ME

• I use spiritual regret in your life to bring you back to me.

MY PRAYER TO GOD

Thank you, Lord, for the deep conviction of sin that you bring into my life. A guilty conscience proves you love me, and it points me back to you. I want to respond to your convicting work with humility and repentance. Keep me from the snare of being sad about sin's unpleasant consequences, but not sorrowful over the sin itself.

day353

GOD'S DEVOTION TO YOU IS UNCONDITIONAL

If we are faithless, he remains faithful, for he cannot disown himself.   2 TIMOTHY 2:13

What's your favorite hymn or praise song? Why is it your favorite? Is it the music you like, the lyrics, or both?

In 2 Timothy 2, the apostle Paul quoted some lines from what most scholars believe was an early Christian hymn. Perhaps Paul and Timothy had sung it together on various ministry trips. Or maybe Paul remembered its special meaning to Timothy. Whatever the case, the soon-to-be-executed missionary used these lyrics to challenge his young friend to keep walking with God—even in life's hardest moments.

The last line, the one quoted above, is important. It's a reminder that even when our commitment wavers, God remains fully committed to us. Our faithlessness does not in any way alter God's faithfulness. Instead, his faithfulness can motivate us to respond in kind.

God is not going anywhere—he's with us to the end. What a comforting promise for fickle followers. And what a motivation to sing our favorite hymns of praise. ✤

GOD'S PROMISE TO ME

- I will not turn my back on you—no matter what.

MY PRAYER TO GOD

Even when I am unfaithful, Lord, you are not. I praise you for being my faithful God. Nothing can cause you to give up on me. You always keep your promises. O Father, let me live to your glory today in the realization of your perfect love and care.

GOD'S LOVE FOR YOU IS FOREVER

Who shall separate us from the love of Christ? Shall trouble or hardship or persecution or famine or nakedness or danger or sword? . . . No, in all these things we are more than conquerors through him who loved us.　　　　　Romans 8:35,37

One of the fascinating subplots in the Oscar-winning movie *Rocky* is the way in which the shy and homely Adrian blossoms in response to the title character's awkward affection. The result is a vivid picture of the transforming power of unconditional love.

This is not just Hollywood fantasy. This is actually the promise of the gospel. Believers are chosen by God. In Christ, we are fully accepted. As God's children, we are absolutely cherished. The inspired words of Paul above assure us there's not a thing in the universe that can alter this stunning fact.

God's love gives us supreme confidence. It not only provides a safety net, but it also gives us wings. We have nothing to fear.

Regardless of how things seem right now, you are on God's heart and in his mind. You are the target of his perfect love. ♣

GOD'S PROMISE TO ME

• Nothing in the universe can keep me from loving you.

MY PRAYER TO GOD

Heavenly Father, nothing can ever separate me from your love. This seems too good to be true. Enable me to grasp the reality of your impossible-to-comprehend love. In my darkest moments, keep me going with this truth, one that will transform me.

GOD WILL HELP YOU PRESS ON

Forgetting what is behind and straining toward what is ahead, I press on toward the goal to win the prize for which God has called me heavenward in Christ Jesus.

PHILIPPIANS 3:13–14

Here's an interesting exercise: On a blank sheet of paper, draw three circles—one to represent how you view your past, one to indicate your life right now, and the third to symbolize how you see your future.

If you're like a lot of people, your "past" and "future" circles will be larger than your "present" circle. Why? Because we tend to agonize over our past and/or obsess about our future. So much regret, guilt and shame over what has been; so much fear and worry about what might be—we don't have time or energy left to enjoy what is.

Instead of worry, Christ calls us to a new mindset—forgetting the past and entrusting tomorrow to the one who holds the future. It's similar to when God gave his people manna in the desert (see Exodus 16). They were forbidden to stockpile this heavenly bread. They were not to worry about the next day's food.

God wants you to live in the "now." And why not? Today is all you have. Trust your faithful Father with your uncertain tomorrow. ♣

GOD'S PROMISE TO ME

- I know all your needs.
- I will meet all your daily needs as you live for me.

MY PRAYER TO GOD

Lord, you know all my needs and promise to meet them. I am comforted by the truth that you know every detail of my current situation. Nothing catches you off guard. Help me to seek you first, to trust your promise, to live in the "now" and to stop worrying about tomorrow.

GOD SUSTAINS THOSE WITH DEVOTED HEARTS

The eyes of the LORD range throughout the earth to strengthen those whose hearts are fully committed to him. 2 CHRONICLES 16:9

King Asa of Judah was in a jam. With the armies of Israel bearing down on him from the north, Asa formed a hasty alliance with the godless Syrians. From a purely human standpoint it might have been his best move. From heaven's vantage point it was an act of faithlessness.

Enter Hanani the prophet. He reminded Asa of the above truth and sternly added, "You have done a foolish thing, and from now on you will be at war" (2 Chronicles 16:9).

This avoidable episode is a sober warning to all who face trouble. God is watching. He is looking for those who are "fully committed to him." This Hebrew phrase suggests a mind that is made up, an inner resolve to trust, a steely will that is determined to do only what is pleasing to God. When the Lord finds this kind of fierce devotion he provides strength and assistance.

Don't be a fickle believer who is committed to Christ only when life is easy and good. Discover God's infinite strength by being a faithful follower of the Lord through thick and thin. ❖

GOD'S PROMISE TO ME

- I see all the affairs of earth.
- I strengthen those whose hearts are fully devoted to me.

MY PRAYER TO GOD

You are watching, looking, searching, Lord. You see all things. You see my heart. I pray you are pleased by what you see. You strengthen those with a radical commitment to you. May my problems drive me into your arms where I can find real help.

day**357**

GOD GUARANTEES YOU A WONDERFUL FUTURE

Do not let your heart envy sinners, but always be zealous for the fear of the LORD. There is surely a future hope for you, and your hope will not be cut off. PROVERBS 23:17–18

Play meteorologist for a few moments. Based on your reading of the signs, give a "weather forecast" for your life.

What's ahead? Hazy conditions? Heat advisories? Cloudy skies? Severe thunderstorms? Hail? Tornado warnings?

Whatever uncertainties you're facing, regardless of the ominous conditions looming on the horizon of your life, the promise above offers real hope. Things might get worse before they get better, but they will get better. The Lord guarantees that those who hope in him will have a wonderful future.

Ask God for the insight to see the truth of this promise and the faith to cling to it when the "weather" of your life turns really nasty. ✤

GOD'S PROMISE TO ME

• I have a wonderful future planned for you.

MY PRAYER TO GOD

I do need light, Lord. Help me to see not just my present troubles but the future you have planned for me. Flood my heart with your light. You assure me that a wonderful future awaits.

GOD PROMISED HIS SON

But you, Bethlehem Ephrathah, though you are small among the clans of Judah, out of you will come for me one who will be ruler over Israel, whose origins are from of old, from ancient times." MICAH 5:2

In the eighth century BC, "because of the sins of the people of Israel" (Micah 1:5), God stirred up an obscure prophet named Micah to speak stern words of warning and judgment.

As with all the other Old Testament prophetic books, it's hard to read these seven short chapters without wincing and cringing. And yet the inspired Micah includes a few promising notes of hope. He reminds us that while God is holy and just, he's also gracious and faithful and loving.

One promise that would have been precious beyond words to Micah's original audience? The one above—that from the tiny, insignificant village of Bethlehem would come a ruler with origins from before time. A king who would shepherd the nation with great strength (see 5:4). A king who would bring ultimate security (see 5:4) and personify peace (see 5:5).

Can you use divine strength and peace this Christmas season? Trust in the King who was born in the manger of Bethlehem. ✤

- I am faithful even when my people are faithless.
- The child of Bethlehem is the King of kings!

Father, this Christmas I praise you for loving me enough to send your Son. Help me to focus on your divine strength and peace.

day359

GOD'S SON CAME TO REIGN FOREVER

You will conceive and give birth to a son, and you are to call him Jesus. He will be great and will be called the Son of the Most High. The Lord God will give him the throne of his father David, and he will reign over Jacob's descendants forever; his kingdom will never end. LUKE 1:31–33

The word *angel* means "messenger," and the angel Gabriel delivered a message of immense magnitude to the young, unsuspecting Mary. Though a virgin, she would become pregnant. Her newborn son was to be named *Jesus* (which means "The Lord is salvation"). And finally, her child would not be an ordinary child. He would be the Son of God. He would be King over an eternal kingdom.

Today is the day we (ostensibly) celebrate the birth of that king. Though we talk much about the wise men who brought kingly gifts, though we sing, "glory to the newborn king," yet how easy it is to forget that Jesus Christ came to rule and reign.

Indeed, the first words Christ spoke when he began his public ministry were, "The kingdom of God has come near" (Mark 1:15). Who else but a king can make such a claim?

The angel's promise could not have been clearer. Christ will reign forever. Isn't it fitting that he reign today—this Christmas Day—in our hearts? ❖

GOD'S PROMISE TO ME

- Jesus is my Son.
- Jesus will reign forever.

MY PRAYER TO GOD

King Jesus, as I remember your birth this Christmas day, let me celebrate with great hope and joy. You rule the universe. Please reign also in my heart.

GOD HONORS YOUR FAITH

We remember before our God and Father your work produced by faith, your labor prompted by love, and your endurance inspired by hope in our Lord Jesus Christ.

1 THESSALONIANS 1:3

With coaches and teammates shouting instructions, the five-year-old in the over-sized batting helmet swings with all his might, sending the T-ball rolling slowly toward third base. After several seconds of wild cheering, running and throwing, the batter sits on first base in a cloud of dust—safe!

Then an interesting thing happens. The kid scrambles to his feet and scans the crowd anxiously. Suddenly he beams. He spies his proud dad in the bleachers giving an enthusiastic "thumbs up" sign.

This hunger to please our earthly parents is a reminder of the truth that we were created ultimately to honor our heavenly Father. Exercising simple faith helps us do that.

Paul commended his "children"—the believers of Thessalonica—for their faith. He knew that when we seek the Lord in hard times and trust him to see us through, we bring glory to him. He promises to honor us too. ❖

GOD'S PROMISE TO ME

• I will honor your faith in me.

MY PRAYER TO GOD

Lord, real faith is demonstrated by seeking after you. Give me a sincere heart, Lord, and a faith that pursues you. Living for you is the great hope of my soul.

day**361**

GOD REWARDS THOSE WHO HONOR HIM

Fear the LORD, you his holy people, for those who fear him lack nothing. The lions may grow weak and hungry, but those who seek the LORD lack no good thing.

PSALM 34:9–10

What does the phrase "fear the LORD" mean? Are we expected to cower with fright in God's presence or live in continual terror and dread?

Fear in this sense is the appropriate response of rebellious unbelievers who flaunt God's decrees. Having rejected Almighty God as a merciful Savior, they now face the grim prospect of meeting him only in his role as the holy Judge of the universe. One the other hand, for the beloved children of God—those whose sins have been forgiven by Christ—"fear the LORD" has a different connotation. The idea for believers is that of awe or stunned admiration in the presence of a great and good Creator. The implication is submissive reverence before a loving Lord, to worship God above all other things. It involves, in the words of the passage, the commitment to "seek" him.

Notice that the promise to those who fear the Lord is that all their needs will be met. Or, as God puts it in another place, "Those who honor me I will honor" (1 Samuel 2:30). ✤

GOD'S PROMISE TO ME

- I meet the needs of those who honor me.
- I make sure my followers have good things.

MY PRAYER TO GOD

You meet the needs of those who treat you with reverence, Lord. Forgive me for the times I fail to honor you. You are the majestic king of the universe—high and lifted up. As I trust in you, you fill my life with good things.

day**362**

GOD IS BIGGER THAN YOUR DILEMMAS

I am the LORD, the God of all mankind. Is anything too hard for me? JEREMIAH 32:27

Your situation is grim. You feel lost in the dead end of a dark maze. You ran out of options and solutions a long time ago. You are past the point of exhaustion. Despair hovers over you like a flock of hungry buzzards.

What you'd like is outright deliverance from your difficulty. But at this point you'd settle for less spectacular help—a fragment of wisdom, a speck of patience and strength, a small bit of peace. You need grace for one more day, the ability to endure without complaining. In short, you need the sustaining touch of God.

If that describes where you are, the divine promise above—with its bold rhetorical question—is the verse you want rolling around in your head, heart and soul. The obvious implication is that nothing is too difficult for God—not your external situation and not your internal confusion. Lost causes are God's specialty. ✤

GOD'S PROMISE TO ME

- I am the sovereign, almighty God.
- Nothing is too hard for me.

MY PRAYER TO GOD

Lord, when my faith is shaky, remind me of your power. Give me a fresh glimpse of who you really are. Nothing is impossible for you. Increase my faith. Supply the confidence I need to believe fully in this promise—especially when I am facing hopeless situations.

GOD PROMISES YOU PEACE

Do not be anxious about anything, but in every situation, by prayer and petition, with thanksgiving, present your requests to God. And the peace of God, which transcends all understanding, will guard your hearts and your minds in Christ Jesus.

PHILIPPIANS 4:6–7

What's the solution for someone whose gut is in knots? Alcohol? Valium? A vacation at the beach? A weekend full of amusements and fun?

Such common remedies might offer temporary relief from stress, but the long-term, ongoing answer for anxiety is simple prayer. Pouring out your heart to God. Honestly sharing your needs with him.

It's not like you're telling God things he doesn't know. And you're not guaranteed everything you ask for. But what you do get when you pray is God's ear and his heart. And if you linger long enough in his presence to get his perspective, you'll find his perfect peace (see Isaiah 26:3).

Prayer isn't magic. But when you talk to God honestly and in simple faith, it's pretty close. ♣

GOD'S PROMISE TO ME

- If you pray about your concerns, I will give you my peace.
- My peace is too wonderful for you to comprehend.
- My peace will guard your heart and mind.

MY PRAYER TO GOD

God, keep me praying instead of worrying. You promise peace—wonderful, supernatural peace—to those who look to you. In an anxious world, this is a blessed promise—the promise of peace.

day364

december 30

GOD IS INVOLVED IN YOUR LIFE

Guide me in your truth and teach me, for you are God my Savior, and my hope is in you all day long. PSALM 25:5

As we navigate our way through days filled with pain or sorrow or uncertainty, here's the truth: There are no secret "keys," no spiritual techniques, no super-duper prayers (not even the prayer of Jabez in 1 Chronicles 4:9–10) that can guarantee us a Disney-esque happy ending in this life. That's because God's goal for us is not earthly bliss, but something grander: his glory brought about through our maturity.

We would do well in tough times to forget about nonexistent magic wands and quick fixes, and to focus on promises like the one above. Look at it closely. Notice what it claims: God, our Savior, guides us. All we have to do is hope in him.

Even so, we will not fall. At least not fatally. When we do stumble, the Lord is there to pick us up and lead us farther down the road. ❖

GOD'S PROMISE TO ME

- I will guide you in my truth.
- I am your Savior.

MY PRAYER TO GOD

I would love an easy life, Lord—free of all trouble and grief and confusion. But you have never promised such an existence. In fact, the testimony of Scripture is that I will go through hard times. Thank you for promising to direct me in your truth. Give me wisdom and courage so that I am willing to walk with you wherever you lead.

GOD HELPS YOU THROUGH GREAT TROUBLE

This is what the LORD says—he who created you, Jacob, he who formed you, Israel: "Do not fear, for I have redeemed you; I have summoned you by name; you are mine. When you pass through the waters, I will be with you; and when you pass through the rivers, they will not sweep over you. When you walk through the fire, you will not be burned; the flames will not set you ablaze. ISAIAH 43:1–2

God sent the prophet Isaiah to his rebellious people to speak stern words of judgment and wonderful words of hope. Consigned to Babylonian captivity because of their sin, the Israelites needed to be reminded of God's continual love and care. In the midst of great trouble and suffering, the people of God needed comfort and courage.

The words of this Old Testament prophecy echo through the pages of the New Testament. God is always with us (see Hebrews 13:5). He is our Savior (John 3:16). He loves us with an affection that we cannot begin to fathom (Romans 8:35–39).

What deep waters and fiery trials are you facing just now? Remember you are precious to God, and he loves you. ♣

GOD'S PROMISE TO ME

- I am with you in times of trouble.
- I am your God and Savior.
- You are precious to me.
- I love you!

MY PRAYER TO GOD

Lord, you are always with me in times of great trouble. Thank you for your presence, protection, and peace. You are the one true God, and the only One who can save.

SCRIPTURE INDEX

SCRIPTURE	DATE	PROMISE
Psalm 10:17	January 24	God Doesn't Always Answer "Why?"
Psalm 16:11	February 2	God Wants You to Experience Eternal Life
Psalm 16:11	November 10	God Gives You Supernatural Joy
Psalm 22:28	July 9	God Is Tender Toward You
Psalm 23:1	July 2	God Is Your Shepherd
Psalm 24:1	September 27	God Is the Source of Your Wealth
Psalm 24:3–5	March 6	God Blesses His People
Psalm 25:1–3	September 18	God Spares the Faithful From Shame
Psalm 25:8	June 12	God Is Good
Psalm 25:5	December 30	God Is Involved in Your Life
Psalm 30:4–5	September 25	God Turns Sorrow Into Joy
Psalm 30:5	February 18	God Cares for You Through Hard Times
Psalm 30:5	September 7	The Lord Will Dry Your Tears
Psalm 31:13–15	January 30	God Sets You Free From Terror
Psalm 32:3–4	January 13	God Disciplines His Sinning Children
Psalm 32:8	March 27	God Watches Over You
Psalm 33:5	July 18	God Is Fair With You
Psalm 33:13–15	October 9	God Knows All About You
Psalm 34:4	August 6	God Sets You Free From Fear
Psalm 34:5	April 3	God Delivers the Faithful From Shame
Psalm 34:6	September 6	God Liberates You From Trouble
Psalm 34:9–10	December 27	God Rewards Those Who Honor Him
Psalm 34:17	February 13	God Listens to You
Psalm 34:17, 19	May 14	God Rescues You
Psalm 34:18	October 12	God Is Close to the Brokenhearted
Psalm 35:10	January 21	God Stands Up for the Helpless
Psalm 36:9	July 19	God Brings Light to Your Darkness
Psalm 37:4	February 5	God Fulfills Your Holy Passions
Psalm 37:4	June 11	God Cares About Your Deepest Desires
Psalm 37:5	August 18	God Blesses You When You Trust
Psalm 37:18	December 4	God Will Honor Your Integrity
Psalm 37:23–24	March 28	God Keeps You From Falling
Psalm 37:23–24	July 28	God Orders Your Steps
Psalm 37:30–31	April 9	The Godly Can Give Good Advice
Psalm 39:4–5	December 5	God Has Determined the Length of Your Life
Psalm 40:1–2	January 22	God Rescues You From the Emotional Depths
Psalm 40:17	January 12	God Is Thinking About You
Psalm 45:6	October 18	God's Kingdom Will Last Forever
Psalm 46:1	May 8	God Is Your Refuge
Psalm 46:2, 10	October 6	God Drives Away Your Fears
Psalm 51:16–17	January 16	God Forgives the Repentant Soul
Psalm 55	October 5	God Hears Your Pleas of Distress
Psalm 55:22	January 9	God Takes Care of the Godly
Psalm 56:8	January 11	God Is Aware of Your Sorrow
Psalm 56:8	September 7	The Lord Will Dry Your Tears
Psalm 57:2	December 3	God Has a Plan for You
Psalm 59:9–10	August 2	God Comes to Those Who Wait
Psalm 59:16–17	October 7	God Loves You in Times of Distress
Psalm 62:1	January 14	God Offers Rest
Psalm 63:1	October 2	God Satisfies the Longing Soul
Psalm 66:18–19	January 6	God Does Not Respond to the Rebellious

Isaiah 43:1–2 . . . . .December 31 . . . .God Helps You Through Great Trouble
Isaiah 43:2 . . . . .May 15 . . . . .God Goes With You Through Trials
Isaiah 43:2, 4 . . . . .August 20. . . . . . .God Helps You Face Your Fears
Isaiah 44:22 . . . . .April 15 . . . . .God Sweeps Your Sin Away
Isaiah 44:24 . . . . .July 9 . . . . .God Is Tender Toward You
Isaiah 46:4 . . . . .August 25. . . . . . .God Sustains You Through Rough Times
Isaiah 46:9–10. . . . . .February 28 . . . . .God Controls Every Situation
Isaiah 49:13 . . . . .May 13 . . . . .God Comforts You
Isaiah 54:7–8 . . . . .September 25 . . . .God Turns Sorrow Into Joy
Isaiah 55:8 . . . . .October 17 . . . . . .God's Plans Sometimes Differ From Yours
Isaiah 59:17 . . . . .May 20 . . . . .God Gives You the Breastplate
of Righteousness
Isaiah 59:17 . . . . .May 23 . . . . .God Gives You the Helmet of Salvation
Isaiah 64:4 . . . . .October 19 . . . . . .God Acts for the Good of Those Who
Wait on Him
Jeremiah 1:5 . . . . .April 16 . . . . .God Knows You
Jeremiah 6:16 . . . . .November 25 . . . .God Wants to Show You the Good Path
Jeremiah 17:6–8. . . . . . . .September 15 . . . .God Blesses Those Who Cling to Him
Jeremiah 17:9 . . . . .August 31. . . . . . .God Changes Your Mindset
Jeremiah 29:11–12. . . . . .January 15 . . . . . .God Promises Good Plans for Your Life
Jeremiah 32:27 . . . . .December 28 . . . .God Is Bigger Than Your Dilemmas
Lamentations 3:22–23 . . .June 14 . . . . .God Is Faithful
Lamentations 3:22–25 . . .June 10 . . . . .God Cares When You Need Hope
Ezekiel 36:26–27 . . . . . . .April 17 . . . . .God Gives You a New Heart
Daniel 11:32. . . . . .November 23 . . . .God Helps You Resist Temptation
Joel 2:13 . . . . .November 1 . . . . .God Abounds in Love
Joel 2:25 . . . . .April 14 . . . . .God Will Redeem the Time
Joel 2:28–29. . . . . .February 24 . . . . .God's Spirit Instructs You
Joel 2:32 . . . . .October 29 . . . . . .God Saves Those Who Call on Him
Micah 1:5 . . . . .December 24 . . . .God Promised His Son
Micah 4:3. . . . . .August 14. . . . . . .The Lord Will Bring World Peace
Micah 5:2, 4–5 . . . . .December 24 . . . .God Promised His Son
Micah 7:8 . . . . .July 28 . . . . .God Orders Your Steps
Micah 7:8–9 . . . . .June 2 . . . . .God Will Bring You Out of the Darkness
Nahum 1:7 . . . . .July 1 . . . . .God Is Good
Habakkuk 2:14. . . . . .August 11. . . . . . .The Lord Will Be Glorified
Habakkuk 3:19. . . . . .July 27 . . . . .The Lord Is Your Strength
Zephaniah 3:17 . . . . .February 22 . . . . .God Rejoices Over You
Zechariah 4:6. . . . . .July 23 . . . . .You Don't Need Might and Power—You
Need His Spirit
Malachi 3:6 . . . . .August 17. . . . . . .God Never Changes
Malachi 3:10 . . . . .July 22 . . . . .When You Give, God Blesses
Matthew 1:23. . . . . .February 11 . . . . .God Is Always With You
Matthew 4:1–11 . . . . . . .May 24. . . . . .God Gives You the Sword of the Spirit
Matthew 4:1–11 . . . . . . .November 20 . . . .God's Word Keeps You From Sin
Matthew 5:5. . . . . .November 15 . . . .God Gives You the Capacity to Be Gentle
Matthew 5:7. . . . . .July 11 . . . . .God Shows Mercy to the Merciful
Matthew 6:6. . . . . .April 19 . . . . .God Rewards Your Quiet Time With Him
Matthew 6:13. . . . . .September 4. . . . . .God Understands Your Temptations
Matthew 6:14–15 . . . . . .April 6 . . . . .Becoming Like Christ in Forgiveness
Matthew 6:26–27 . . . . . .August 13. . . . . . .God Is Concerned for You
Matthew 6:31–33 . . . . . .May 28. . . . . .You Can Trust in God's Provision
Matthew 6:32–34 . . . . . .July 30 . . . . .God Takes Care of Tomorrow
Matthew 7:1–2 . . . . .May 2 . . . . .Do Not Be Judgmental

SCRIPTURE	DATE	PROMISE
Matthew 7:7	March 4	God Rewards Those Who Seek Him
Matthew 7:13–14	December 7	God Provides Satisfaction As You Live by His Word
Matthew 7:21, 24	April 12	Those Who Obey Are Wise
Matthew 11:25–26	October 15	God Reveals Truth to Those With Childlike Hearts
Matthew 11:28–30	May 29	You Can Trust in God's Grace
Matthew 11:29	April 1	Becoming Like Christ in Humility
Matthew 11:29	November 15	God Gives You the Capacity to Be Gentle
Matthew 14:23	September 26	God Can Be Found When You Seek Him
Matthew 16:24–25	March 10	You Can Find True Life
Matthew 17:20	June 3	Nothing Is Impossible With Faith in God
Matthew 18:1, 4	April 1	Becoming Like Christ in Humility
Matthew 18:3	October 15	God Reveals Truth to Those With Childlike Hearts
Matthew 18:33	June 16	God Is Merciful
Matthew 20:26b–27	July 5	God Exalts His Servants
Matthew 20:28	April 2	Becoming Like Christ in Service
Matthew 28:19–20	April 25	You Are Christ's Witness
Matthew 28:20b	February 11	God Is Always With You
Mark 1:15	December 25	God's Son Came to Reign Forever
Mark 6:31	September 30	God Does Not Want You to Burn Out
Mark 6:34	April 7	Becoming Like Christ in Patience and Compassion
Mark 8:35–38	April 5	Becoming Like Christ in Self-Denial
Luke 1:31–33	December 25	God's Son Came to Reign Forever
Luke 4:1–13	September 8	God Gives Success in Fighting Satan
Luke 6:47–48	December 12	Your Life Can Have a Sure Foundation
Luke 10:42	February 15	God Blesses You When You Worship
Luke 12:4	February 12	God Guards You From Evil
Luke 12:7	January 11	God Is Aware of Your Sorrow
Luke 15:11–24	July 13	The Joy of the Lord Is Your Strength
Luke 16:10	November 14	God Promises the Fruit of Faithfulness
Luke 19:10	December 14	Jesus Came to Seek the Lost
Luke 22:69	December 11	Jesus Is Counselor, God, Father, Prince of Peace
Luke 23:34	April 6	Becoming Like Christ in Forgiveness
John 1:12	February 14	God Has Set His Affection on You
John 1:12	July 3	God Is Your Father
John 1:12	December 15	God Has Made You Part of His Royal Priesthood
John 1:14	September 22	The Lord Will One Day Be With Us
John 3:16	July 16	God Gave His Son for You
John 3:16	December 31	God Helps You Through Great Trouble
John 3:36	March 5	God Gives Eternal Life
John 4:14	February 25	God Satisfies Your Deepest Longings
John 4:14	November 29	God Quenches Your Thirsty Soul
John 5:19	January 25	You Can Say No to Ungodliness
John 6:37	October 29	God Saves Those Who Call on Him
John 6:44	December 14	Jesus Came to Seek the Lost
John 8:31–32, 36	November 21	God Has Set You Free in Christ
John 8:36	February 26	God Sets You Free in Christ
John 10:10	November 6	God Wants You to Experience Abundant Life

SCRIPTURE	DATE	PROMISE
John 10:11–14	July 2	God Is Your Shepherd
John 10:15	April 5	Becoming Like Christ in Self-Denial
John 10:27–29	February 12	God Guards You From Evil
John 11:25–26	January 7	God Is Triumphant Over Death
John 11:25–26	June 26	God Promises Resurrection
John 12:25–26	February 23	God Honors His Faithful Servants
John 12:44–46	April 4	Becoming Like Christ in Integrity
John 14:2–3	August 29	God Has an Eternal Place Prepared for You
John 14:2–3	November 4	God Has Given You a New Identity
John 14:6	May 19	God Gives You the Belt of Truth
John 14:6	June 19	Jesus Is the Way, Truth, and Life
John 14:7	November 6	God Wants You to Experience Abundant Life
John 14:21	November 5	God Values Your Obedience
John 14:26	February 3	God's Spirit Leads You
John 14:27	June 30	God Calms Your Troubled Mind
John 15:5	November 8	God Produces Change in and Through You
John 15:7	June 6	God Cares When You Pray
John 15:14–15	March 12	You Are God's Friend
John 15:15	February 1	God Is Intimate With His Followers
John 15:18–19	February 6	God's Children Are Chosen Out of the World
John 15:20	February 18	God Cares for You Through Hard Times
John 16:7	December 1	God's Children Will Face Trouble in This Life
John 16:13	November 2	God Gives You His Spirit
John 16:20–22	September 25	God Turns Sorrow Into Joy
John 16:33	January 1	God Is Bigger Than Your Worldly Troubles
John 17	July 14	The Son of God Prays for You
Acts 1:8	February 3	God's Spirit Leads You
Acts 10:34–35	March 26	God Does Not Play Favorites
Romans 3:11	December 14	Jesus Came to Seek the Lost
Romans 3:22	May 23	God Gives You the Helmet of Salvation
Romans 3:22–24	July 4	God Frees You From Sin
Romans 3:23	June 12	God Is Good
Romans 3:23	July 11	God Shows Mercy to the Merciful
Romans 5:3	January 10	God Uses Problems to Shape You
Romans 5:3–4	December 14	God Grants You Overcoming Power
Romans 5:8	June 12	God Is Good
Romans 5:8–9	June 21	God Showed You His Love Through His Son
Romans 5:8, 10	February 14	God Has Set His Affection on You
Romans 5:10	July 10	God Has Rescued You From Sin and Death
Romans 5:10	October 3	God Adopts You
Romans 5:12	September 29	God Will Deal With Death—Forever
Romans 6:4	August 12	God Gives You Real Power Over Sin
Romans 6:22	December 13	God Is Making You Holy
Romans 6:23	July 11	God Shows Mercy to the Merciful
Romans 6:23	October 13	God Has Saved You From Eternal Death
Romans 8:1	July 21	God Delivers You From Condemnation
Romans 8:15	February 14	God Has Set His Affection on You
Romans 8:16	February 16	God Has Made You His Heir

2 Corinthians 5:19–20	February 7	God Has Made You His Ambassador
2 Corinthians 5:20	December 15	God Has Made You Part of His Royal Priesthood
2 Corinthians 6:4–7	June 18	God Empowers You to Build His Kingdom
2 Corinthians 6:14–16	March 15	You Are God's Temple
2 Corinthians 7:5–6	August 4	God Encourages the Discouraged
2 Corinthians 7:10	December 18	God Uses Sorrow for His Purposes
2 Corinthians 12	September 25	God Turns Sorrow Into Joy
2 Corinthians 12:8–9	May 25	You Can Trust God's Strength in Your Weakness
2 Corinthians 12:9–10	September 12	God Makes You Able
Galatians 2:19–20	April 24	You Can Live by Faith
Galatians 3:29	February 14	God Has Set His Affection on You
Galatians 4:4–5	October 3	God Adopts You
Galatians 4:7	November 27	God Gives Confirmation That You Are His Child
Galatians 5:13	April 2	Becoming Like Christ in Service
Galatians 5:16	February 3	God's Spirit Leads You
Galatians 5:16–17	November 3	God Has Given You New Longings
Galatians 5:22	November 9	God Gives You the Ability to Love
Galatians 5:22	November 10	God Gives You Supernatural Joy
Galatians 5:22	November 11	God Gives You Wonderful Peace
Galatians 5:22	November 12	God Gives You Unearthly Patience
Galatians 5:22	November 13	God Supplies You With His Kindness and Goodness
Galatians 5:22	November 14	God Promises the Fruit of Faithfulness
Galatians 5:22–23	November 15	God Gives You the Capacity to Be Gentle
Galatians 5:22–23	November 16	God Gives You Self-Control
Galatians 6:1–2	March 25	You Can Help Others
Galatians 6:7	August 27	God Lets You Reap What You Sow
Galatians 6:9	September 16	God Assures Triumph If You Don't Give Up
Ephesians 1	August 23	God Blesses the Righteous
Ephesians 1:3	August 1	God Has Given You All You Need
Ephesians 1:3	November 24	God Has Provided All You Need
Ephesians 1:4	June 17	God Is Holy
Ephesians 1:5	October 3	God Adopts You
Ephesians 1:13–14	June 25	The Holy Spirit Guarantees Future Promises
Ephesians 1:18	August 28	God Guarantees You a Wonderful Future
Ephesians 2:8	July 10	God Has Rescued You From Sin and Death
Ephesians 2:8, 10	April 30	God Empowers You to Do Good Works
Ephesians 2:10	February 4	God Has Changed You
Ephesians 2:10	February 9	God Equips You to Help Others
Ephesians 2:13	November 17	You Were Bought by the Blood of Christ
Ephesians 3:9	July 9	God Is Tender Toward You
Ephesians 3:19	August 20	God Helps You Face Your Fears
Ephesians 3:20	September 13	God Wants to Do More Than You Think
Ephesians 4:7–12	May 1	God Calls You to Use Your Gifts
Ephesians 4:11–13	August 19	God Promises to Build His Church
Ephesians 6:1–3	March 13	God Blesses You When You Obey Your Parents

Ephesians 6:6–8 . . . . . . .July 6 . . . . .God Rewards Your Hard Work

Ephesians 6:12–13 . . . . . .May 18. . . . . .God Helps You to Stand Firm

Ephesians 6:14 . . . . .May 19. . . . . .God Gives You the Belt of Truth

Ephesians 6:14 . . . . .May 20. . . . . .God Gives You the Breastplate
of Righteousness

Ephesians 6:14–15. . . . . .May 21 . . . . .God Gives You the Shoes of Peace

Ephesians 6:16 . . . . .May 22. . . . . .God Gives You the Shield of Faith

Ephesians 6:17 . . . . .May 23. . . . . .God Gives You the Helmet of Salvation

Ephesians 6:17 . . . . .May 24. . . . . .God Gives You the Sword of the Spirit

Philippians 1:6 . . . . .January 2 . . . . . . .God Has Given You All You Need
in Christ

Philippians 1:6 . . . . .September 28 . . . .God Is Slowly Changing You

Philippians 1:10–11. . . . .April 23 . . . . . . .Filled With the Fruit of Righteousness

Philippians 2:3 . . . . .February 9 . . . . .God Equips You to Help Others

Philippians 2:5, 7 . . . . . . .April 1 . . . . .Becoming Like Christ in Humility

Philippians 2:12–13 . . . .March 31 . . . . . . .God Gives the Desire and Power to Obey

Philippians 2:13 . . . . .September 19 . . . .God Provides Supernatural Strength

Philippians 3:13–14. . . . .December 21 . . . .God Will Help You Press On

Philippians 3:20. . . . . . . .November 4 . . . . .God Has Given You a New Identity

Philippians 4:6–7 . . . . . .May 10. . . . . .God Exchanges Peace for Worry

Philippians 4:6–7 . . . . . .December 29 . . . .God Promises You Peace

Philippians 4:7 . . . . .May 21. . . . . .God Gives Us the Shoes of Peace

Philippians 4:8–9 . . . . . .April 26 . . . . . . .Your Thought Patterns Can Change

Philippians 4:12. . . . . . . .May 5 . . . . .You Can Find Contentment

Philippians 4:13 . . . . .August 5. . . . . . . .God Grants You Persevering Power

Philippians 4:18–19. . . . .December 17 . . . .God Supplies Everything You Need

Philippians 4:19 . . . . .February 10 . . . . .God Helps the Weak

Colossians 1:16. . . . . .November 18 . . . .You Were Created for God

Colossians 1:21 . . . . .July 10 . . . . .God Has Rescued You From Sin
and Death

Colossians 1:21 . . . . .October 3. . . . . . .God Adopts You

Colossians 1:22 . . . . .June 17 . . . . .God Is Holy

Colossians 1:24 . . . . .February 18 . . . . .God Cares for You Through Hard Times

Colossians 3:2 . . . . .August 16. . . . . . .God Gives Peace to People of Faith

Colossians 3:3–4. . . . . . .August 12. . . . . . .God Gives You Real Power Over Sin

Colossians 3:15 . . . . .September 11 . . . .God Gives Peace in Crazy Times

1 Thessalonians 1:3 . . . . .December 26 . . . .God Honors Your Faith

1 Thessalonians 5:14 . . . . .April 7 . . . . .Becoming Like Christ in Patience
and Compassion

1 Thessalonians 5:23 . . . .September 9 . . . . .God Will Purify You

2 Thessalonians 2:13 . . . .June 17 . . . . .God Is Holy

2 Thessalonians 3:2–3. . . .May 12. . . . . .God Protects You

1 Timothy 1:15–16 . . . . . .September 17 . . . .God Is Long-Suffering

1 Timothy 4:3–4 . . . . . . .May 3 . . . . .You Can Enjoy God's Gifts and Be
Thankful

1 Timothy 4:4 . . . . .May 4. . . . . .Do Not Be Tied to the World

1 Timothy 4:7–8 . . . . . . .July 8 . . . . .God Is Most Concerned With Your Heart

1 Timothy 6:6–8 . . . . . . .September 5 . . . . .God Can Make You Happy With Less

1 Timothy 6:17–18 . . . . . .September 27. . . .God Is the Source of Your Wealth

2 Timothy 1:7. . . . . .April 28 . . . . . . .You Have Power

2 Timothy 1:7. . . . . .July 12 . . . . .God Gives You the Will to Keep
Doing Right

2 Timothy 2:3 . . . . .December 15 . . . .God Has Made You Part of His Royal
Priesthood

2 Peter 1:3–4 . . . . March 9 . . . . You Can Live a Godly Life

2 Peter 1:4 . . . . February 4 . . . . . . God Has Changed You

2 Peter 1:6 . . . . November 16 . . . . God Gives You Self-Control

2 Peter 3:9 . . . . September 17 . . . . God Is Long-Suffering

1 John 1:5 . . . . July 19 . . . . God Brings Light to Your Darkness

1 John 1:8–9 . . . . May 27 . . . . You Can Trust in God's Forgiveness

1 John 1:9 . . . . March 1 . . . . God Uses Pure People

1 John 1:9 . . . . April 29 . . . . You Can Confess Your Sins and
Receive Mercy

1 John 1:9 . . . . October 4 . . . . . . God Restores the Humble in Spirit

1 John 3:1 . . . . February 14 . . . . . God Has Set His Affection on You

1 John 3:2 . . . . June 28 . . . . God Promises That You Will Be
Like Him

1 John 3:2 . . . . October 1 . . . . God Will Destroy This World and All Its
Troubles

1 John 4:1 . . . . March 21 . . . . God Will Give You Discernment

1 John 4:16, 19 . . . . November 9 . . . . . God Gives You the Ability to Love

1 John 4:16–18a . . . . June 20 . . . . God Is Love

1 John 4:18 . . . . November 11 . . . . God Gives You Wonderful Peace

1 John 5:12–13 . . . . March 5 . . . . God Gives You Eternal Life

1 John 5:14–15 . . . . June 6 . . . . God Cares When You Pray

Revelation 1:5–6 . . . . December 15 . . . . God Has Made You Part of His Royal
Priesthood

Revelation 3:20 . . . . July 25 . . . . God Longs to Be Close to You

Revelation 4:11 . . . . December 16 . . . . God Created Everything to Bring Him
Glory

Revelation 21:3 . . . . September 22 . . . . The Lord Will One Day Be With Us

Revelation 21:4 . . . . September 7 . . . . . The Lord Will Dry Your Tears

Revelation 21:4 . . . . September 22 . . . . The Lord Will One Day Be With Us

Revelation 21:5 . . . . June 29 . . . . God Promises to Make All Things New

Revelation 21:10–11 . . . . . October 1 . . . . God Will Destroy This World and All
Its Troubles

Revelation 21—22 . . . . . . August 28 . . . . God Guarantees You a Wonderful Future

Revelation 22 . . . . September 22 . . . . The Lord Will One Day Be With Us

Revelation 22:12 . . . . September 2 . . . . . The Lord Will Return and Bring Rewards

TOPICAL INDEX